Ancestry of
Experience

Aloha e, Steve and Daira:
What a gift it has been to
know you two! We will
never forget how you two
initiated Ivan into ocean
swimming. And our time
in Tahiti together was
priceless. We're so glad
our friends on Huahine
got to meet you. Those
dinners at your place and
our meals on the
catamaran were definitely
treats -- for the body,
and for the soul!
        Me ke aloha,
             leilani

For those who came before us.
In hopes that we act on behalf
of your bones.

Ancestry of Experience

A Journey into Hawaiian Ways of Knowing

Leilani Holmes

University of Hawai'i Press
Honolulu

Library of Congress Cataloging-in-Publication Data

Holmes, Leilani.
Ancestry of experience: a journey into Hawaiian ways
of knowing / Leilani Holmes.
    p. cm.—(Intersections)
Includes bibliographical references and index.
ISBN 978-0-8248-3129-5 (hardcover: alk. paper)
1. Hawaii—Civilization. 2. Oral tradition—Hawaii.
3. Holmes, Leilani I. Title. II. Series: Intersections
(Honolulu, Hawaii)
DU624.5.H59 2013
305.89'9420092—dc23
[B]
                    2012004807

ASIAN AND PACIFIC AMERICAN
TRANSCULTURAL STUDIES

David K. Yoo
Russell C. Leong
General Editors

University of Hawai'i Press books are printed on acid-free
paper and meet the guidelines for permanence and
durability of the Council on Library Resources.

Designed by Ivan Holmes

Printer-ready pages were prepared by Linda Lockowitz.
Printed by Sheridan Books, Inc.

This Book is in Memory of

Ali'i Sir Wayne Keona'anamanu Davis, C.K.:
kahu Moʻokūʻauhau nui
for The Royal Order of Kamehameha I

you are sorely missed
yet at dawn I hear your voice
through the trees on your mountain

Aunty Philomena Keali'i Waine'e Aranio:
kumu hula, Hālau o Hale Loke

I miss you always
yet when I dance your *hula*
I feel your hands trace the *ʻāina*

Acknowledgments:

George J. Sefa Dei *(OISE, University of Toronto)*,
Steve Derné *(State University of New York)*,
Kauka De Silva *(University of Hawai'i: Kapiolani
    Community College)*,
Lisa Kahaleole Hall *(Wells College)*,
Mary E. Leslie *(Grossmont College)*,
Stephanie Mood *(Grossmont College)*,
Noenoe Silva *(University of Hawai'i)*,
Geoff White *(University of Hawai'i)*,
and Masako Ikeda *(University of Hawai'i Press)*,
    for your kind, generous support and
    insights.

Malie Wahine Ke'ali'i o ke Kai,
    from Pūpūkea
And my wonderful *'ohana,*
    for your loving hospitality.

Ivan Holmes,
    my husband, designer, and vision-keeper
    for your healing and transforming love.

Contents

Photos

Here is a list of names, settings, and approximate time frames for most of the images in this book. Because the images are meant to be evocative rather than representational, some of them were created using image-editing software. The images are listed by page number.

Preface

How to Read This Book

As I began to write this book, I discovered that two voices were emerging from my "self"—often speaking simultaneously. I realized that in the furthest reaches of my memory, these two voices have always existed. I thought back and found that many times in my life I acted on the intentions shaped by one or the other, but not necessarily by both of these voices.

One voice seemed to hold the shape of my rising and falling breath, sometimes seemed to enfold all my experiences into loving acceptance, yet at other times seemed to come from a place of dimly understood pain or non-integration. This voice seemed to be the privileged interpreter of experience and ancestry as a source of knowledge.

The other voice seemed to try to represent itself, wanting to categorize and explain, delighting in the process of abstracting, containing, and sometimes obscuring my experience. This voice constantly fought for closure and enjoyed grappling with every theory that could in any way explain my current reality.

In listening to these two voices I realized that over time both of these voices had developed in peculiar ways. One voice developed into my personal "self-talk" voice; another developed into my public or school voice. True, sometimes they overlapped or visited one another, or found a close harmony, maybe even a passage or two in unison. But often these voices sat up at night arguing, fought over my intention or behavior, struggled to choke one another out, even lied to one another.

Worse yet, sometimes these voices simultaneously discussed two entirely unrelated topics. At those moments I could always silence one of the voices. Or I could occupy the place between the voices, searching there for a connection between them. The place between those two voices was not a comfortable place to occupy.

As I wrote this book, I decided to let these voices do what they usually do. They tend to speak as separate voices, sometimes estranged from each other, sometimes echoing one another, sometimes simply co-existing. I decided that it would be important for them to do that. It seemed that my "grappling, struggling voice" had developed into the voice I write with when I write academically. Maybe the academic world has offered an outlet for that sometimes distanced voice. That voice tends to take over; it focuses on trying to win arguments.

My "self-talk" voice usually appears in the left column of these pages, which is also sometimes occupied by letters, the voices of others, or journal entries. My academic voice usually appears in the right column and spills over into endnotes. In fact, endnotes have become a way to try to contain that voice. As I interview people, their voices take over the left column entirely. Their voices take the place of my "self-talk" voice, as they offer clues to experience, ancestry, and the source of knowledge. At those times I limit my "analysis" to the right column, because the meanings I construct in the right column are dependent on the definitive voices of those I interviewed in the left column. This relationship reflects the way that the voices of those I interviewed continue to manifest in my life.

The left and right columns of this book comprise two descriptions of the journey I have taken, and what I learned on the way. There is also a place that lives between those two columns, those two voices. It is where transformation occurred, and it is inhabited by dreams and symbols. In this book that place shifts. Sometimes it arrives on the left, sometimes on the right, sometimes on both sides. That place is without words and communicates through images or silent, empty space.

Shutting out either voice would silence that place in between those two voices. It would obscure the threshold I occupy. That threshold is a state of knowing and not knowing, of looking in and looking out, of feeling grounded and feeling adrift. I realize that this offers you, the reader, a difficult challenge at times. There isn't always a tight fit, or closure between these two voices, and the "space in-between" can be a frustrating space to occupy.

Enter this text any way you wish. One voice may seem boring, or obscure, or over-emotional, or stilted. Whenever something doesn't make sense, just let it go by. Read only what you wish to read. You may end up only on one side, or only reading sections of this text. That is probably for the best. This book was not written to be a closed, integrated whole. That would misrepresent the nature of the journey. I hope that in entering this text in whatever way you decide, you find something, some voice or some silent place, which draws you.

Introduction

This book is about my attempts to understand how certain Hawaiian *kūpuna* (elders) talk about knowledge and transformation. It is about how their knowledge led me into my Hawaiian ancestry, which, for most of my life, I believed I would never find. It is about interviewing *kūpuna* and about the transforming power of their knowledge. As long as their knowledge connects us to those who are no longer living, our ancestry can never truly be lost.

Trying to understand the words of certain *kūpuna* has been a journey for me. If I were to write as I wrote during most of my graduate work at University, only an incomplete road map of that journey would emerge. My dreams would not be in the story.[1] The story of how my learning transformed my life would be left out.[2]

On the other hand, to write as if this story were only a story of personal transformation would exclude certain theories or stories about social change that I grappled with at University. My conversations with those theories were an important part of my life transformation.

According to Pukui and Elbert's 1986 Hawaiian dictionary, *kupuna* means: "Grandparent, ancestor, relative or close friend of the grandparent's generation" (186). Although Hawaiian *kūpuna* traditionally passed down knowledge in their families, many *kūpuna* also share certain types of knowledge outside their families.

In recent times the word *kupuna* has often been used to refer to elders or those of the "grandparent generation." However, just being of a certain age is not the only determiner of who seems to be called *"kupuna."* This term is often used for older people who are expert in Hawaiian culture.

Many *kūpuna* engage in activities associated with groups such as churches, Hawaiian civic clubs, *hālau hula* (schools where Hawaiian dance or *hula* is taught), state-sponsored school programs, and sovereignty organizations.

Although it is hard to track how their knowledge is taken up, it is certain that many *kūpuna* are esteemed because of their wisdom. This is not to say that all *kūpuna* are leaders, or are wise, but it can be said that their voices are invoked by others in cultural and political realms.

It is strange to live at the confluence of stories of those *kūpuna* and stories I heard at University. Certainly, each sort of story offers a particular genealogy of knowledge and of knowledge production. Alone, each story has the capacity to distance me from a part of myself or from a community I enter. I harbor a sense of this distance; yet as I write, I also harbor a sense that I am being carried along by my ancestors.

Intensive recovery of language and culture is taking place among Hawaiians. Hawaiians are also retelling and interrogating history. These powerful trends are intertwined with the drive for sovereignty in Hawai'i.

The voices of *kūpuna* are pivotal in many undertakings, threading through complex and contested discourses. These discourses, in turn, weave through the varied and fluid terrain of Hawaiian communities, urban and rural, on- and off-island.

In this book are the voices of a few *kūpuna* and people whose lives they touched. I thank those who shared their knowledge and helped me begin to understand where I come from and where I am going.

1 Searching Through Texts

Texting Memory

I did not meet my birth mother, and she seems to have kept my birth secret from everyone, so no "true" memories of my birth are given to me. Throughout my childhood I did have a recurring dream. It is not verifiable by others, so it is safe to say that it cannot be a memory. Rather, it is inauthentic, a stand-in for memory. Its pedigree unconfirmed, it hides behind my eyes, its own feral eyes glistening, its fangs bared. It is just a dream.

I have just been born. I am on my back being wheeled in something: four empty straight sides, a bed, a table, moved by a hand. I look up at white walls, am almost blinded by a bright, harsh light overhead.

A Hawaiian woman with marcelled hair and white clothing looms over me, looking ahead, hands on the bars of this cart that contains me. Occasionally she looks down at me. Light seems to stream out of her head, blurring her face. On my right, the edge of a face, a man's face, passes, floating by. Footsteps. He is wearing white. Light from behind him makes his edge-face look flattened out as he walks away.

A particular kind of history can be told about Hawai'i—a history governed by dates, events, and material processes. This history has an academic pedigree, and comes with footnotes. It is not "passed down" through tears or rage. Many minds, schooled in objectivity, have a part in continually shaping, contesting, and consequently reshaping it. The authenticity of this history is resistant to challenge. It is less likely to be called "imaginary" or "invented." This history, however narrowed, might be less painful to hear than a history shaped by storylines, the fangs of memory and identity, or a need to set a course for the future.

Prior to 1778: While governed by the *ali'i* (chiefly class), *'ohana* (extended families) share food from the land through a system of communal land use (McGregor 1996, 5). Genealogically, *ali'i* are viewed as descending from the gods (Kame'eleihiwa 1992, 40). A complex system of law, the *kapu* system, sets *ali'i* apart as a class (Herman 1996, 83). Chant and *hula* tell of creation, history, genealogy, the deities, and people's deep relationship to the cosmos.

I wait. I am aware that someone, or something, is floating away from me. I already remember being held up by a hand, another edge of a face nearby. The face, moving away, beginning to flatten out. Laughter or crying, or both, a sobbing sound. A thought or emotion bubbles up in me that I cannot name.

For most of my life, the story of my birth has not had the status of a "story." It is not an account of a series of events that we are certain happened, nor is it a statement of "known facts." The story of my birth is actually more like the anthropological notion of an "origin myth." It is not verifiable, perhaps imaginary, perhaps explaining something that is, at its core, inexplicable. I prefer to call it an "origin myth" since for most of my life it has been a fiction that (like a myth) has served to organize my worldview.[1]

During our life together, my adoptive parents told and retold their version of events which eventually led to my adoption:

It is the 1930s or 1940s. My adoptive-mother-to-be is a tall Texan woman, blonde, thin, laughing. She works in clerical jobs. She is sweet, thoughtful, smart as a whip. She meets my adoptive-father-to-be. He is a pianist, talented, witty, urbane. They fall in love.

She discovers that she cannot have children, at about the time that he proposes to her. She must have her uterus removed. She breaks up with him and goes off alone to have the operation. She plans to remain single. He finds her in the hospital, tells her he loves her and can't

1778: Captain Cook "discovers" Hawai'i. While in the islands Cook's men engage in *kapu* violation repeatedly and with impunity. This causes both *ali'i* and *maka'āinana* (commoners) to begin to question sacred law (Kame'eleihiwa 1992, 67). Cook's visits also involve attempts to impose European laws, based on the centrality of private property, onto Hawaiian society (Herman 1996, 81–87).

1795: Kamehameha I unifies the islands. The years between 1778 and 1820 are a period of global mercantile capitalism in Hawai'i, involving the fur and sandalwood trades, then whaling (Kent 1983, 16, 19; Merry 2000, 23).

1820: American missionaries arrive and English, a language ill-equipped to articulate Hawaiian values, grows to dominate public life (Buck 1993; Trask 1993). A resident merchant community of non-Hawaiians emerges. Hawaiians experience a population collapse.

1843: Hawai'i is recognized by England and France as an independent state. The *kapu* system governed by the *mō'ī* (king) and *ali'i* begins to shift to a system of Anglo-American common law and the missionaries advocate individual land ownership (Merry 2000).

1848: In the Māhele, government lands are opened to foreigners. By 1897, foreigners own most of the land and dominate the economy (H. Trask 1993). Land shifts from control of Hawaiian leadership and communal use to private ownership based on a capitalist model. Hawaiians are dispossessed.[2] Through immigration and land use policies, sugar planters avoid U.S. tariffs and protect profits.

give her up. He tells her they can adopt a child. They marry.

In my adoptive mother's story, last told just before her death, the two of them are living in Honolulu. She is bored, lonely, wants to have a child. They agree it is time to adopt an infant. She visits Child and Family Services, where I have recently returned from a stay with a foster family in Mānoa Valley.

When she sees me at Child and Family Services, she recognizes me. She knows me, has always known me. She chooses me.

1859: *Hula* is banned by law (Silva 2000, 29) and goes underground into Hawaiian *'ohana.* A foreign-dominated economy centering on large sugar plantations and mills results in further dispossession of Hawaiians from the land and disruption of communal economies.

1887: King David Kalākaua is forced by a covert group of mostly Caucasian-American annexationists to sign the Bayonet Constitution. This document eliminates the King's power over the legislature, imposes a property qualification on voting that prevents many Hawaiians from voting, and extends franchise to foreigners. The King is reduced to a figurehead. Hawaiians organize in protest (Silva 1998, 45).

1891: King Kalākaua dies. Lili'uokalani becomes Queen.

1893: After attempting to promulgate a new constitution, Queen Lili'uokalani is deposed by a "Provisional Government" (American sugar interests) backed by an occupying force of Marines. In 1894, the Provisional Government declares itself to be the Republic of Hawai'i.

1895: The Wilcox rebellion, an attempt to reinstate Lili'uokalani, is thwarted.[3] The Queen is tried for treason, found guilty, and imprisoned in her palace. She abdicates under duress, never to be restored to power. A rich legacy of Hawaiian response to these incursions survives both in texts and in Hawaiian oral tradition (Silva 2004).

This version of my origin myth was told to me by my adoptive parents:

I was born in Honolulu in 1952, when Hawai'i was still a territory of the United States. My birth mother was part Hawaiian. She was connected with some sort of royal Hawaiian society, which met in Nu'uanu at the place where our relatives were buried. My birth mother claimed to be of royal Hawaiian blood. She was a theater usherette.

My birth mother gave me up to foster care. I lived at a foster home in Mānoa Valley until I was adopted at the age of seven months or so.

The instructions for my care, that were given to my adoptive mother, are now fragile, yellowed documents that she saved. They verify her story that I once lived in Mānoa:

Child is used to Manoa weather (just above Punahou School) and has slept nights with a light blanket. . . . Holding her seems to encourage kicking around a lot and spitting up milk. She is used to being left in crib with bottle propped up.

Easy as it is to find my geography in these yellowed pages, it is harder to find my self. Depending on how I choose to read these pages, I am either a self-sufficient, independent infant, or an infant who already does not know how to be held.

Later, when I am becoming part of the household, my new mother tries to communicate with me, to teach me "yes" and "no." I don't respond to the angry tone in her voice when she reprimands me. She experiments, having heard that my Mānoa Valley foster

1897: The United States unsuccessfully attempts to annex Hawai'i through treaty. Hawaiians organize resistance against annexation and over 90% of them sign a petition against annexation (Silva 2004, 123–163).

1898: The U.S. Congress passes a joint resolution to annex Hawai'i. Hawai'i becomes a colonial territory. Hawai'i, a plantation society, is now an economic satellite and strategic military outpost of the United States.

1900: The Organic Act unilaterally imposes U.S. citizenship on Hawaiians.[4] Executive power is vested in the governor of Hawai'i, who is appointed by the president of the United States (Andrade 1996, 189–190).

1921: The Hawaiian Homes Commission Act allots nearly 200,000 acres of the poorest, most underdeveloped and inaccessible agricultural lands to Hawaiians (H. Trask 2000a, 10). This legislation distinguishes Hawaiians of 50% blood quantum as beneficiaries, reducing the number of potential beneficiaries (Kauanui 1999a, 127; H. Trask 1993, 71).

Mid-1950s: The U.S. military conducts test bombing on the island of Kaho'olawe. Tourist resorts and land developers rapidly encroach on Hawaiian lands. Hawaiians are recruited as labor, along with new immigrants.

1959: Through a process that is essentially illegal under international law, Hawai'i becomes a state.[5] Tourism ties Hawai'i to global corporate structures. Hawaiian culture, particularly *hula*, is used to attract tourists (Buck 1993; H. Trask 1993, H. Trask 2000b). *Hula kahiko* (ancient *hula*) continues to be nurtured in Hawaiian families and communities.

family was Chinese. She admonishes me one day, imitating a tonal language, letting her voice swoop up and down. I listen, and seem to hear her; I respond.

In one photo taken by my new mom, my new dad lifts me up against the blue sky. My mouth is frozen in a delighted scream. My baby-edges feather into the clouds behind me.

When he was in his mid-80s, my dad flew his car off a mountain embankment, flipping it over and crash-landing upside down at the bottom of a ravine. As he later described how he hung, uninjured but bemused, by his seatbelt in the totaled car, I unaccountably remembered him holding me, swinging me up into the air, up, down, safe in his arms.

Hundreds of photos from my infancy with my adoptive parents should provide tangible evidence of something. Yet they seem as amorphous as my parents' memories. Sometimes I seem to blur into the scenery, and I invoke no memories. Other times my image seems sharper and I focus in on the photo, using it to conjure up pseudo-memories or to color my present-day feelings for my parents.

Mid-1960s: Hawai'i's economy is dependent on the American military and tourism. As land prices soar, many Hawaiians can no longer afford to live on their own land. They organize resistance to development. Others go off-island to the U.S. continent to find jobs and affordable housing.

Early 1970s: Land development, tourism, and military expansion become intolerable for many Hawaiians. Pig farmers, *kalo* (taro) farmers, tenants, fishermen, and small landowners resist eviction with varying degrees of success. Others become homeless "beach people." Businesses concerned about the effect of "beach people" on tourism re-evict the "beach people" from the beaches.

Mid-1970s: Beliefs in the sacredness of land, communal ways of life, and Hawaiian self-determination are shared by groups dedicated to sovereignty. *Protect Kaho'olawe 'Ohana*, dedicated to the termination of military test bombing on Kaho'olawe, articulates the belief that Kaho'olawe is the goddess Hina's home. *The Pele Defense Fund*, dedicated to the prevention of geothermal drilling on the volcano Kīlauea, articulates the belief that Kīlauea is the goddess Pele's home. A Hawaiian delegation to the U.S. Congress enters a bill for reparations for losses sustained as a result of the overthrow of the Queen and subsequent annexation. No action is taken.

1978: OHA (Office of Hawaiian Affairs) is established as a state agency to administer Hawaiian lands. OHA later broadens its scope, advocating for self-government and encouraging dialogue on Hawaiian sovereignty. A "Hawaiian Renaissance" or cultural revival intensifies as people embrace Hawaiian arts, language, history, and music—particularly chant and *hula kahiko*. The past and historical memory become increasingly powerful for Hawaiians.

One story my father tells about our early years in Hawai'i describes a trip we took to the fire pit at Halema'uma'u on the Big Island (the island of Hawai'i), where the goddess Pele lives. Photos from that time, perhaps another form of evidence, perhaps not, show me, for once, without a smile. I take these photos to be my history.

My father says that as they drove away from Halema'uma'u, he and my mother experienced an odd sense of anxiety. Later, driving on the saddle road, they saw a red light appear ahead of them on the road. The light stayed ahead of them a distance, and moved steadily forward. Eventually when the road curved around, the red light continued moving and went straight into the forest, where no road or path could be seen. Then it disappeared.

This story, which I first heard as a child, has always captivated me. Many times, as a child, I asked my parents to repeat it for me. As an adult, until recently, I only shared it with others who were very close to me. I never asked others to help me interpret it. I have always believed that it somehow resists interpretation.

So, why do I rehearse it, amplify it in my own mind? Maybe because it is a story about the presence of powerful forces who are usually undetected. Or maybe I imagine it as a story about how I was somehow watched over, or protected. Or maybe it allows me to sustain some notion of ancestry, so crucial to my origin myth, whose tangled, fragile threads could so easily unravel.

1980s: The environmental and social consequences of tourism and its place in Hawai'i's future are hotly debated. Hawaiians continue to migrate to the continental United States to escape economic hardships. Restitution from the American government and Hawaiian formation of a land base become core issues in the sovereignty argument. Hawaiian sovereignty is argued by defendants in eviction court cases and taken to international forums such as the United Nations.

1990s: The proliferation of pro-sovereignty organizations and differences in philosophy and practice among them generate debate about the form self-determination should take and the means to achieve it. These groups assert the ethics of *aloha 'āina* (love of the land) and *mālama 'āina* (protection of the land). They contest non-Hawaiian versions of Hawaiian history, engage in traditional cultural practices, file legal claims, stage mass demonstrations and occupations, and support people resisting eviction due to land development. Hawaiian beliefs, images, and practices, such as *hula kahiko*, continue to sustain political activity.

1993: Public Law 103–150 (U.S. Congress 1993) is passed, constituting public recognition that the overthrow of the Hawaiian Kingdom was illegal. In this formal apology to the Hawaiian people the United States admits governmental complicity and support of the overthrow. It also acknowledges that the Hawaiian people never relinquished claims to their inherent sovereignty. Hawaiians continue journeying toward some form of self-determination as public debate and cultural practice intensify.

2000: The U.S. Supreme Court rules in *Rice versus Cayetano* that the ancestry qualification for voters of the Office of Hawaiian Affairs is unconstitutional. This ruling threatens to unravel OHA's role as a form of self-government for indigenous Hawaiians and to unravel programs that benefit indigenous Hawaiians (Osorio 2001).

My parents' stories and photographs constitute only one version of the story of my birth, my origin myth. Unlike my recurring dream, these stories are verifiable by my parents to some extent. They can almost be confirmed, so they are almost authentic. They are domesticated, without fangs. They are safe.

Other, more specific, versions of the story exist, in the hands of people I do not know. Most probably these other stories that exist about my birth are not told. For my birth mother, and perhaps others, these stories have fangs, are not safe.

In the photographs of my new mom and me, we are in perpetual motion, wind whipping through our hair. Sun and sand filter into one another, and she floats in her cotton dress. She is radiant, sun shining from the inside out. Her face, hair, are incidental to her mom-self that bursts my middle-aged heart.

This version of Hawaiian history is brief. It only barely describes precolonial Hawai'i and emphasizes the effects of colonization. Another version could emphasize the many years of Hawaiian self-rule and minimize colonization as a temporary recess in Hawaiian history.

This version of Hawaiian history centers around the effects of a cash economy (or capitalism) on Hawai'i, de-emphasizing the continuity of Hawaiian culture. Another version could emphasize the continuity of oral tradition and continuing relationships to the land on the part of Hawaiian families.

This version of Hawaiian history names the sources of social change as the incursion of capital and people's responses to that process; humans are the sole actors in this story. Another version could emphasize the behavior/intentions of ancestors, deities, stones, other Earth beings, or the cosmos itself.

I actually remember only the sound of the rushing waves and the feel of the sand, shifting beneath my feet. It could be that this is not a memory, but instead just the way my body invokes emotion. Now that my mother is dead, when I look at these photographs it seems we are gasping for breath, gasping for time, beached on the shore, spinning.

While my new parents' photos offer no confirming evidence about who I am, they do offer testament about who my parents are. Whether they hold me or simply occupy the same space, they exist in these frames not as my "adoptive parents," but as my parents.

Yet just now, my birth parents have no real identities. They are named by me with qualifiers: birth mother, birth father.

Unlike my birth parents, my parents emerge in every photo. If I seem alone it is only because they are out of sight, behind the lens of the camera. These parents, who named me as their daughter, exist for me as one word: mother or father. Their feelings peek out at me through the tiny testifying lens of their camera. The trails of all other histories are for the moment written over, scratched out.

This version of Hawaiian history is a commonly heard and said version. It is only one version of the story of Hawai'i. Other versions of the story exist.

In particular, this version of Hawaiian history does not include Hawaiian land as a presence. Only in passing does it recognize a relationship between the land and the indigenous people of Hawai'i. Further, the idea that this relationship was ruptured by colonization is not posited, nor is a notion of how that rupture might be healed.

Histories and theories emerge from particular kinds of stories and their telling can be viewed as a kind of practice of storytelling. Like the personal stories we tell, histories and theories reproduce our worldviews.

This version of Hawaiian history is a story about indigenous "destiny" told from a point of view outside Hawaiian indigenous knowledge. Dei (2000) describes indigenous knowledge as grounded on the long-standing spiritual relationships that indigenous peoples have with Earth. Worldwide, indigenous peoples speak of a protective relationship to the earth, which has ruptured, and which must be healed.

Berry (1991) describes humans as autistic—locked away from a conversation with Earth. For me, the language used in this version of Hawaiian history has that autistic quality. Earth is not included as a conversant. In this version Earth has been written over, scratched out.

In these early photos, I am rarely surrounded by Caucasians or *haole*. Every once in a while a *haole* pops up, a visitor from the mainland, a dignitary visiting a church service. For the most part, other than my parents, the arms that hold me, the faces that lean toward mine, belong to local people, of non-Caucasian descent.

Through a policy of listing the adopted child's ethnicity as that of the adoptive parents, which existed when I was born, I was listed as Caucasian on my birth certificate. In fact, on paper, I am more like my new parents than the local people who encircle me in these photos. I like to believe that this information would probably not be relevant or even plausible for the local people who inhabit these photos.

My father got a job in Cleveland, Ohio, and our family moved there. I was about four years old. I have a photograph taken just before my trip on the *Lurline*, an ocean liner traveling to the mainland where I would live with my parents. I cling to my mother's skirts as she stands with a couple of other *haole* women.

In my version of this story, this particular photo is pivotal. It is important to me that my "self" in this photo does not visually match the information on my birth certificate. I choose to imagine that the people in this photo know and are even thinking about "what" I am *not*. In my version of this story, I stand on the threshold of a new set of relevancies. From within my version of this story, I look at the photo and imagine my face drawn inward, my body motionless, waiting.[6]

Stories are always subject to formatting and reformatting. As a *kupuna* tells a story about a personal experience, that *kupuna* formats the experience for the listeners. I may reformat it to fit my own needs, employing practices I learned at University or from my community. Some ways of reformatting might distance me from the teller's intent. Other ways may spiral me down deeper into that intent.

My constant reformatting of my own stories or the stories of others links them to my present-day intentions. These links between narrative and intention have no place in the imaginary world of truth value because that world is imaginary. Yet these links have consequences.

Both personal stories and theoretical paradigms in a given academic discipline sustain cosmologies. So what languages do we—*kūpuna*, professors, students, listeners—choose to use? What are the consequences of the languages we choose?

I remember very little of our early days in Cleveland. I remember the biting cold and the crunching sound that snow made underfoot, like bones. I remember the hallway of the hotel we stayed in had a musty smell, which I then associated with "old ladies." I remember making, then hiding in, elaborate caves in the huge snow banks that accumulated in our front yard.

My parents have a story about our move. They remember that I had problems wearing shoes after being continually barefoot. I spoke some Hawaiian or pidgin words as if they were common English. Snow was strange to me. Shortly after our move to Cleveland I became ill. Nobody knew what it was. It lasted for almost a year: fevers, weeping, and flu-like symptoms. My parents took me to a variety of doctors who were unable to diagnose it. Finally, they took me to a doctor who just talked to me. After that I was fine.

Although *The Kumulipo*, or Hawaiian creation chant, has been interpreted by various researchers, I'd like to talk here about my process of "reading it" rather than their interpretations. I'm not an interpretive authority on *The Kumulipo*, but I can describe voices emerging from my own heart in response to its narrative.

The hearts and minds of those who produced *The Kumulipo* are unavailable to me. Their language and its referents live in an inaccessible world, outside my experience. It is hard to explain their language using categories existing in my own language: English. Although the English version of *The Kumulipo* I read is a translation by Lili'uokalani, it is nevertheless a translation, already distanced from the mother chant.

Further, an academic language that might make *The Kumulipo* accessible to a particular audience might also write over its references and deeper layers. So I do not intend to discuss this work using writing on Hawaiian epistemology, or any set of fixed interpretations.

I have no memory of this time except for that of the large, freckled white face of the doctor. At the time, and until I was about thirteen or so, freckles and orange hair fascinated me. This is how I remember the doctor, tattooed in freckles, orange hair sprouting like sunrays around his round face. I remember that his face loomed over me, as he spoke to me in a calm voice for what seemed like hours.

The suburb of Cleveland where we lived was mostly "Caucasian," with only a few Asians. My parents, being of non-Hawaiian extraction, were not in a position to help fulfill my hunger to know about Hawaiian culture.

My birth story changed when I was ten years old. I had been reading "Nancy Drew" spy stories voraciously, one after another. I still remember their plain yet inviting webbed, dark blue covers. My mother received them either free or cheap from somewhere, and they stacked up like cords of wood on the ledge in my bedroom.

Somehow, as part of the fantasy world created in these texts, I invented for myself an identity. I decided that my real name was Amy Nolan. Like Nancy Drew, I had a task to "get to the bottom of things," find the truth, and tell all interested parties the news about "Amy."

I also had dreams where an old, Asian-looking face looked down at me, murmuring "Eemee, eemee." That face, hovering over me like a glowing moon, thin, wrinkled, and weathered, comforted me at night, moving me to tears. White bedroom window curtains fluttered, opening out into darkness and spongy

Instead, since I have limited knowledge of Hawaiian culture and language, it is most useful for me to describe my struggle to understand *The Kumulipo*, noting the gaps in my understanding and what I have learned from those gaps. I can also describe parts of *The Kumulipo* or themes emanating from it that move me, as a learner rather than an expert. These thoughts may say as much about where I come from as they do about where *The Kumulipo* seems to come from.[7]

From the overthrow until the annexation of Hawai'i to the United States, Queen Lili'uokalani labored over her translation of *The Kumulipo*. Her title page reads:

An Account of the Creation of the World according to Hawaiian Tradition: translated from original manuscripts preserved exclusively in her majesty's family by Lili'uokalani of Hawai'i; . . . for Ka Ii Mamao, from him to his daughter Alapai Wahine, Lili'uokalani's Great-Grandmother, composed by Keaulumoku in 1700 and translated by Lili'uokalani during her imprisonment in 1895 at 'Iolani Palace. . . . (Lili'uokalani 1978, frontispiece)

This title page is a difficult read for me; I want to skim it because it specifies events distanced historically, not only from my present, but also from Lili'uokalani's present. This points to how she framed *The Kumulipo* in relation to her genealogy and to its displacement by outsiders. Her introduction states:

front lawns where streetlights made tentacled shadows. When I imagined Eemee Face, and her high-pitched murmurings to me, I could be pulled out of fear, into sleep.

Oddly, Eemee Face was related to the perky Nancy Drew mysteries that I devoured by flashlight under the bedcovers. In one story Nancy and her faithful girlfriend George tracked down eerie night cries and ghostly manifestations, contradicting boys who wouldn't believe their stories. I read this story over and over again.

I told my parents my story and described Eemee Face. Then they told me that my name in foster care, before my adoption, was Amy Notley. They told me they believed that while I was in care of a Chinese-Hawaiian family that lived in Mānoa, the grandmother had held me, cared for me, and had called me "Eemee," her version of "Amy."

Early on I believed that after giving birth to me, my birth mother died. In this version of my origin myth there was no one to care for me, no one I belonged to, so I had to be adopted out. This version of my origin myth was a hungry poem, an imaginary history to recite.

I remember wondering about my birth mother as I sat in my Ohio bedroom. I was probably about ten years old at the time. The clock downstairs struck every fifteen minutes, and its ticktickticking was by turns irritating and consoling, a constant wordless mantra. I remember dust motes floating through the air, visually amplified by the sun filtering in through a snowy window.

There are several reasons for the publication of this work, the translation of which pleasantly employed me while imprisoned by the present rulers of Hawaii. (ibid., Introduction)

It should not surprise me that Lili'uokalani made it clear that her work occurred during an intense political struggle, yet this is "news" for me. I think it is "news" because I have been schooled to believe in a pristine or "authentic" Hawaiian culture, "untainted" by political intentions. In reality, it should not be hard to imagine Lili'uokalani trapped in her palace fighting for her Kingdom and taking refuge in and perhaps deploying an ancient text.[8]

Lili'uokalani wrote of *The Kumulipo* as offering a "souvenir" of her life, the genealogy of her line, allusions to Hawai'i's natural history and "the folk-lore or traditions of an aboriginal people" (ibid., Introduction).

I falter in my reading as she calls it a "souvenir" of her life, since it is not about her life, but reaches into events which predate her life. It is as if her life, on some level, is an expression of historical memory.

It also surprises me that Lili'uokalani used the term "aboriginal," positing an indigenous identity for Hawaiians in the late 1890s.[9] I find myself again reflecting on my schooling and the notion that indigenous people only have a conscious sense of identity when they have "almost completely acculturated." Lili'uokalani states that *The Kumulipo* was chanted by High Priest Puou to Captain Cook:

I truly believed my birth mother was dead, a spirit already. She rattled around, echoing in my head. We conducted ghost conversations that I invented. I imagined her reaching toward me from beyond death, and I think I sometimes cocked my head towards her voice, reaching for her, behind my eyes. This didn't happen often. I did try unsuccessfully to reach her once on my ouija board, but I don't recall being disappointed at our failure to connect.

My aunt told me this story:

I am taking a bath. My mother is outside the bathroom talking to my aunt. I call to my mother: "If I wash really hard, will my brown come off?" My voice sounds matter-of-fact. According to my aunt: "You didn't know what you were saying." My mother leans against the door to my room and says: "No. Why would you want to do that?" Her eyes fill with tears. My aunt's story ends here.

My mother told me this story:

I am outside on the driveway playing with a child who is calling me "nigger." My mother pauses at the window to hear what will happen next. I tell him that I am Hawaiian, from a faraway island. I am a princess, I tell him.

I have no memory of either of these incidents. I do remember trying to get even with a kid who called me "nigger" by running up behind him to yank him off his bike. I remember a number of incidents like that. I also remember running away from a little boy who was in love with

. . . whom they had surnamed Lono, one of the four chief gods, dwelling high in the heavens, but at times appearing on the earth. . . . Captain Cook's appearance was regarded by our people then as a confirmation of their own traditions. For it was prophesied by priests at the time of the death of Ka-I-i-mamao that he, Lono, would return anew from the sea in a Spanish man-of-war or Auwaalalua. (ibid., Introduction)

This statement describes historic events as confirmation of prophecy suggesting that history comprises sequences of admonitions and lessons.

Lili'uokalani refers to her ancestors, particularly those for whom this chant was composed. Her way of naming her lineage is hypnotic, yet hard to follow. Frustrated, I try to untangle what I believe for Lili'uokalani was the simplest naming of genealogical relationships. I need a chart to understand these connections. Lili'uokalani experienced herself as the end of a royal lineage tracing itself back to the mating of sky with earth to create life. I have difficulty understanding this profound sense of belonging, or connection, so central to her introduction and to *The Kumulipo* itself.

The term *kumulipo* can be translated as "origin genesis, source of life, mystery" (Pukui and Elbert 1986, 182, 208).[10] It is a progression of naming which centers around the reproduction of life, beginning with male and female principles, then detailing the births of species before the entrance of humans. Males and females of

me, climbing innumerable hospitable oak or apple trees, nibbling on mint or honeysuckle, catching bees or fireflies in a jar, picking wild roses near the railroad tracks, building forts behind the garage, and trying to fry an egg on the sidewalk in summer.

Apparently there were no Hawaiians in our community. Although I knew that I was Hawaiian, I had very little idea of what that meant. When I was in grade school, on International Day I was to have my photo taken for the town newspaper. I remember my mother looking for plastic flowers to shape into some facsimile of a *lei* and sewing a long flowered dress that could "look Hawaiian." I was dressed up in the *muumuu* she made, and wore her plastic *lei,* and people took pictures of me. I remember enjoying the attention and feeling special. I also remember feeling that she was somehow struggling with the materials she had, to put it all together. It was a little like Halloween for that reason—involving an effort on my mother's part, to help me put together a costume.[11]

In geography class in fourth grade I became obsessed with volcanoes and wrote a report on Kīlauea complete with a crayola illustration of a brilliant orange, exploding island.

My parents never took me back to Hawai'i. Outside of an old Kamaka *'ukulele*, a thin, yellowed book of "pidginized" fairy tales, monkey pod artifacts, photos, and a few record albums, I had no connection with things Hawaiian.

I dreamed constantly of an elderly man in white and of a middle-aged woman in a

various species emerge and bear offspring of related species.

The repeated phrase: "A night of flight by noises, Through a channel; water is life to trees; So the gods may enter, but not man" (Lili'uokalani 1978, 2) evokes in me an image of movement in the night. Water appears here as the essence of life. In the word "channel" I find myself predictably referencing the birth canal.

What stands out for me in many of these phrases is that there is no human presence, nor is there the presence of a specific being that creates plant and animal life. Instead plant and animal life manifest themselves and give birth. Species from the ocean are paired with species of like name on land, to guard them (ibid., 2).

Fish are named and paired in poetic specificity. Creatures that occupy specific structural categories are not named together. Rather, disparate species whose names seem to be poetically related are linked.

Along with the repetition, this strikes me as a mnemonic device for the chanter. However, as I read this text, it also seems to represent a way of seeing the cosmos.

This way of naming earth creatures connects them, not through structure, but through protective or genealogical relationships. The cosmos is seen as a series of interconnected protective relationships. My own lack of connection with these creatures is evidenced by my desire to skim over these passages. These creatures, predating humans, experience intent:

long black dress. They looked like photos of Hawaiians I had seen, so I figured they must be Hawaiian. I thought they were ghosts. He appeared at night, and she appeared when I was ill.

I would often dream about walking into a lush rainforest. I could hear the dew dropping, and periodically rain would rush gently down onto the leafy branches. I would do nothing in this dream but walk and walk. It seemed in these dreams that I could not stop moving.

Occasionally as I turned to follow the path, I would suddenly see eyes peering out at me from behind every leaf. They would blink and disappear. I walked in a forest of silent eyes. I could awaken at any time, but the forest of eyes would still remain pressed to the backs of my eyelids.

Sometimes I thought that my birth mother was gazing at me from those eyes. Sometimes I felt that I stared out at myself from those eyes. Eventually I grew to believe that my birth mother was the silent forest itself, inhabited by eyes but no mouths. The inhale and exhale of the forest matched her heartbeat. But beyond that steadily beating heart, there was only empty observation.

There were a few other "people of color" at my high school and at my friends' high schools, so I found sources of deep identification with other "minority" kids. At some point during this time I was shown my birth certificate, and learned that I was listed as Caucasian. This knowledge connected me to nothing, held no referents or meanings for me.

The train of Palaoa (walrus) *that swim by*
Embracing only the deep blue waters,
Also the Opule *that move in schools,*
The deep is as nothing to them . . .
(ibid., 11)

My impulse is to skim over this writing, since it does not focus on "acts" like the stories or histories I'm used to, but instead focuses on beings who are manifesting. Yet I am captured by the poetry at another level, transcending meaning. As I utter the words, I am pulled into the rhythm of the Hawaiian language. For me, this process of naming becomes a path to a transcendent state. I am not sure that it is necessary to know the exact meaning and referents for each word to be transported into this state.[12]

If I read *The Kumulipo* without relying on outside commentary, I feel a constant tension. This tension lies in my feeling that its meaning does not lie solely in the words and referents attending the written text. My reading seems to be a "modern" one which doesn't foreground the auditory power of the text. Committing this chant to memory, chanting, and hearing it were probably profound ways of knowing it. Ronald Silvers (1994, 1) states:

Some summers I went to Wind River Indian Reservation in Wyoming with a volunteer group that taught pre-school children and painted buildings there. When I was with my Indian friends, I felt as if I finally blended in. I felt at home.

What I remember of myself at my mostly white high school is my bitterness. I have kept my journals from English class. My writing seems so far from what my English teacher must have wanted. It is too embarrassing for me to read. I write cynical scenarios involving a laughing, manic Charlie Chan; an imperialistic, clueless Lone Ranger; an embittered Tonto; a jaded, racist Abraham Lincoln.

I can talk of nothing but racism. Am I obsessed with it? Do I imagine it? Or is it there, sitting on my back, digging its knees into my kidneys? Some of my "minority" friends from that time remember a shared siege mentality, a sense that we were being marked or seen as separate. One Caucasian friend from that time says that I suffered imagined slights and carried a chip on my shoulder. My story unravels here and meaning escapes me.[13]

. . . The importance of sound and therefore orality . . . may overtake (the) meaning of words and their objective referents; . . . words may . . . intensify their significance for the reader when the reader occupies a particular mode of consciousness. The reader must read aloud rather than silently to enter that universe; . . . the sounds of the words are found in the "indissoluble unity" between the words and their objects.

Thus to use words is to call their meaning into being. . . . To read them silently and within a context of a referential linguistic meaning (a meaning beyond their immediacy) is to take a text from its own grounding and thereby violate its presence.

When I was a senior in high school, the Concert Glee Club from Kamehameha Schools in Hawai'i performed in Cleveland. My parents decided to host a Hawaiian girl and take me to the event. The girl came home for dinner, spent the night, ate breakfast with us, and left the next day. She seemed shy. The silences were awkward. We had nothing to talk about. My parents talked to her. I did not know where to begin, and said very little.

As the sea washes the land, beings who seem to be gods or half-god, half-animal emerge; and the motif of the birth of male principles is repeated.

Two types of beings emerge from the mating of Sky and Earth: the human and the *kalo* (taro). From the *kalo* (the elder sibling to humans) are reproduced insects and birds of the land and sea. Humans do not exist outside the *kalo* plant, but are connected to it. They seem to have the

My parents and I went to the Kamehameha Schools Concert Glee Club performance. Classical pieces were part of the concert, but *hula kahiko* and *hula 'auana* (ancient *hula* and modern *hula*) were also performed.

I was stunned. I sat still, stiff with misery. *Hula* after *hula* unfolded before my eyes. I felt like crying as their voices drifted across the auditorium towards me. These were kids my age who were a part of something and were proud of who they were. I couldn't name this feeling then, but now I would describe it as a feeling of rootlessness, of intense loss.

When we got home I was furious at my parents, yet secretly guilty about my rage. I remember I asked them why—given all the places they took me—Mexico, Canada, Florida, Texas—why had we not returned to Hawai'i? I could barely speak. My father still remembers this and wonders what got into me. I remember how hurt they seemed, how silent and icy I became that night. Even today it is difficult to explain.

For several days afterward I looked over the Concert Glee Club brochure. On it were the names of all the Concert Glee Club members. I was suffused with rage and self-pity. Any one of these kids could be a relative of mine, a relative I would never meet, never touch, never know. I imagined a relative who would never know of my existence, would never acknowledge our common blood. I believed that I would always feel this way.

Several times I threw the brochure in the trash. In a ritual that went on for days, then weeks, then months, I threw it in the trash and later fished it out. I remember that during those

same destiny as other beings—to increase. Their names are given, but narratives are not woven around them. Lili'uokalani's translation reads:

> Then came the children of Loiloa [Lo'iloa],
> And the land grew and spread,
> And the goblet of wish was lowered,
> Of affections for the tribe of relations,
> Of songs that grasp of Oma's friends
> Till relations are enrolled
> from Kapokanokano . . .
> (Lili'uokalani 1978, 20)

There is the sense that in this long night, everything emerges, is alive, is named, and is tied to this "goblet of wish." This feeling connects to the notion that every being, no matter how small, has intent or character, and has a name that must be named:

> There in hollow places the parent rats dwell,
> There huddle together the little mice.
> It is they who keep the changes of the month.
> (ibid., 21)

This verse catches in my throat, bubbling up like the emotion that I, like my infant self, in my story that is not a memory, cannot name.

days, weeks, and months, I would occasionally see my image in the mirror over the dresser as I fished the brochure out. Sometimes I looked angry at myself; sometimes I looked resigned; sometimes I just looked emptied of emotion—blank.

It didn't matter how I felt. The brochure always ended up back on my desk.

By the time I was attending a college in Ohio, I still had never visited Hawai'i. I was dreaming often of dolphins and islands. During college my birth story changed, when my parents verified that my birth mother had not died. This notion of her death had been my own convenient fiction. I slowly came to terms with the idea that she had given me up for adoption. I imagined her, unable to support me, weeping as she reluctantly let me go into another's hands. I do not remember thinking of her often.

There were many reasons not to think about such details from the past. Various jobs, involvements with local social issues, learning from dynamic, committed professors, friendships and romances occupied my present.

In college I became interested in the political economy of Hawai'i, in particular the replacement of communal land use by a market economy. I read the story of Queen Lili'uokalani and the loss of her kingdom. This story seemed alien to the romantic and paradisical image of Hawai'i I had carried with me in Cleveland. Yet as a narrative about betrayal, theft, dispossession, and heartbreak, it somehow seemed to work better for me.

After college, I moved to San Diego, Cali-

The Kumulipo is a powerful poetic description of creation as a sacred process of reproduction. It is also a practical, historical, and personal text, taking people, particularly *ali'i*, back to their "roots." Its original purpose was to instruct the child of Lonoikamakahiki as to her identity.

However, her identity and that of all humans are as progeny of the mating of sky and earth, sibling to the *kalo*, the sacred food of the land, and an unimportant moment in the ongoing reproduction of life.

The Kumulipo was chanted at moments of birth and death, moments of articulation in the reproduction of a lineage. It was chanted at the arrival of Cook, marking momentous political/cosmological change.

My desire to skim passages detailing specific paired species and my lack of interest in the nature of each relationship betray my way of reading *The Kumulipo* and my language as anthropocentric. Even though I am reading an English translation, English, my first language, does not offer within it the tools to sustain those connections. Nor do I daily live those connections. Worse, I do not have the tools to judge the accuracy of the translation.

fornia with my husband, whom I had met in college. He had been accepted to graduate school there, and I got a series of clerical and then technical jobs. More importantly, in San Diego I became part of a Hawaiian community for the first time.

I studied *hula 'auana* and *hula kahiko* from a learned *kumu hula* from the Big Island. Her name was Philomena Keali'i Waine'e Aranio and we called her Aunty Mena. Her stories, advice, and prayers had an incredible impact on me.

After eating *mahimahi* one night, I dreamed that the fish came to me, told me he was related to me, and forgave me for eating him. For days after this dream I walked around in a kind of fog. When I told my *kumu hula* about the dream, she advised me that this fish was probably my *'aumakua* (family god, or guardian spirit).

I also I met a young woman whom I'll call Kalo. She had grown up in Hawai'i, and now worked where I worked, also in a clerical job. Kalo drew me further into the Hawaiian community and the local Hawaiian club. Hawaiian friends, mentors, and *kūpuna* voiced theories about my genealogy and encouraged me to search for my birth parents. I started with the names and clues my parents had given me. Local *kūpuna* who had grown up in Hawai'i suggested other names and leads.

I looked at lists of names in phone books at local libraries. I looked through microfilm records of old Honolulu newspapers, for records on marital dissolution. I searched

My gaps in attention or understanding represent the edges of *The Kumulipo*'s world, a world I cannot access. My tendency to expect "historic" events featuring "individuals" as "actors" betrays my anthropocentrism. As I read it silently, I want to skim through parts of it, yet when I read it aloud, my focus and its meaning seem to intensify.

In *The Kumulipo* all beings possess life, intent, and agency. Life manifests itself in every instance, in a constant act of reproduction by the cosmos.

For Lili'uokalani, this continuing cosmic event manifests her lineage—those who have come before her in her genealogy and those who will come after her. This text not only names the cosmos, but inscribes particular ways of knowing, and a particular way of using language. The language used in *The Kumulipo* fixes the power of lineage in the life of the land.

Samuel Manaiakalani Kamakau, who wrote *Ka Po'e Kahiko* (The People of Old) and *Na Hana a ka Po'e Kahiko* (The Works of the People of Old), also references particular ways of knowing, and using language. These two works originally appeared in Hawaiian newspapers in the 1860s and 1870s. In these works, Kamakau discussed the society, the family and *'aumakua* (family gods, guardian spirits), the spirit world, transfiguration, medical practices, and what was commonly called "magic" or "sorcery." He discussed the spiritual aspects of societal and familial hierarchies.

Although Kamakau (who converted to Christian belief as a boy), denounced the "evil" of old ways, he also explained and normalized Hawaiian religious practices which are outside Christian practices (Barrère in Kamakau 1964, viii). Kamakau detailed chiefly ranks and the *kapu*

through maps and phone books for the cemetery where my relatives might be buried. I researched the few last names that I could, from the Concert Glee Club brochure I had saved from High School. I cross-referenced names from old genealogical records with all the leads I had. I got nowhere.

Kalo continually provided balance by listening, her arm around me, as I poured out my frustrations. She told me, over and over: "It doesn't matter if you can't find them, even if they don't want you, or don't want you to know them. I am your 'ohana."

I took my first trip to Hawai'i in the mid-1970s. There I felt an intensified presence of the man in white, who had first arrived in my childhood dreams.

There are ghosts still around . . . especially (the) one who looks Hawaiian. I think he's a relative. . . . (JOURNAL: 1977)

While I was on O'ahu I visited the church where my dad had worked and on whose grounds my parents and I had lived. There, I experienced sudden, intense memories of the grass, trees, and the porch of the house where we had lived.

When I was on the leeward side of Māui, the North Shore of the island of Hawai'i, and

system (system of religious laws) accompanying those ranks. He discussed the *kahuna* (priestly orders) attached to the chiefly class, the gods to which the orders belonged, and *heiau* (temple) rituals. These complex hierarchies were related by lineage and wove together the social order, the religious order, the *kapu* system, and genealogy.

Kamakau described the *kapu* system as a given, discussing how everyday knowledge of the *kapu* system was necessary. To break a *kapu* was to threaten the continued increase of all beings and of the land itself. The *kapu* system seems to fuse the social, material, and sacred worlds. An everyday task was to uphold the sacred, thus sustaining the cosmos. This gives humans tremendous responsibility in the universe story.

Kamakau (1964, 7) discusses the *papa kaula* or order of prophets who foretold events. He later relates prophecies:

. . . The last prophet was Kapihe, who uttered his final prophecy near the end of the reign of Kamehameha I(st),

the windward side of O'ahu, some of the people I met were convinced we were related, and talked for long stretches of time with me, discussing my origin myth.

. . . it's weird to see all of the things represented by my race and culture that are good; . . . after more than twenty-one years of struggle, I feel at home here and have no desire to find my "biological" parents. Sending good thoughts to my birth mother, wherever she is . . . I am sure I will find out what I'm meant to find out. (JOURNAL: 1977)

At Lahaina, on Māui, I walked to the Waiola Church and its nearby cemetery. Over and over again, I found myself at one particular part of the cemetery, where I felt surrounded by my ancestors:

A sense of paying my respects to long lost ancestors in some way—I felt protected somehow. A feeling of eternity and the weightlessness of time. . . . My roots are within my own heart and will never be destroyed no matter what happens. I feel my life running a cycle: As I grow intellectually and spiritually, I strengthen my roots. As the years go by, the pieces of my life fall together. . . . The seed carries its own roots within itself. (JOURNAL: 1977)

During this time, I had more "fish" dreams:

I was a dolphin of some sort beached on the shore. I was translucent with purplish freckles around the top of my skin. I didn't seem to be "all dolphin" since under the translucent skin there seemed to be my more brownish skin and muscles showing

saying . . . "The islands will be united, the *kapu* of the gods overthrown, those of the heavens (the chiefs) will be brought low, and those of the earth (the common people) will be raised up." (ibid., 7)

(The Hawaiian kingdom) . . . would be overthrown and the ruling family and the chiefs of O'ahu would be set aside and the ruler over the people would "belong to the sea," those who came from across the sea. . . . Not a hundred years have passed . . . and his (Ka'opulupulu's) famous prophecy for the kingdom of Hawaii is being fulfilled upon the Hawaiian race. (ibid., 89)

These prophecies predict colonization and the restructuring of the social hierarchy. They relate this process of change to the overthow of the *kapu* system. The political and the sacred do not exist in separate realms—the overthrowing of the *kapu* system and the demise of chiefly power are related. The *kapu* system and prophecies predicting colonization frame social change as a sacred process.

Prophecy contains the European presence as only a moment in the confluence of time and cosmic intention. The existence of prophecy, as knowledge given to Hawaiians by the cosmos, qualifies European knowledge as partial. This empowers Hawaiian people and the Hawaiian cosmos.

Kamakau discusses the coming of foreigners as a cosmic rather than a political event. According to Kamakau, some of the gods became angry and demanding during the period of spiritual chaos prior to Christianity. By the time the first wave of missionaries arrived in 1820, the *kapu* system had been overturned as the result of a series of religious and political events.

through. I was beached with two other dolphins who seemed to be "all dolphin," one on each side of me. I began to rise up into the sky. When I got high enough I could see a lot of water in different areas. I started my dive down on the other side of a continent. At the last moment I arched my back and fell in the water in a perfect dive. The water was beautiful, transparent, and cool. (JOURNAL: 1978)

I was a fish . . . (in a lake that) seemed to be all cement (blocks) fitted carefully together. No, not cement—cold, hard stones, the bottom and side walls were stones. . . . (JOURNAL: 1978)

Feeling a sense of déjà vu I reread my journals from college and found descriptions of dreams from that time:

(I found myself in) shallow water and a fence within which . . . some older men were feeding some fish that were big; we could see the fish. My friend and I hung onto the fence and talked to a man. . . . Suddenly my friend was shot in the head. I felt a bullet pierce my brain. I was dying. A man, like an old grandfather, lifted me up and carried me somewhere through the shallow water. I was saying that I could feel darkness closing in on me. I was dying and I was scared. He was consoling and holding me, saying I would be all right. My mind was slipping away and I felt calmer. Right before I died some voice, from where I would be when I died, said "Life on earth is bittersweet." (JOURNAL: 1972)

By 1981 Kalo had moved back "home" to O'ahu. Some time after I returned home to

With the advent of Christianity, according to Kamakau, the ability of the gods to work for humans and the balance of the spiritual order were further lost. The gods became less responsive because people did not call on them as much, or with the same care as before the *kapu* system was overturned.[14]

Kamakau stated that without the *kapu* system Hawaiians were lost. Despite his Christian upbringing he mourned this loss. Kamakau stated that when the *kapu* system fell, people were overtaken by meaninglessness, pleasure-seeking, and disbelief, until the missionaries came. In his view the missionaries brought a viable, yet flawed replacement for the loss of the gods.

Kamakau mentioned human sacrifice as part of a larger discussion on the laws of the gods. I am struck by Kamakau's language as he described how thousands of people watched as the gods came down to receive these burnt offerings. He seemed to take for granted a relationship between gods and humans, for which human sacrifice was necessary and central.

Can we trust the "accuracy" of a story told by a Christian convert? I am not sure that the "accuracy" of Kamakau's story is as important as the nature of the cosmos that he narrates. Christian conversion may have rendered his stories inaccurate. Did it really completely reshape the cosmos that lies behind the eyes of the teller?

Generally sacrifice could be said to "bracket" or set aside an activity as sacred. As a convert, Kamakau should *not* honor a Hawaiian notion of the sacred. Yet his story constructs sacrifice as a deep form of communication comprised of a powerful, complex set of sacred meanings. I find that the shape of the cosmos that Kamakau narrates is not Christian. The cosmos he narrates, the connections and meanings in his story of sacrifice, lie far outside my own experience.

Kamakau described the physical features of the cosmos and technologies related to cultivation and fishing (1976). The

San Diego from a stay with Kalo in Hawai'i, I contacted her to tell her that I was pregnant. My husband and I were happy that we were starting a family, and I was happy that I would meet my first blood relative. Then I became ill with what doctors diagnosed first as flu, then incipient miscarriage, then an ectopic pregnancy. Finally I wrote Kalo:

Dear Sister,

So much has happened since we last talked. But don't be alarmed by my news; . . . the first thing I must assure you is that I am all right. But I was indeed pregnant—it was [an] ectopic pregnancy. You know . . . I knew I was carrying the little guy but I knew it wasn't right—that something was wrong. Deep down I was prepared to lose him. I had funny dreams, pain, and bleeding. My body tried to protect him by building tissue around him, and tried to protect me by sending all its energy to him, and even tried to warn me by showing me dreams. I knew my mana *was off. I was under the weather for three months. Then I quit my job as I'd planned and went into emergency on the spur of the moment.*

It's good to be home. . . . I sit in the sun and read . . . play guitar when the early sun filters through our windows. Listen to the bird and cricket sounds from the field adjacent to our house, feel the breeze wafting through our big windows. Ku'ulei gave me laua'e *and* tī *[Hawaiian plants], which thrive in a pot in our bedroom. The house is full of plants and Hawaiian implements. I'm working on featherwork and 'ulī 'ulī [feather rattles] from Aunty Helen's legacy of Hawaiiana to me. So I am very satisfied here.*

I'll be calling that lady about my adoption situation. I may initiate legal proceedings to open the

multiple names for the cardinal points, sky, earth, space above and below the sky, and land divisions inscribe the power of words. Kamakau stated that *ka po'e kahiko* "gave a suitable name to each thing . . . according to the nature of that thing" in explaining the propensity for naming (ibid.,7).

Kamakau spoke of the *kūpikipiki'ō ka po'i ana* (swells that twist about and break here and there in an agitated manner) and the *'ale wiliau maka lae* (swells which break agitatedly against points or capes of land). As I read these names, I feel the pull to allow "nature" to guide or shape my own emotions.

As described by Kamakau (1964), healing *kahuna* included subclasses who read omens from the sky, clouds, earth, and other sites in the cosmos. Medical or healing *kahuna* included subclasses who did such things as induce pregnancy, deliver babies, and cure childhood ailments. A class of *kahuna* were sorcerers, and another branch counteracted sorcery. One branch "treated" the spirits of illness.

Subclasses of *kahuna* diagnosed illnesses in various ways, such as using pebbles, through the ends of their fingers, by palpation, "at a glance," "through the eyelashes," through insight, or through critical observation. This list describes various ways of knowing—not only classified by what is known but also by how one knows.

Kamakau distinguished between non-Hawaiian and Hawaiian medical knowledge, stating that in some countries medical practitioners "rely on their own skill" and "visual proof" while in Hawaiian medicine, prayer and the "mana of god" were central elements.

He described how, for non-Hawaiian medical practitioners, bodies are cut up in study:

case files or apply pressure via some loopholes. Ectopic pregnancies are sometimes hereditary and had I known my family's medical history . . . we may have pinpointed the problem earlier.

I'm doing fine. It was a release and a relief to be operated on . . . and though I miss the little guy, what happened had to happen in that way, and my faith is strengthened. Someone was watching over me and protecting me—I felt it. (LETTER FROM JOURNAL: 1981)

My memories from this time are mainly of the dreams that clotted my sleep during my illness. In these dreams I searched through rainforests where *tī*, fern, and *laua'e* swayed and murmured. Something watched me, then darted deep into the forest; the air seemed to mist up with its breath. The jungle would inhale, pause, exhale. Sometimes, at the end of these dreams small hands would fly up to touch my face; sometimes I was like a fern myself, reaching tendrils out to touch someone.

Looking back on these dreams I think this is when I began to mourn something dying, whether it was the oncoming death of my marriage to my first love, or to some other honey-brown softness inside me, tender with unspent love. It was certain that something could not grow inside me.

I do remember worrying that perhaps my only "blood connection," a baby-to be, was not ever to be born. I worried that my body, in some sense, like me, had turned a gift of life from my husband into something petrifying, dying. Something that would need to be expelled.

A body is cut to pieces, inside and out, and sections . . . are examined to find out what remedies to use. . . . (ibid., 107)

Kamakau (1964) stated that in Hawaiian healing, gods came first, as the foundation, prayer second, diagnosis of diseases third, remedies fourth, the art of killing fifth, and finally, the art of saving.

Kamakau discussed how children whose parents or grandparents were in a *kahuna* (sacred) profession were also taught or consecrated into that particular profession. Reading omens, selecting sites, home-building, studying the earth's or stars' configurations, deep-sea fishing, and engaging in rituals were *kahuna* subprofessions. People experienced medium possession, visions, and dreams.

All forms of instruction were apparently sacred and took the form of a life-long apprenticeship. As a child was introduced to a system of knowledge, the child's body was placed under various *kapu* regarding such things as sex, diet, and cutting one's hair.

Kamakau said that the *kahuna* who consecrated the child always knew if the child committed a wrong at some level beyond conscious communication. I automatically think of knowledge available by way of the senses: seeing nonverbal cues or hearing a guilty tone of voice, for instance. Kamakau did not cite such options.

These descriptions offer a theory of knowledge. Knowledge is connected to the sacred dimension of

I began to pass like a ghost through my own life and my own marriage, creating ways to feel unloved, unwanted. When people told me they thought I was beautiful or intelligent, I was inwardly consumed by rage: I did not want that knowledge.

During an earlier stay in Hawai'i with Kalo, I had visited Aileen Kawahara, a Child and Family Services social worker, to request information from my files. At a government office I had tried unsuccessfully to get legal records pertaining to my adoption. Afterwards I had waited outside for Kalo to pick me up:

I'm waiting by the Kamehameha statue for Kalo to pick me up. All day I was hassled by bureaucrats . . . searching for my birth parents. My mother. When I don't associate it with Mom, that is, my adoptive mom—it becomes a sadly alien term . . . not one tie. What a hollow feeling. I did all I could fighting the bureaucracy—cold eyes, colder questions, that feeling of disassociation and separation . . . . Aileen Kawahara . . . is still trying and can get nothing done for me, insists that we continue the search even after I go to the mainland. . . . Wanting to sit alone and cry. So here I sit under a tree—strange, disembodied, alienated. . . . (JOURNAL: 1980)

As I had waited for my return flight to San Diego, I had called Aileen from a pay phone at the airport. In the middle of a noisy, bustling crowd of fellow travelers, I had leaned in towards the phone, trying to create a quiet, calm cocoon. Aileen's voice, precise and com-

life and comprises practices such as reading omens or engaging in rituals. Those who are introduced to a system of knowledge take on life-long responsibilities to that knowledge. These responsibilities are sometimes marked by the act of consecration. Not only do we come to knowledge; knowledge comes to us.

Kamakau made it clear that prayer was the foundation of knowledge. Prayers were taught to pupils of the *kahuna*. They learned to concentrate prayers in ways that would result in physical changes, such as the crumbling of a cliff or the death of a person.

He also noted the types of *'aumakua* or ancestral/family gods whose names had to be invoked in order for prayers to be heeded. I am struck by the many lines naming *'aumakua*. Kamakau (1964, 28) described the *'aumakua* as:

. . . the ancient source gods "from time immemorial". . . the gods from whom the ancestors implicitly believed they had come (personified natural phenomenon), or from whom they had actually descended. If a god had mated among them, and a human had come forth, this god was an *'aumakua* of theirs. . . .

The theme of the power of the word, and in particular, the word as a means of contact with *'aumakua* are apparent here. Kamakau (1964) quoted prayers for contacting *'aumakua*, so families without a protective family god could enlist one. The idea of sacred borders and the role sacrifice might offer for transit between those borders, captures me in these lines:

[O] 'Aumakua *at the rising and the resting*
places of the sun,

passionate, had confirmed certain parts of my origin myth. Yet the knowledge I had was pathetically incomplete:

How strange to know actual facts about myself. It suddenly makes me aware of the parts of me that are mysterious: the dreams, the visions, sudden bursts of energy, the intensity of it all. Something in my blood cries out. I will put this journal away before it becomes painful. Pull it out when the experience has drifted into the background. (Journal: 1980)

After I had returned to San Diego, I had written Aileen Kawahara at Child and Family Services. I had felt that my meeting with her had been a transforming experience, and because she had held (and withheld) important knowledge I had felt strangely connected to her.

Dear Aileen:
. . . Speaking to you and realizing I had a file gave me a strange sense of completeness I had never had before. I suppose I had always felt as if I was "found" rather than born. I had never had details surrounding my actual birth that weren't second-hand information.

I also felt hurt when I spoke to you, for it was as if the key to my past was held in the hands of a friendly stranger — who was unable to hand it to me. What an incomplete and frustrating feeling, alleviated only by your sympathetic and helpful attitude. Of course I understand the rights of my birth mother to confidentiality. Yet my own claim to a family history, ancestry, and sense of roots somehow gets lost in the shuffle.

From that sacred border to this,
Here are the offerings and sacrifice. . . .
(ibid., 30)

An example of the potency of the word in prayer is contained in Kamakau's quote from a chant: "Establish the inviolability of the utterance." Literally, the translation is "set up the sacred drum of the voice" (ibid, 14). The question of meaning enters here as a question about knowing. Was knowledge of meaning necessary to knowing?

Kamakau (1964, 36) said that the word has the power to create or destroy:

Before Christianity came to Hawaii there was no death-dealing . . . equal in *mana* [supernatural, divine, or miraculous power] to the *mana* of praying to death in broad daylight. . . . Solid rocks were melted away by the *mana* of the prayers, and thunder and lightning vibrated. . . . That was through the *mana* of the prayer.

In prayer, men, women, and children inhabited different ritual spaces. Kamakau (1964) viewed Christianity, within which men and women prayed together, as disrupting the purpose, structure, and potency of prayer. Like *The Kumulipo*, Kamakau emphasizes the importance of reproduction. He does not construct similarities between humans and plants, but rather fuses their identities.

Kamakau scorned the idea that the cause of the Hawaiian population collapse was sin. Rather the insertion of Christian practices and mingling across sex and age disrupted the efficacy of prayer, the reproduction of human bodies, and cosmic balance:

After our last long talk I was elated for a few minutes at having my own birth-history (to a small extent) verified. . . . Then depression set in and I cried, wishing that I could know my whole past and be somehow complete. . . . Thank you for your kindness and support. You may hear from me if I decide to pursue my past any further; . . . every step seems a bit painful somehow. . . .

When I try to enter this letter to Aileen, the feelings that I described in that letter surge back over me. Oddly enough, outside of that I am unable to really "think" about the letter. When I try to write my feelings my words are inadequate. All I can remember is the bitterness that bloomed inside me.

By the early 1980s, as a full-time technical worker at a local University in San Diego, I was entitled to take tuition-free graduate classes. My initial plan was to use the classes to make me eligible for a promotion. However, I found myself taking history, anthropology, and sociology for an M.A. focusing on Pacific Island area studies.

I also became increasingly involved in *hula*, particularly *hula kahiko*. Our *hālau hula* performed at Hawaiian and Pacific Islander events, as well as non-Hawaiian venues such as parties and cultural festivals. As a member of a local Hawaiian club and editor for its newsletter, I found myself listening to older Hawaiians as they talked about Hawaiian culture and history.

Symbols, themes, and stories circulated among all these settings in weird ways. I might

Ka po'e kahiko used to pray ritually . . . that the race might increase, and flourish, and sprout from the parent stock. Thriving seedlings *ka po'e kahiko* bore; great gourds filled with seeds they were. But today they are poison gourds, bitter to the taste. Because of some wrongdoing, it is said. Well, now they pray to God in a congregation. What ruler of old would allow a mixed gathering of men, women, and children to pray together to the gods? None! (ibid., 99)

Kamakau listed chiefly spirits or *'aumakua* and their various names, as well as those of the gods. Kamakau described the practices people could engage in for their dead to become a volcanic manifestation of Pele, who was originally from Kahiki ("the firmament" or "Tahiti").

Transfiguration, according to Kamakau, was still common at the time of his writing. He spoke of people who have *kuleana* (ancestral plots of land) in the firepit of Kīlauea, since they are related through ancestry to the Goddess Pele, saying, "The god recognizes that blood kinship and clings forever to his descendants in the living world" (ibid., 66).

Kamakau discussed how the appearance of certain *mo'o* (serpent) forms foretold events or revealed hidden things, suggesting that *'aumakua* or forces of nature lead humans to knowledge.

perform *hula* for an anthropology class, or use information from my class to deepen my understanding of a *hula* text. I might hear about a history text at a Hawaiian club gathering, then end up mentioning that conversation in my history class.

Soon I was ending my ten-year marriage and was embarking already on a new, doomed relationship. My words and life events somehow seemed to loop back into themselves; it seemed there was some code I could not understand. The relationships I created were incomplete trails: they unwound, veered away, somehow fell short. I created new trails, then stamped them out, naming countless imperfections in myself and others. My gestures and words were inadequate, rang false.

Yet it seemed that in *hula kahiko* the words, chanted and gestured by our bodies, created in me a layer of knowing that sat outside meaning. It was a knowledge that flourished outside the chaos that I was creating in my life. The movement, the vibration of our *kumu hula's* voice, the *pa'i* (pounding) of the *ipu* (percussive gourd), seemed to create a constellation of unexplainable feelings. Oddly, I felt, in my body, in my bones, a safe haven, a connection to my ancestors.

A dream seemed to provide a metaphor for what I was actually doing through *hula*, and seemed to be about connection:

I am living in a low house, very open, shoji screens . . . a perfectly manicured garden. I am living with my parents. . . . I go outside and care-

He also spoke of sharks, who, though deadly, could be loving *'aumakua.* Kamakau stated that many sharks who became supernatural beings were people who had been transfigured into the forms of their shark ancestors. A very dense passage about the relationship among sharks, gods, and people (if these can be said to be separate) follows:

Most of the sharks who had become supernatural beings . . . were people who had been changed into forms of their shark ancestors. . . . These ancestral sharks . . . were not beings deified by man. . . . They got their shark forms from the god. Nor did their angel forms remain permanently in sharks—but when they showed themselves, it was in the form of sharks. They did not show themselves in all sharks, but only in those which had been given distinguishing marks . . . known to their *kahu* (humans who acted as guardians of the *'aumakua*) and offspring, and known to their descendants in the world of light. If a *kahu* were in trouble and in danger of death on the ocean, he would call upon his own shark, and that shark would come and get him, and so he would escape death. (ibid., 74)

Discussing transfiguration from human to shark, Kamakau (1964, 79) creates complex protective connections between humans and nonhumans:

His body assumed that form, and the remembrance of him was on the shark, without his spirit living permanently in the shark. It was the same with other forms—a volcanic

fully plant a row of tī plants at the entrance. The next day . . . they are replaced by bamboo. My mother comes out and says: "Your father wanted bamboo there." I am very angry and open the garbage pail. There are the uprooted tī lying in the trash, already sprouting roots. I pick the rooting orphan plants out of the trash and carry them to the backyard to find a small patch of earth to put them in. (JOURNAL: 1981)

I thought often about two images I had found at Bishop Museum. These images seemed imbued with feelings of connection:

God Image: Kawaihae, Hawai'i:
This stone image was dug up about 1900 by a Hawaiian man who said a dream guided him to it. He identified the image as the fish god: Kāneikōkala. I put my hand on this image. I could feel the image . . . talking back to me, coming in loud and clear—an explosive burst of energy rocked me. I touched his eyes, mouth, face, forehead. It was very hard to say goodbye.
(JOURNAL: 1980)

Fish God: Kāne'ohe, O'ahu:
This naturally formed stone was named "Ka-wahine-ka-hala-o-Puna." It was considered a habitation for the spirit of the fish god. I saw this stone in the garden, knelt down, felt it, kept my hand there. The mana *came through into me.* (JOURNAL: 1980)

fire, a bird, or whatever the body had been changed into to live again. The spirit would become strong and would return and possess [*noho*] his parents, relatives of his own generation, or other relatives perhaps. Then it would say: "My bodies are such-and-such and such-and-such. When you are in trouble, in sickness, and near death, and you see such-and-such, it is I. You can ignore the trouble; there is no trouble. If you hear that a relative is in danger of death elsewhere and you see this thing, it is I; you can ignore the danger; there is no danger."

These passages, which for me are very difficult to read, seem to describe the intertwining identities of deities, humans, and other creatures. These identities manifest themselves in the process of transfiguration and in the protective relationships between beings. The specificity of these relationships and the fact that in *The Kumulipo* and in Kamakau's work they seem to elude categories are notable. They point to the fact that the hierarchies of beings in the Hawaiian cosmos, lying in the interstices between god, human, animal, plant, and geological or meteorological formations, are still impossible for me to recapture.

My Master's thesis was called *Music and the Maintenance of Hawaiian Identity in San Diego.* I focused on field research and analysis of Hawaiian cultural production. I felt that the practice of *hula kahiko* (ancient *hula*) was fast becoming a political statement about identity and history on the part of Hawaiians.

I tried to explain to my thesis advisor that at times, my body seemed to make me remember something that wasn't in my past, a connection to *'āina.* I grew to view these moments as expressions of sovereignty. I could not validate this claim to the satisfaction of my thesis supervisor, so my thesis ended up being mostly descriptive.

Now I would explain this by saying that when I performed *hula kahiko* my body became a site for powerful pre-contact rememberings of *'āina.* Because these rememberings recovered the disconnection from land brought by colonization, I would now assert that in a way, they were an expression of sovereignty. I would say that by taking up identity as a link between the body and *'āina, hula kahiko* enacts a powerful cosmology for sovereignty. But back then I could not find the words.

For our *kumu hula,* every place, every subject that we danced, held a story, and one story led to another. Knowledge was certainly not a set of categories, frames, or paradigms. Rather, knowledge was simply her stories and chants.

It seemed to me that in the texts of *hula kahiko* the subjects of intentional action were not usually human. We performed their subjectivity. It was like the bonding behavior of babies in response to their mothers—mom nods her head, baby nods her head. Like a

Kamakau often describes matters that I might define as sacred in his discussions of everyday matters. Kamakau stated that before Christianity, even if the bones of evil persons were hidden, they would be exposed, and defiled somehow. The imposition of a system of juridical, rather than religious law changed this state of affairs.

Kamakau (1964, 37) talked about how by law, the wicked were punished while they were still living, suggesting that as a result, the bones of the wicked were not defiled:

Today the bones of the wicked are safe: No difference is seen between the bones of the wicked and those of the righteous.

Kamakau believed that the power of the Hawaiian gods could also affect non-Hawaiians. Kamakau told of a non-Hawaiian doctor who took the bones of a dead person for transport to England for study. The bones were later destroyed by a mysterious outbreak of fire. Kamakau hypothesized that the fire broke out because the bones were going to be publicly "belittled." He says: "We see what trouble can come from abusing the bodies of the dead" (ibid., 43).

The importance of one's bones, or *iwi,* enters Kamakau's description of secret preparation of bones for burial. In their definition of the term *iwi,* Pukui and Elbert (1986, 104) say, "The bones of the dead, considered the most cherished possession, were hidden, and hence there are many figurative expressions with *iwi.*" The bones of chiefs

mother, *'āina* coded itself into my body, into my bones, where it sedimented in layers of feeling and image.

During this time my *kumu hula* told us about Waipi'o, where, she said, Līloa had built a *heiau*. She told us about the great falls of Hi'ilawe, where the bones of Līloa and Lonoikamakahiki were placed.

My *kumu hula* taught us a chant about Waipi'o, using the version that she had learned and then transcribed from her *kumu hula* many years ago:

A-e: Aia Waipi'o, no paka alana.
Here is Waipi'o, waterfalls fall from great heights.

Aia Waipi'o, no paka alana.
Here is Waipi'o, waterfalls fall from great heights.

Pae pai kapu ia, o Līloa.
To praise the sacred father of 'Umi (Līloa).

Ua pe'e pa kai a ulu, o Waimea.
Hiding place of sprouting, increase in Waimea.

Ua ola i ku'u kai, ke ola ewa e.
Peaceful waters of health at peace from wandering.

He aloha ka wahine, pi'i ka Pali.
Greet the Woman Pele, rising up the mountain.

Pu'ili ana, i ka hua u lei.
Picking berries, with which to make a *lei*.

as receptacles of *mana* were preserved in sennit caskets. *Mana*, or supernatural, divine or miraculous power is in the bones, and also in the *hā* or breath (Pukui and Elbert 1986, 235; Pukui 1974a, 43, 151). *Hā* means "to breathe, exhale; to breathe upon . . . after praying; . . . breath, life" (Pukui 1974a, 41). Kamakau described how the *hā* as it was passing out of a dying parent would be breathed in by the first-born child (1964, 44).

Like Kamakau, John Papa Ii also describes sacred matters in his work, *Fragments of Hawaiian History*. Ii spent much of his childhood with the ruling Kamehamehas for whom his uncle was an attendant. Kamehameha II sent Ii to study under the Reverend Hiram Bingham to observe and report the effects of missionary teachings. Ii narrated Hawaiian history from his particular vantage point as a Christian convert and as a loyal supporter of the Kamehameha dynasty.

For Ii, the history of the Kamehameha dynasty is a story of sacred practices. He describes these, as well as orders and classes of *kahuna* (1983). Ii, like Kamakau, wrote in detail of ceremonies that included human sacrifice. His tone imbues it, however "un-Christian" in Ii's framework, with a sense of great importance, describing it as a "fearful activity" (ibid., 43). Ii's description of these ceremonies connects them to the maintenance of the *kapu* system and the socio-cosmological hierarchy. As I read Ii's description of the terror involved and invoked, the precise practices required, and the length of the ceremonies, time—past, present, and future—seem to momentarily fuse for me.

This same feeling emerges when Ii tells of his childhood, describing the children of Nānākuli, who chanted in unison:

The sun sends a streak of light on Maunaloa,
The clouds go scurrying by,
There is a rumble on the mountain top

I ka ai mo'a, i ka lau la'au.
Eating chicken, cooked in leaves.

Ho'o la'au mai, o ka welo welo.
Nearby, a flying streak (firebrand) overhead.

He inoa no . . . Kamehameha.
(A name song for Kamehameha.)

(translation, personal notes)[15]

Although I had never been to Waipi'o, this chant, and dancing it, brought up strong emotions in me. Perhaps this is because through *hula*, my physical self was made to embody Waipi'o.

In learning to dance this chant, I remember repeating the motions over and over in order to correctly model the behavior of the falls at Hi'ilawe. Usually it seemed that the point where our *kumu hula* exclaimed that we had got it right was a point where my mind was no longer an active part of the process. In order to get it right again, I would simply have to lose my mind in the same way, again. At such moments, my interior world seemed full of the outer world of Waipi'o. Waipi'o was a presence that spoke to and within my physical self.

Every time I danced that *hula*, my body amplified my sense of communion with Waipi'o, while my mind emptied out. My mind emptying out, and Waipi'o displacing the self that resided in my body, was a feeling of both disassociation and ecstasy.

I grew to think of Waipi'o as containing

That echoes from the mountain of Kona, the calm.
Hilo stands directly in the rain.
(ibid., 29)

In this poetry, there is no inclusion of a human voice commenting on places or phenomena. It is the phenomena themselves, the "nonhuman" workings of the cosmos that are used to elicit human emotion. Perhaps, for me, it is these "nonhuman" workings that serve to fuse time.

The familiar non-Hawaiian categories of "human versus nonhuman" and resultant way of seeing things are not helpful to understanding Hawaiian cosmology. The categories I find myself using—humans, gods, animals, geologic formations, and land—are not categories that arise in *The Kumulipo*, the works by Kamakau, or Ii's work. Categories like "species" or "nature" fall short.

The way in which chant voices this cosmology emerges in Ii's work. Ii discussed how chanting was central for the chiefs and might continue through the night until dawn, with different chants marking different times in the night such as midnight, dawn, or the coming of day. He described how his playmates and relatives expressed sadness at parting by chanting name chants (ibid., 108). Ii also talked about the *hula*, deriving obvious pleasure in it, despite the fact that Reverend Hiram Bingham, Ii's teacher, once denounced *hula* as "an abomination."

As Ii discussed the Kamehameha line, he used chant to demonstrate the meanings of events. I am struck by

historical memory. By embodying Waipi'o it seemed that I was remembering, or perhaps re-membering that place. It was as if Waipi'o had appropriated my body as a site for expression of itself, and of historical memory. My body became a container for that place.

Later, when I first visited Waipi'o, it was already coded into my body. I saw where, according to my *kumu hula,* Līloa had built a *heiau.* And I saw the great falls of Hi'ilawe, where my *kumu hula* had told us the bones of Līloa and Lonoikamakahiki were placed. I had danced the places that stood before me. I did not need a mother, at that moment. I was *in* that place and *of* that place. Displaced as I was, my body belonged to that place. And, as I turned to leave, I felt the presence of that place at my back, and I wept.

the interrelatedness among chiefly genealogy, history, and chant in Ii's accounts. Also I am struck by the way that creatures and features of the universe actively set the stage for human emotion and human relationships. The death of Queen Kamāmalu, at age twenty-seven, is com-memorated in this chant:

> . . . *The rain scatters the* hala *fruit*
> *of Kanakea,*
> *The young bracts*
> *of the* hala *blossom fall too,*
> *The overripe fruit, bruised,*
> *sends forth a fragrance,*
> *The sweetness reaches the* lehua *blossoms beloved*
> *of the birds.*
> *I am bruised and wounded by grief.*
> *I hurt to my innermost depths. . . .*
> (ibid., 175)

2   Viewfinders

View from Outside

During a stay in Hawai'i, I found the name of a burial place in Nu'uanu and tried to connect with somebody there. I was returning to San Diego soon, and nobody had answered my calls yet. Between errands, I stopped at a pay phone to call one more time.

This time, the caretaker of the burial place answered the phone. I asked if the place was open, and she said it was closed for renovation. Then she asked me why I wanted to visit. I wasn't sure about the nature of the place and felt at a loss to explain. I told her that I was following up on a rumor that I had relatives buried at that place, or somewhere nearby.

It was pouring down rain, and I fumbled in the small booth, with my notes, the phone, my purse. As the rain streamed down the four glass sides of the phone booth, I felt a faint chill. I couldn't tell if it was the sudden rain, the emotions I was feeling, or something else.

She asked my family name, and I said I was adopted, so I didn't know. I asked her if

The Hawaiian literature I've discussed tells stories about *earth*, *practice*, *destiny*, and *knowledge.* It voices a powerful worldview, describing human-cosmos relationships and ancestry.

In this literature, Hawaiians, descendants of Earth and Sky and younger siblings to *Kalo*, are genealogically connected to the universe and all its creatures and features. Humans are the extended body of nature, and spirit manifests matter. This literature narrates the transforming power of the cosmos.

In this literature, life is in a constant state of sacred reproduction. Abundance is the result of right action or ethical *practice*, occurring when humans "tap into" other forms of consciousness in the cosmos. Every life form in the cosmos, including humans, is tasked to guard and protect other species. Every creature and feature of the cosmos manifests emotion, intent, and purpose.

she knew of some royal Hawaiian society that had met at the place where she was caretaker. She paused, and then said, "No." Then, after another pause, she suggested that I visit her. I was surprised and grateful at her kindness in letting me visit.

When I arrived, I was astonished to discover that the burial place was not just a small cemetery. As the rain beat down, I walked past the manicured grounds and a mausoleum and then arrived at the caretaker's house. When the caretaker met me at her door, she said I looked familiar to her. Although she seemed to be examining me, her eyes were warm, and she welcomed me in.

At her request, I repeated what I had been told about my biological family. She asked me about my dreams, reassuring me that someday I would find "my people."

I also told her that there were people on O'ahu and Māui who said I looked familiar, and she asked me where those people happened to live. She mentioned family names, saying, "Maybe they are your people." These names were all unfamiliar to me, and I was too abashed to write them down. I felt touched that she was taking time to search her memory for my family.

After we had talked for some time, she left the room for a few minutes and came back with a sheaf of paper. She said it was a list of all the people buried on the grounds. As I left, she hugged and kissed me and told me to keep searching and to pray. We had talked for

History or social change is a sacred process that may live outside human agency. *Destiny* is related to protective relationships among all beings. Colonization is the separation of Hawaiians from the land and the overturning of cosmological relationships. Social change (as predicted by prophecy) is dependent on cosmic intention.

We may come to *knowledge*; knowledge also comes to us. Words may be sacred, may fly through the air, and are causal agents. The first element in knowledge is prayer. Lineage and bloodline are at the core of identity and are central to knowledge-making.

The Hawaiian literature I've discussed contains stories about earth, about the cosmos. These texts trace the contours of their own discursive worlds. They cannot, as texts, imagine the discursive worlds that they will someday visit—that will someday receive the stories that those texts tell.

These texts cradle ideas about ancestry and experience, imagining a line of descendants who will be cradled by their words and by the cosmos. They cannot, as texts, imagine the discursive worlds that those descendants will visit—the discursive worlds that will someday receive the stories that those descendants tell.

what seemed a long time. I was shaken and weeping.

When I returned home from Hawai'i, the list, comprised of pages and pages of vault locations for *ali`i*, seemed to take on weight. I searched through the names, uncertain how to proceed. I also searched through books and found information about the living descendants of the families she had mentioned. I read and reread the brochure, as if clues were hidden in its straightforward text:

The Royal Mausoleum: Nu'uanu
They say the custodian is traditionally a descendant of the great chief Ho'olulu who hid the bones of Kamehameha I. In pre-European times the bones of chiefs were hidden in caves or other secret places so they could not be found; later, wooden caskets became popular and a mausoleum on the 'Iolani Palace grounds held royal caskets until 1865. In 1863 the Mauna 'Ala site was chosen for the new Mausoleum. (PARAPHRASED FROM VISITORS' PAMPHLET: JOURNAL: 1980)

Finally I put all the materials aside, to pull out and read through once in a while. When I read them, certain memories would come back to me. I would remember the rain, and the warmth in the woman's face, as she paused in her doorway. I would remember the sense that I wanted to sit in her room for a long time. I would remember the weight of the papers, so full of meaningless names, that she placed in my hands. These papers were not clues, but merely artifacts—representations of what I did not know.

The literature of political economy (historical materialism) and a debate on the invention of tradition in the Pacific also tell stories about human-cosmos relationships and ancestry, voicing a worldview. Critiques of these literatures address their validity and applicability as constructs. I believe that these literatures circulate not only as constructs, but as cosmologies, or discursive worlds.

In this chapter, I will discuss political economy and the invention of tradition. I will not question the validity of their claims, but I do want to talk about the stories about *earth, practice, destiny,* and *knowledge* that they tell. These stories and the images that they evoke are not just artifacts of their claims. They are like mnemonic devices, reproducing the cosmologies they represent.

These cosmologies constitute the discursive worlds now visited by the Hawaiian literature—the discursive worlds that receive their stories and the stories of their descendants. From within these discursive worlds scholars evaluate and publish information about present-day Hawaiian cultural practices—about Hawaiian ancestry and experience.

In 1985, Child and Family Services sent me more information. Aileen had contacted my birth mother, because I had requested medical information that was missing from my file:

Dear Leilani:

Per your request for background information of your birth mother, I have read and reread her record and have come up with very little information.

According to the record, your natural mother was born on July 5, 1922, was about 5 feet 2 inches tall and of German, French and Hawaiian extraction. She reported that she was a granddaughter of a Hawaiian princess.

Your natural mother was described as an exotic, attractive young brunette, fastidiously groomed, and dressed in excellent taste. Her long, dark wavy hair was worn in a large bun at the back of her neck. She was an exceptionally good-looking woman.

The natural mother completed the ninth grade and left school because she did not care for academic studies. Her employment covered a wide range of positions from a theatre usherette, file clerk, waitress in a bar or restaurant to sales clerk. She had no training for any specific job and worked only a few years prior to her marriage.

Natural mother was divorced in October 1951 and had three children from the marriage. She had exaggerated fears about people learning of her pregnant condition and repeatedly needed reassurance about the confidentiality of records and protection from identification at the time of confinement.

The writings of Marx and Engels offer core claims of political economy, inscribing certain beliefs about *Earth.* Although Marx and Engels didn't discuss Hawaiian society, in discussing the preconditions for capitalism they did describe pre-capitalist societies. Marx notes that in the "primitive" relationship with nature in pre-capitalist societies, humans, the proprietors of Earth, are barely able to modify it (Marx 1964).

Capitalist societies are said to present an evolutionary advance beyond this state, where humans are able to modify nature to a much greater (albeit incomplete) extent. Finally, under communism, technology will be freed from the bonds of capitalist relations, and humans will dominate nature completely (Grundmann 1991).

For Marx, Nature, stripped of emotion, intent, purpose, and agency, holds meaning for humans only as they expropriate value from it. Earth is described as essentially dead, as "man's inorganic body." In effect, Earth is separated from humans.

Humans "invent" spirit, and generate meaning as they exert control over Nature. Spirit cannot animate matter (Marx and Engels 1981). For Marx, capital conditions the human spirit as it transforms the pre-capitalist relationship with Nature.[1] As I read Marx and Engels, I feel a powerful pull to view capital as possessing the sort of agency and transforming power with which Earth is imbued in the Hawaiian literature.

Due to this feeling of a need for complete confidentiality it is understandable how she reacted when contacted regarding your inquiry. . . . I will briefly summarize my contact with her and her reactions to my call: The natural mother was shocked to hear from us and was angry at our tracing her after 30 years. She stated that she had an agreement with us to provide her complete secrecy. She accused us of going back on our word and felt that we were not worth dealing with. She felt that a wound, which had dried, was now being reopened.

She asked questions about your need for the information and I explained that you were especially interested in your Hawaiian heritage due to your study of the ancient hula. *She wondered if you didn't ask about your Caucasian background. She felt too that we were accusing her of being responsible for your life-threatening situations when I told her that we wished an updating of her medical information. . . .*

The natural mother appeared to be quite disturbed about the whole issue of our breaking confidence with her and tracing her and calling her. . . . It appears that she will never be ready for any kind of contact. . . . I am sorry that we were not able to assist you more fully in your quest. . . .

Sincerely,
Child and Family Services

When I received this letter, I set it aside and tried to forget about it. It was too painful to address the issues it dredged up for me. I was unable to discuss these issues with anyone—even those close to me.

For Marx and Engels (1981), through *practice* or productive human action, humans transform the world. Consciousness is assigned only to humans. Subservient to Nature, people in pre-capitalist societies possess a "sheep-like or tribal consciousness" (ibid., 68). Progress, or growing control over Nature, is emancipation from the scarcity that typifies pre-capitalist societies (Hobsbawm 1964, 13).

The goal of humans is not to protect Nature, but rather to use technology to actively transform it (Grundmann 1991). The dissolution of the pre-capitalist human relationship to land is inevitable, caused by the evolution of economic exchange. The "herd animal" moves beyond an animal existence and becomes an individual whose labor is no longer directly related to the land (Marx 1964).

Destiny, or social change, is shaped by utilitarian interest. In this evolutionary notion, pre-capitalist societies lack historical movement, and await the transforming power of capital, the prime mover of destiny (Marx and Engels 1981). Capitalism signals the end of human relationships to land, and the beginning of history.

History or social change is shaped only by humans, as they use technology to transform Nature. Only humans possess emotion, intent, purpose, and the ability to shape destiny. Humans, the sole shapers of destiny, are in conversation only with themselves.

After four years had passed, I was ready to address those issues again. It did not feel as if meeting my birth mother ("natural mother?") was important, or even desirable. It was my ancestors, the ones who visited me, whom I wanted to find. I felt that my birth mother, and a social service apparatus, stood between me and my ancestors. In 1988 I wrote Aileen again:

. . . I am sure you don't remember me but I am enclosing a letter you wrote me approximately three years ago. . . . I am so disturbed that I cannot find out my genealogy or even (get) an accurate accounting of my ethnic background other than hearsay. . . .

I am sure you know how important it is for many people who have a bit of Hawaiian blood to know what their roots might be. I have NO desire to know the mother who was described in your letter. . . . But (please excuse the perhaps misplaced sentimentality) . . . I wish I knew my ancestors. Sometimes things happen or I dream things, which make me feel a link, which I cannot define. What else can I do to find out my background?

. . . Since I've come into my thirties this search has taken on new dimensions and significance in my life. I am really not sure how to resolve it . . . and I hope that we can meet or correspond again.

Aileen wrote back:

I certainly do remember you. I wonder about you periodically when I refer to your situation in telling people some of the experiences we have had in trying to arrange contact among members of the adoption triad.

Marx and Engels viewed *knowledge* as conditioned by productive forces and material conditions in society. Relations of production of knowledge—the way we "do knowledge," or express our lives, are articulated with a mode of production, or the way we make products.

Knowledge does not come to us from nonhuman sources; rather, we create it in service of our present-day relations of production. Ideology refers to the attitudes, values, and ideas representing the interests of a particular (usually dominant) group or social class. Their every expression is ideological.

Analyzing ideology involves discovering how specific ideas are tied to the interests, needs, or identities—in short the material conditions—of those who create them (Ollman 1993). Productive forces and material conditions actively set the stage for human consciousness and knowledge.

I know that it is important for you to know your roots and yet due to the birth mother's feelings of keeping her identity confidential, I am unable to further pursue anything with her. . . . I am sorry that we are unable to help you.

By this time I was going in for surgery for acute intestinal obstructions, and also seeing a *kahuna.* My meetings with him were characterized by a profound sense of nurturance and connection. It is hard to recollect my feelings from this time. I do remember a conviction that my history was controlled by strangers, who held documents to which I had no access. I had no access to my history, or to my ancestors.

All that I can recollect of my feelings is several occasions where I broke cups. If I was thinking about my "origin myth" I would just grab a coffee cup and shatter it by throwing it to the floor.

By 1989 I was teaching sociology and cross-cultural studies at a local community college, and reading about teaching and learning across cultures. The more deeply felt lessons for me happened within the *hālau hula,* yet it seemed that I could not actually name what I was learning. During this time, I had dreams about *hula:*

. . . I was at a function to do hula. *. . . I suddenly realized that Aunty Mena (my* kumu hula*) was there, sitting in the audience. Someone else began discussing how we would raise up this dead child by doing* hula. *Messages came in from this child, who was (asking) for help for his soul.* (JOURNAL: 1989)

Sahlins (1976) and Povinelli (1995) open up a space to consider political economy as a cosmology, or discursive world, in relation to indigenous cosmologies. Sahlins discusses knowledge created about pre-capitalist societies from the point of view of political economy. He notes that if, as Marx says, humans' worldviews emerge as they materially transform the world, then Marx's ideas are themselves symptoms of those transformations. They represent the "self knowledge of capitalist society" (ibid., 18).

In capitalist society a "classificatory grid" of the marketplace is imposed on the total culture. Distinctions about persons, time, and space that exist within capitalist relations of production are reproduced in the rest of society as well as the study of "other" cultures (ibid., 220). The disconnections between people and products, or people and each other that exist in capitalism are assumed to exist in pre-capitalist societies.

Human-to-human and human-to-Nature relations are "reified as economic relations" and it is assumed that practical activity, driven by utilitarian interest, drives society (ibid., 18, 52).

Povinelli (1995, 507) notes that political economy divides human life from animal or object existence through the assumption that only humans are capable of "subjective intentionality and appropriation." She suggests that this division is unhelpful in understanding the shared belief among aboriginal people in Australia that nonhumans are capable of intentional actions.

I also continued to be visited by the "lady" and "ancestor-man." The visits of the Hawaiian-looking lady were not only in the form of dreams, but also visions. These visions came only when I was ill, so I usually wrote them off as a by-product of illness. Yet sometimes I felt that she came to help me to heal. She seemed to be middle-aged, with placid eyes and a half-smile. Her face held in its shape a familiar look.

The man also continued to visit me, unbidden, in my dreams. These visitations usually had nothing to with what I was doing or how I was feeling at the time. They just came. He had a face like withered leaves, and intense eyes with yellowish whites and burning pupils. Unlike her, he did not stand by silently. He spoke to me, but I usually had no memory of what he had said once I woke up.

By late 1989 my mother was dying of cancer. They had given her half a year, and during that time uterine cysts began to blossom in me like lucky oranges. An operation to remove my uterus kept me off work for a semester, and there was time to be with my mother. She drew me pictures to tell me where to find things when words failed her. She worried about being "addlepated" and told me how lonely dying felt.

Despite her loss of memory, my mother continued to try to complete *New York Times* crossword puzzles. In my childhood her pen had scratched in the answers, each grid so complete that I never realized that the task was difficult. As my mother weakened, the boxes began to empty out. Although my dad tried to fill in her answers, eventually the puzzles went blank.

Like Sahlins, Povinelli suggests that a preoccupation with scarcity and the uncertainty of the "natural world" leads to an incomplete assessment of human-environmental interaction and connection. She notes that the result is a "cultural organization of Western disbelief" that obscures and silences indigenous practices and beliefs (ibid., 506).

Political economy is a useful theoretical approach, indispensable in its analysis of the effects of capitalist economic formations on indigenous societies.[2] Yet, while the Hawaiian literature is saturated with the presence of Earth, Earth is leached out of the anthropocentric language of political economy. Analyzing Hawaiian cosmology (or cultural production) using its inverted "other" as a theoretical base seems ill-advised.

Perhaps the literature of political economy can be regarded as "just another story." In my case, this story does not necessarily have the power to seep into one's bones like the *hula*, so it may not command the same sort of authority as the voice that speaks through the texts of *hula*.

My mother and I sometimes sat peering into twilight or dawn together, in her living room. This time together carried a special sort of clarity for me. We talked about my childhood. She reviewed her life, and we reviewed our life together as mother and daughter. She told me about the difficulties she had experienced as a tall blond mother of a short, dark child—comments made about her, assumptions imposed on her by others.

When I was a child, for a time my mother had made a point of dressing us in "twin dresses" made for us by her mother. As a child this had deeply disturbed me, and I had felt myself to be a bizarre visual parody of my mother. Now, as we pored over photos of us together, all that came to me was the courage and selflessness that marked her love for me. Our twin dresses struck me now as her own powerful visual telling of our connection. Toward the end, my mother saw visions of her ancestors standing behind her chair, and at times she felt that she could see beyond the materiality of her living room to some invisible world beyond. Often we sat together in comfortable silence, at sunrise or sunset, as red blossoms of light suffused the room.

Yet the "story" of political economy also constitutes a cosmology, which names and authorizes a particular sort of universe. Its invisibility as a construct makes it difficult to detect and contain its voice. This voice avoids everyday circles, so while it may trivialize or marginalize other voices, it may escape trivialization and marginalization. It is a voice that permeates Western scholarship. When scholars interpret texts or discuss people's practices, political economy is often the voice they choose to make their claims.

At the beginning of the nine-month process of my mother's death I wrote her a letter:

Dear Mom:

I thought I'd share with you a dream I had about you the evening after I came from the hospital. . . . I feel it was a . . . message to me about you from my deepest . . . self.

Anthropologists have written prolifically on virtually every aspect of Hawaiian culture.[3] In the 1970s, apace with Pacific Islander indigenous self-determination movements and cultural revivals, anthropologists began to explore ethnic identity and cultural/political practice.

By the late '80s and early '90s, a debate about the "invention of tradition" and "creating the past" (or cultural construction) had emerged, primarily in the fields of

The dream: I am talking to Mom about the difference between one side of the island we are on and the other side. The island is lush . . . tropical. I have discovered that either side appears more pleasant to the inhabitants of the other side, although the island is beautiful all around and the sides are almost interchangeable. However, on the side we are on (Mom and I) I can go down deeper into the ocean. . . .

The hidden implication in our discussion is that I can on this side go deeper into the world of the unconscious, or the metaphor. We talk at length and with great pleasure about the beauty of the island. . . . We speak of the same places, places we've shared together, for we are essentially traveling the same path.

When I wake up from such dreams I usually write the first thing that comes to mind:

Knowing you is better for me than living in Hawai'i with my "birth mother" could ever have been. . . . In this life, with you, I am going down deeper into myself. In many ways I credit you for the different types of learning which have taken place in my life, the ways my life has opened up for me. . . . You were and are, for always, my mother. Love as always,
Me

I remember one dream in particular that I had about my mother:

I am in an apartment somewhere, in the future, writing a dissertation for my Ph.D. I am walking back and forth with sheaves of paper. My mother sits on a stool at a high table off to the side. She is smiling peacefully at me and as I pass she takes a sheaf of paper from my hands. She says, "Here,

anthropology, history, and Pacific studies. In some ways we can see these debates as a response to local self-determination movements and cultural revivals.

Early discussants implied that present-day Pacific Islander cultural identity is largely a reconstruction, which is sometimes inaccurate.[4]

The invention of tradition debate arose at a particular historical moment in anthropology and Pacific studies. Although the invention of tradition debate is "over" and the discussants have moved on, it is important to note that this debate reproduced the scholarly worldview or cosmology of political economy. In particular, certain ideas about *Earth, practice, destiny,* and *knowledge* are embedded in the language and stories of early discussants such as Keesing, Linnekin, and Hanson. Although the debate involved much discussion, at the time only a few discussants (in particular, Sahlins, Trask, and Friedman) approached the invention of tradition as a cosmology.

Keesing (1994) felt that unnuanced anthropological constructions of culture, focusing on the essential, timeless differences of the exotic Other, did not take into account the effects of global capitalism and mass culture on the lives of individuals under study. He was concerned with his and other anthropologists' romanticization of the past and "the power of the pastoral vision" (1989, 30). Keesing noted that these ideas had passed into popular thought—in particular into postcolonial nationalist political rhetoric.

I think this is probably ready for me to type." As always, I'm very relieved. Her word-processing, editing, and critiquing skills are immense and she has always helped me.

I look down at her hands and suddenly realize she is naked, swollen, red, and looks exhausted, with IV needles and tubes in her arm.

I am shocked and frightened. "Mom, you're sick, you can't do this," I say. Her face is glowing, happy. She says, in the firm, no-nonsense voice she uses when she will not change her mind, "Oh yes I can."

The dream ends this way. I don't want to tell her that she's dying and my heart clutches up, because I realize that if I ever write again, she will not be beside me. She looks deep into my eyes and I realize that although her body is in this state, she is not aware of it—she is not hurting. Gently she says, "Give it to me," and I do. Then I wake up.

He urged Pacific Islanders to be skeptical of such faulty anthropological notions. Keesing's representations of *earth* were nested within, and perhaps conditioned by his focus on political rhetoric:

The symbolic themes Pacific Islanders use to assert their unity and identity have also been shaped by struggles against domination, as is most clearly manifested in the pervasive elevation of "land" as a political symbol. While I do not doubt that in precolonial times many Pacific peoples had a deep identification with and reverence for their land, this identification has become radically transformed in the course of political struggle and histories of conquest and land alienation. . . . Land has become a powerful symbol of identity and a site of contestation. An ideology of attachment to and spiritual significance of the land could achieve such prominence only in a historical context of invasion and colonization (ibid., 29).

I go back in the journal and realize that the end of my dream as I wrote it, right after I dreamed it, was actually very different:

I tell her to please stop—that it is OK for her to die, and that I don't need her to do anything. She says "OK" and I hold her and we kiss each other. I wake up knowing that mom is dying now. (JOURNAL: 1989)

On her last night at home before she left for the hospital, I gave my mother a shower and was flooded with the memory of sitting as a five-year-old in the bathtub with her. It had seemed her body was the world, and the world would last forever. Now, in the shower, her trusting eyes were large in her shrinking face, and there was a radiance about her.

As I hugged her goodnight it seemed that she journeyed away from me. Her inner loveliness was intensifying, a light filling her eyes. A wish for her healing stayed with me, like a small bubble continually bursting in my chest.

I stayed overnight with her in the hospital, after she went into a coma, and we knew that she would not regain consciousness. I remembered being an eight-year-old grump, sick and silly with fever on Halloween Eve. She had made marshmallow people with bony tooth-pick legs and arms, clove smiles, noses, and eyes. Now, I held her cooling hands and gazed at her softening, cloudy eyes.

I felt her slipping away from me and said, "It's all right, you can leave, we'll be OK," but I didn't really feel that way. When I slept on the cot at the foot of her bed she came to me in dreams saying, "Honey, everything will be all right," just as she had on that Halloween Eve, and many times since.

My father and I were each holding one of her hands, and had finally admitted we would be OK without her, when cancer called her bones home. As we felt the life go out of her hands, the room suddenly seemed to be full of her. I thought: "She is my mother; she recognized me; she knew me and chose me, from the very first."

Keesing asserted that Pacific ideologues "reconstructed ancestral pasts characterized by Mystical Wisdom, One-ness with the Land, Ecological Reverence, and Social Harmony" (ibid., 30) and populated by "imagined ances-tors": "Wise Ecologists, Mystical Sages, living in harmony with one another, cosmic forces, and the environment . . ." (ibid., 29).

Keesing's concerns about the creation of an idealized past serve to constrict the discursive space for contemporary talk about aloha 'āina and mālama 'āina. A result is the conditioning disbelief in the idea that stories might pass down through ancestral lines. Ancestral connections to land are contained in the past, and marked off from the present.

Keesing implied that the experience and class positions of present-day "Pacific Island elites" negated the possibility of ongoing relationships with their own communities, or with the land. He said that these "Westernized elites" were separated from the village communities and ancestral cultures that they invoked (ibid., 31). Keesing said that they used symbols of the past in order to deny their alienation and mask issues of class interest and noted:

Squarely situated within the establishment and sustained by institutional power and bourgeois life-styles they share with white colleagues, they are separated from their rural poor cultural cousins by wide gulfs of class interest, political power, perception, life experience, and material circumstance. (1991, 169)

After my mother was pronounced dead, I prepared her body for a healing. It felt light, it was losing volume, and my hands traveled over her bones, moved over her face, as if her face were my own. My hands found, in her face, the light, blossoming. I packed her bags, placing them in the window, and then I sat on her bed, holding her hands, feeling the light stream from them and leap into the room, and it was sunrise or sunset, a blossoming, a beating of wings, a healing.

Shortly after my mother's death I was in the hospital again with another intestinal obstruction. I dreamed of the *heiau* (ancient temple) at Pūpūkea, near Waimea on Oʻahu. There, at Puʻuo Mahuka Heiau, I had always felt the presence of my ancestors and relatives. The man who appeared in my dreams visited me again:

I am in an emergency room: "Old man" approaches me saying, "Pūpūkea is where the ancestors will meet you." I am suddenly at Pūpūkea. I search among the guava, and something in my stomach clenches, then unclenches. Trees inhale lazy spattering rain while frantic nurses dart, tubes dangling from their hands, murmuring into the forest. The small hairs on my neck puff up and I strain up the hill to the temple, to the heiau.

Up there, I look out onto surf and the rocks below. Then I am in room four-sixteen, in the hospital; then I am looking down at myself, in surgery, as my guts clench, then blossom under a scalpel. I smile through sobs and suddenly feel my mother's hand, cool on my forehead. (JOURNAL: 1989)

Reading Keesing (1989, 1991) I notice an invitation to imagine "Pacific Island elites" as bereft of elders, family stories, and cultural practices. It is difficult to imagine their lives before they went to college—in fact, it is their college experience that is easiest to imagine. Their lives are lightweight, one-dimensional, stripped of ancestors, stripped of experience. Land plays no part in their lives—either in their lived experience or as the subject of stories passed down. They are represented as genealogical and ecological isolates.

The disconnection that Keesing theorized into their lives allowed them very little authority to speak about land, or about lessons their ancestors passed down. The stories of their ancestors will not be authorized.

Keesing's discussion of ideology was aimed most particularly at Pacific islander ideologues and Westernized "elites." Yet I believe that a structure of feeling emerges, denying the plausibility of anyone who speaks of a relationship to ancestors, *ʻāina*, or the cosmos. This reproduces a Western "organization of disbelief" in the idea that land could possess or activate knowledge. Its focus on ideology, class, and alienation reproduces the cosmology of political economy. Earth has been written over.

Another dream occurred shortly after my mom's death:

I saw myself in a bed in a room with old furniture and light beaming up through the floorboards. I was conversing with my mother who looked like she was in her thirties. She was glowing with health.

Then I remembered she was dead. I turned to her almost angrily and said, "Wait a minute . . . you're dead. We can't be talking like this."

"No, I'm not dead," she said, and we went back and forth for a while, until I was really angry. I said, "You are dead, and I'm going to wake up in my bed in a few minutes, alone, and begin to cry, realizing that this was just a dream, and you're dead."

At that moment I woke up, alone, crying, realizing my mother was dead. Then, just as suddenly, I was back in the room with her, with the light shining up through the floorboards, and dust motes filtering through the light.

My mother was sitting beside me again. She said, "You see? This is real." She then pointed down through the floorboards, indicating my waking hours and said," That is the dream." Then I woke up. (JOURNAL:1989)

During this time, my second marriage began a slow slide into disintegration. Despite a core of caring and a deep intellectual connection, my husband and I were inciting in each other our worst selves. Revenge for real and imagined hurts, and real and imagined pasts raged through me. I positioned myself as a victim in my relationship and in relation to my past. I found it impossible to leave my marriage or to come to terms with my past.

Linnekin inscribed ideas about *practice* in her contributions to the invention of tradition debate. In her study of a Hawaiian community (1985) Linnekin rooted Hawaiian tradition in Hawaiian notions of family, relatedness, and exchange. She focused on exchange through giftgiving, contrasting it with articulating the value of *aloha 'āina* or engaging in Hawaiiana (traditional crafts and performance arts). In a piece on the politics of culture in the Pacific, Linnekin described Hawaiiana as "a way for Hawaiians who do not otherwise take part in nationalist activities to assert their identity" (1990, 163).

Aloha 'āina and *mālama 'āina* appeared in Linnekin's formulations as selective reappropriations of Hawaiianness for political ends (1985). In contrast, true Hawaiianness was seen to involve engaging in exchange and maintaining the land. Urban, part-Hawaiian Nationalists who didn't speak Hawaiian and whose families were "long separated from rural life" maintained a variable relationship to past practices. They contrasted sharply with those whose practices of exchange and giftgiving had "demonstrable links to the past" (ibid. 2, 9).

For Linnekin, economic practices were actual practices, while cultural practices were a form of representation. Dynamic economic exchange was contrasted with static representation of culture-as-product. This obscures the relationship that practices other than economic exchange might open up between humans and land. Linnekin described Hawaiians who work in the tourist industry:

The house we lived in burned almost completely to the ground. Among the few items left were my Hawaiian possessions, particularly old artifacts and *hula* implements that had been given to me. In one instance the flames shot down a fairly long hallway, only to stop at the back wall, inches away from a portrait of Ka'iulani that had been given to me by my mother.

We moved into another home for more than a year. After we moved back into our rebuilt home, there were two more fires; smaller, but still disturbing. Then I was diagnosed with breast cancer. My husband, despite our crumbling relationship, led my stumbling body into chemotherapy. By the time I was recovering and in radiation, we were occupying different areas of the house and I was making plans for my departure. Our marriage was over. Meanwhile, the dreams continued:

I was with dear, old friends sailing to Tahiti where we had a mission. We succeeded in the mission, which involved "liberating" an area for dolphins and other "water beings." (JOURNAL: 1992)

I was in Hawai'i, on a point. Wind, sea, mountains. There was a road, wide, long, leading through a long, long row of trees. Leading to a house. A kahuna *lived there. I was walking down the road, toward the* kahuna's *home. I was not afraid: I was very calm.* (JOURNAL: 1992)

As I prepared to leave my husband, I was fearful of the future and angry and sad about the end of the relationship. For perhaps the first time, it seemed that my feelings of sad-

Their indigenous lifeways apparently destroyed long ago, many modern Hawaiians are recruited by the tourist industry to participate in the manufacture and sale of "Hawaiian culture" for commercial ends. Certainly the pursuit of a real Hawaiian tradition is difficult in this context, where authenticity seems so easily invented, and the premise of continuity may seem farfetched in the face of wholesale change. (1985, 239)

For Hawaiians in the tourist industry, the moment of sale was the central context, and peoples' knowledge and experience were compressed into the realm of products. This makes it difficult to address how these workers might pursue "a real Hawaiian tradition" in noncommercial contexts.[5]

How do we view the practices of a *kupuna* who demonstrates *lauhala* weaving for tourists? It is difficult to imagine her collecting her materials or talking story with a *mo'opuna* who drops by. How do we view the practices of a young *hālau hula* member who dances for tourists? It is difficult to imagine her practicing *hula kahiko* in her *hālau* or studying the text of a chant.

In the lives of many tourist industry workers, we might find a rich confluence of intersecting texts, intentions, and practices, connecting humans to the land, and to one another. Linnekin's description limited this possibility, reproducing Marx's assertions about the transforming power of capital.

Linnekin recounted a story a *kupuna* told her about a burial cave that opened to this *kupuna*'s husband. This *kupuna*'s husband was told to leave an article of his own; then he might be permitted to take something. However,

ness about my birth mother's two rejections of me (at my birth and in my adulthood) "shape-shifted" into an all-encompassing rage that I could not shake. In 1993 I confronted my feelings and wrote another letter to Aileen Kawahara at Child and Family Services:

. . . You were most helpful to me when we last corresponded and spoke. However, my life events have caused me some reflection on the issue you wrote of in your 1985 letter. I desire no contact whatsoever with my birth mother—it seems to me she must have her own emotional issues.

However, I wish to know my family history. . . . I wish to know my family name. I will sign any document stating that I'll never contact my natural family if this is necessary. I feel that if she wishes to remain confidential that is fine. However, denying me knowledge of my lineage is not at all fair. I am sure you understand the value of lineage, particularly as it relates to being part Hawaiian.

When you contacted my birth mother, she felt that my presence in her life was as a wound that was being reopened. She wondered if I didn't ask about my Caucasian background. She felt that she gave adequate information regarding my medical history (and also felt as if others were) accusing her of being responsible for my life threatening situations. In 1985 I was ready to let this all drop, despite the incredible feelings of loss which resulted from . . . her words.

I certainly don't feel my existence is a wound, am curious as well about my Caucasian background, and, particularly in light of my last illness, can only describe her attitude about my medical history as impervious. . . . I want to know her medical background and certainly am unwilling at this point to go with "no medical information."

before he could return, his friends told others of its location, and *the cave sealed again, forever.* The *kupuna* explained that *the cave would open only to her husband* because he was probably related to those who were buried there (italics mine). The *kupuna* also said that you must be related to take something, and you must "leave something of your own as offering" when you depart (ibid., 40–41). Linnekin used the story to construct Hawaiian identity as residing:

. . . in the wide and unknowable extension of relatedness, the mutual, enduring obligation established by kinship, and the mandatory nature of exchange. (ibid., 40–41) (italics mine)

Was *the mandatory nature of exchange* actually a strong theme in this story? What entity opened and sealed the cave? Was the extension of relatedness actually unknowable? What entity was aware of the "wide and unknowable extension of relatedness"?

If we ask these questions, we might consider Hawaiian identity as residing in the wide extension of relatedness, which, in this case, the cave (or *'āina*) knows, and *acts upon*, the mutual, enduring obligation to follow the lessons that the land gives us.[6] Perhaps it is not the practical nature of mandatory exchange, but the daily choice to follow the lessons of the land, that is important in this story.

The cosmology that attends Linnekin's retelling of this *kupuna's* story limits access to the idea that land is the teacher, and humans are learners. Her work reproduces the discourse of political economy regarding human practice. There is little discursive space for suggestions that Earth activates practice, or is capable of being activated by practice.

Please tell me what I may do, and what my rights may be in this matter. . . .

As I was recovering from cancer and divorce, I talked at length with my father. Although Child and Family Services had sent me no new information, my father was convinced that someday I would find out about my family and even meet them. He urged me to forgive my birth mother.

He was also certain I should take a trip on a freighter, which departed from Pape'ete and traveled from island to island throughout the Marquesas. He felt that my mother, now dead for three years, was urging him to persuade me to go on this trip.

I was reluctant to go, since I was saving money for graduate school. The community college where I taught had granted me a sabbatical for the following year. I had been accepted to a number of universities to study indigenous knowledge, but understood there were not necessarily professors interested in that topic. I was also accepted at the University of Hawai'i at Manoa, but felt, on reflection, that my questions about my "origin myth" were too upsetting to deal with during a long stay in that setting.

I envisioned a Ph.D. as possibly leading to an interesting option of teaching and research at the university level. I was also wanting to pursue a degree while *not* working full time. If I spent my money on a trip to the Marquesas, that opportunity might be lost. I could not see any value in going to the Marquesas.

Linnekin (1983, 1985), Keesing (1989), and Hanson (1989) inscribed ideas about *destiny* in their contributions to the invention of tradition debate. To varying degrees, they suggested that the impact of colonization and capital in the Pacific was the pivot around which culture was constructed. They suggested that Pacific Island peoples assimilated, then externalized Western concepts of culture as (at least partially) a response to colonization and the "penetration" of the market economy.

Linnekin attributed much less vigor to capital than Keesing or Hanson. Discussing the community where she worked, she said that despite the "penetration" of a market economy over a hundred years ago, "the egalitarian ethic of village social relations has persisted" (1985, 245).

Keesing deployed Gramsci's discussion of hegemony to construct invasion and colonization as activating the "ideology of spiritual significance of the land" (1989, 29). His work generated images of acculturated natives—"Pacific Islander elites" alienated from their indigenous roots (1991, 170).

In the context of New Zealand (Aotearoa), Hanson (1989, 893) privileged the impact of colonization, noting that Maori "traditions" were the internalization of foreign representations and Western scholarly ideas of "racial greatness." Hanson also generated images of acculturated natives—Maori activists "moved by their own political agendas to appeal selectively and creatively to the tradition of their ancestors" (ibid., 898).[7]

My father finally purchased my ticket himself, and drove me to the airport to board a plane bound for Pape'ete. On the way to the airport, I fell apart. I knew that my life was going to change and I was terrified. I arrived in Pape'ete, deep in thought:

What am I doing here? What is my interpretation of my illness? I needed to get over the lump. The lump in my throat. The lump in my life. . . . (JOURNAL: 1993)

Shortly after boarding the freighter I met Ivan, a graphic designer, living in Toronto. The trip included hikes on the islands, and Ivan's presence seemed to be part of a healing journey for me. Following my inner voices, on those hikes I divested myself of items that symbolized my past, letting go of my history.

On the first hike, Ivan cheers me on, giving me water. After the hike I feel I have beat the cancer. In the clearest of pools there is a waterfall. We float up under it. I feel healed.

On the second hike we slog over muddy stones and ford streams. Sheer cliffs, caves, burial sites, waterfalls. Ivan helps me hide artifacts of my past: Mom's clock, Aunt Ricey's crystal, in secret places, in these islands. He takes photographs of the places where we have placed them. There are many sacred places here.

Just yesterday I was in chemotherapy. Just yesterday I stood with Ivan at the bow, watching dolphins making camp out on the open sea, watching them cap out of the waves. It seems like there are no accidents, no coincidences.

Given these formulations, the years before contact with the West, and other sources of historical movement recede into the background. It is easy to assume that Western contact, colonization, and the "penetration of a market economy" drive destiny.[8]

How did the invention of tradition debate approach *knowledge*, ancestry, lived experience, and everyday talk (or stories)? Keesing positioned knowledge-making as a reaction to the disconnections of Western culture, using Gramsci's notion that dominated peoples internalize the premises and categories of those who dominate them.

He told a story about how Polynesian students and faculty at the University of the South Pacific positioned *mana* as a central thread in an "ideology of a common Polynesian cultural heritage and identity." Keesing informed them that *mana* was not "a crucial concept" in a number of regional variants of Polynesian religion. Their notion of *mana* was based on wrongheaded anthropological interpretations (1989, 34–35). Keesing noted that these scholars internalized the mistaken premises and categories of scholarly work done by dominant peoples. Their knowledge was ideological, emergent from their material conditions, rather than their experiences or ancestral stories.

As we hike across this mountain-island, walls of fragrant jungle obscure our view. Tī plants dip and wave in a desultory hula, *vines and flowers extend lazily, dew falls in leafy silences. Fragile gingers lean subtly toward us in the misted wind. Fallen, half-eaten mangoes lie on the road. These are signs planted along the way. Stones alongside the road chant, procreate, acknowledge us without words. We too speak without words. The secrets of our hearts sprout shoots.* (JOURNAL: 1993)

If these scholars' sources were accurate scholarly research, would their indigenous identities be questioned? Would the fact that they are "squarely situated" in an academic space disauthenticate their indigeneity? If their sources were ancestral stories, would their scholarly identities be questioned? Would the fact that they are telling ancestral stories disauthenticate their scholarly rigor? Keesing's story shapes a narrowed discursive space for ancestral wisdom in the academy.

On the freighter there were Europeans, North Americans, and Polynesians.

I was talking to this guy from the Tuamotus and we talked about gods that we have in common. In the middle of this, the tour guide, who is German, came by and slipped him a book she had picked up for him at Bishop Museum in Honolulu. It was a volume of ancient Tuamotuan stories and chants as recorded by an anthropologist.

He was excited and said something like, "This is where I can find more knowledge, now that the last generation of stories is dying off." He told me he wasn't sure but thought one of the "informants" was in his family. He talked for a while about how old people were dying and younger people weren't getting the information. (JOURNAL: 1993)

As we traveled from island to island, for every new daybreak arrival, I felt compelled to go up top before dawn, and dance *hula kahiko* at the deserted bow. It seemed that there was some odd greeting taking place, beyond the reach of words. As I danced, I would gaze at the island, which seemed to be approaching me. As I gestured to the land, it seemed that the land moved toward me. It was as if the ship was not there.

At my first *kāhea* (recital of the first lines of the chant) the island was usually just a darker shape looming in the dark. Slowly the deep black-blue of the island would shade into purple-blue, then velvet-blue, then blue-green. This process, this journey into light, would take the length of the chant. Then it would be day. The island would loom up, walls of deep, singing green. Its wise presence would overwhelm me. At these moments, I sometimes felt

Later in the invention of tradition debate, discussants argued about the consequences of their own academic formulations, exploring issues about *knowledge* and power. Some insisted that the invention of tradition debate was innocuous, circulating only in academic circles. Others said that the debate had important consequences in big stakes issues.[9]

However, for the most part, the discussion of knowledge and power constructed *those who create knowledge in their everyday talk* as either ideologues or as victims of scholarly Western ideologies. In either case, it was assumed that indigenous people, who possess lived experience, their own ancestral stories, had little power in relation to Western scholars or the Western world.

Lindstrom and White (1995) asserted that the discussants rarely theorized Pacific Islander cultural production or everyday practices as knowledge production. They noticed a focus on national and international rhetoric rather than everyday talk (ibid., 208–209).

A notable exception was Briggs (1996), who rooted his critique of the invention of tradition literature in everyday talk. He examined indigenous discursive techniques, comparing them to those of scholars. He then described how invention of tradition scholarship "undercuts the discursive authority of native elites" (ibid., 461–462).

jury-rigged and useless walls inside my brain, dislodging, crashing down.

After the ship arrived back in Tahiti I spent some more time there with Ivan and prepared to say goodbye. On our last night together a great raging tropical storm gathered over Pape'ete and rain shimmered in the air outside our rooms.

The next morning we said goodbye and I left Pape'ete to catch my plane. As my taxi cruised into the outskirts of Pape'ete, I glimpsed Ivan, running in the rain, with his friend. Some reservoir of pain released itself, let go and flowed out of me. By the time I arrived at the Los Angeles airport I wrote in my journal:

I am ready to let the rhythm of the universe take over my life. I have come to trust that rhythm. (JOURNAL: 1993)

I am embarrassed at the sound of that phrase. Why, when it constitutes such an important turning point?

When I returned home from the Marquesas, I moved in with Linda Rose Locklear, a dear friend who taught Native American Studies. Her family lived in the mountains outside of San Diego in two houses, surrounded by land and rocks.

Pictures of her family and her ancestors inhabited her walls along with feathers, stones, and turtle shell rattles. Sometimes a nearby creek flooded the only access to the road where she lived, allowing me a day off from work. I felt surrounded by the warmth of her family, yet alone and utterly free.

For the most part, the discussants conceptualized cultural production as ideology rather than pedagogy. H. Trask was one of the first exceptions to this tendency. Like other discussants, H. Trask (1991, 1993) used the language of political economy, critiquing anthropologists as part of the colonial challenge to Native cultural resistance.

However, H. Trask also grounded knowledge in land, ancestry, lived experience, and everyday talk of Hawaiians. She described Hawaiians as having a present-day genealogical, familial, and protective relationship to the land, through bloodline and birthplace (1993, preface).

H. Trask told of a debate she had with a historian. She offered the song *"Kaulana na Pua"* and then a story passed down in her family as evidence that the Hawaiian people were against the overthrow of Lili'uokalani, and the historian dismissed these sources as invalid. H. Trask noted:

And so, history goes on, written in long volumes by foreign people. Whole libraries begin to form, book upon book, shelf upon shelf. At the same time, the stories go on, generation to generation, family to family. . . . If it is truly our history Western historians desire to know, they must put down their books, and take up our practices. First, of course, the language. But later, the people, the 'aina, the stories. Above all, in the end, the stories. (ibid., 156–157)

I visited Ivan in Toronto during spring break. There I felt oddly at home. One late afternoon I dropped into the Ontario Institute for Studies in Education (OISE) at the University of Toronto. That department was closed down, and only one faculty member was there, working at his computer terminal, his office filled to bursting with books. His name was George J. Sefa Dei, and one of his areas of interest was indigenous knowledge.

I applied for admission at OISE, but was informed that the decision was delayed. Later the admissions committee said they would read my application anyway. As time began to run out and my going-away party loomed, I told people I was going to go to the University of Toronto. They never bothered to ask me if I had

Another influential exception was Hau'ofa (2000, 455), who critiqued political economy's use of the term "capitalist penetration" and the notion that Pacific history began with the arrival of Europeans. He privileged everyday talk:

Our histories did not begin with the coming of Europeans. If we continue to rely for the reconstructions of our remote pasts mainly on the works of archaeologists, botanists, zoologists, and the like, we will still be trapped with our pasts as prehistory. We must resort very seriously to our ecologically based oral narratives. (ibid., 457)

been accepted, and I never thought that I might not attend there.

Ivan invited me to live with him while I was in Toronto. Despite the fact that we had known one another for so little time, I impulsively decided to move in with Ivan. I had my going-away party and moved my things to Toronto, then flew there, although I had not yet been accepted and had spaces waiting for me at other universities in the United States. Those spaces were in sociology departments, while at OISE, in the Department of Sociology in Education, George J. Sefa Dei was exploring the role of indigenous knowledge in the academy.

After about a month Linda Rose called me to say that she had received a call from the University of Toronto for me. I immediately called the University of Toronto from my new home just down the road. The individual whom I called told me I was accepted to the University of Toronto, and asked me when I could be there. She was shocked when I told her "in about twenty minutes." When I told her I was already in Toronto, she asked, "What are you doing in Toronto?" "Wishful thinking," I said, suddenly realizing how crazy that sounded.

George J. Sefa Dei became my faculty advisor, and later, my dissertation supervisor. There were several students working on the topic of indigenous knowledge. They were from Kenya and Ghana, First Nations (indigenous) students from Canada, and non-indigenous Canadian students who worked with First Nations communities. We became close friends.

Hau'ofa asserted that academic history exclude's orally transmitted and therefore undocumented pasts. He privileged the act of passing down memories as central to "the strengthening of our autonomous identities" (ibid., 463). He also grounded knowledge in land, ancestry, lived experience, and everyday talk.

Friedman (1992b) also posited oral history as an alternative to an academic history which defined Hawaiian culture (knowledge) as a thing of the past. Friedman privileged the continuity of culture as passed down from *kūpuna*. He felt that *'ohana, aloha,* and *aloha 'āina* were values that were continuous rather than invented (ibid., 843).

What were the consequences when discussants focused on Pacific Islander cultural production or everyday practices as ideology rather than pedagogy? What is important here is not what *was* seen, but rather what was *not* seen—not what claims *were* made, but what claims were *not* made.

In this debate, the successful struggle to recuperate Kaho'olawe, the sovereignty movement, and a far-reaching cultural revival were rarely discussed as other than epiphenomena of ideology. Very little (or no) agency was attributed to everyday people who, through their work, created (and continue to create) social change. The possibility that the dedication they brought to their work could be a consequence of everyday talk was not entertained.

I was interested in looking at the pedagogy of Hawaiian cultural practices, which were increasingly linked to political practice and the intensifying discourse on sovereignty. I felt that cultural production, as pedagogy, opened up ways for Hawaiians to engage the past, the present, and the future, in particular ways, propelling social change.

In my dissertation proposal my aim was to explore how Hawaiian cultural practices "teach" people about Hawaiian land and identity. I also wanted to discover how elders' remembrances of the past might structure ties and responsibilities to the past, present, or future.

Although Ivan and I hardly knew each other, our life together was easy, as if we had lived with each other for years. Despite the fact that my decision to move to Toronto made no sense on the surface, I felt guided and protected. Never once, in spite of the rapidity of these transformations, did I question the radiance that was pouring through my life.

However, my relationship with texts I was studying at OISE was not so easy. I struggled with the literature of political economy and the invention of tradition debate. Although necessary for my dissertation proposal and comprehensive examination, it seemed that these frameworks did not deepen my understanding of Hawaiian cosmologies or knowledge-making.

Cultural production and everyday talk were not acknowledged as forms of knowledge-creation.[10] The possibility that knowledge generated in a spiritual context might propel change was not entertained. The spectacular wave of social change that was (and is) shaped and driven by everyday Hawaiians remained largely unacknowledged.

At the time of the invention of tradition debate, in everyday contexts, rich connections could be seen between knowledge, spirituality, and social change. As well, there were powerful claims to be made about the clearly visible agency of everyday people. At that point, from within the debate, these connections were not seen; these claims were not made.

In the evenings that problem, which lived in academic hyperreality, was dwarfed by the very real daily presence of Lake Ontario, shape-shifting outside our windows. Waves billowed, whipped by the wind. Or they disappeared. Or they iced up into static, white surf-bytes. Sometimes the wind howled, sometimes it whispered, sometimes it rattled our windows. Although the days were full of texts, night just next to Lake Ontario seemed to be populated by spirits and metaphors. By the time I was writing my dissertation proposal, this dream came to me:

I'm searching through texts in a very upscale-looking store with Ivan. We are befuddled by all we must do and by the array of things there: books, post office, bank machine, food, store clerks behind counters. It seems we are wandering aimlessly. Finally we leave, and he asks, "Do you want to go to the bookstore?" I envision a big warehouse full of books, and I don't want to go.

Suddenly I'm on a ship, traveling through Polynesia. The tourists on the ship are taking videos of a place that looks like the North Shore of Kaua'i. They are unable to see the heart of the place. They want to duplicate exactly in the video the colors of the island, but they are unable to. They stand before the island, but are transfixed by and perceptually stuck to their viewfinders.

I'm aware that to them, later, it may seem like we were silenced/silent. The "we" is all the islanders at this particular place, which somehow has come to include me. We are aware that these tourists move through the world perceptually stuck inside big, barely permeable bubbles.

What can be said about the literature of political economy and the invention of tradition debate as cosmologies? At certain junctures, the literature of political economy represented an inversion of *The Kumulipo* and works by Kamakau and Ii. At certain junctures the invention of tradition debate reproduced the worldview of political economy.

Political economy constructed a hierarchy of beings, that wrote over any human genealogical connection to Earth, and other creatures and features of the cosmos. It denied the potential of spirit to activate matter. Nature was the extended body of humans.

The invention of tradition debate positioned claims to a genealogical connection to the universe as ideological, reactions to the transforming power of capital. Capital animated spirit. The relationship between Nature/Earth and humans was written over.

Political economy discussed practice by positioning humans in competition for scarce resources. Nonhuman creatures and features of the cosmos were divested of emotion, intent, and purpose.

The invention of tradition debate privileged practice in pre-Contact-derived economic exchange systems. Contemporary attempts to "tap into" other forms of consciousness in the cosmos or promote the role of humans in guardianship of other species were reconfigured as representation.

I go to my quarters and begin packing, dressing for an excursion we will go on—all of us, tourists and islanders. It seems I'm an interface: I'm a tourist in my travels, but treated as an islander. I'm dressing for the outing and am suddenly aware that I have on mainland-style clothes. I look down at myself, surprised and somehow afraid.

I pull the clothing off and begin packing . . . my Hawaiian instruments, made in the ancient style, because I know that the heiau / marae *(temple) will be a place to chant. I've packed my* ipu, 'ūlili, 'ulī 'ulī, pū'ili, 'ili 'ili, niu, *even* 'ohe-hano-ihu. *All are ancient-style "percussive" instruments used for the chant, except for* 'ohe-hano-ihu, *which is a nose flute, a haunting, melancholy-sounding instrument.*

I am suddenly aware this 'ohe-hano-ihu *I have packed is not mine. I don't have an* 'ohe-hano-ihu. *So whose is it? I search back through the bag for it, only to find it is an ancient sennit bag—it is not my bag. All the instruments I had packed as mine, but handcrafted by me or my* kumu hula *twenty years ago have been transformed into ancient instruments. . . .*

The tour guide is (the) kupuna *(and is) standing outside my door. Through the door he sends me the thought: "What is the ancestry of experience?" I have never heard this phrase before, but I know it is important for me. I take his question to mean: How do my ancestors prefigure my experience, in their voices, brought into historical memory that I've heard, danced, coded? But the question means more. There is at least one other layer that I do not yet understand.*[11]

In political economy, destiny was related to the movement of capital and the ability to control scarcity. Colonization was seen as the inevitable incursion of capital and consequent overturning of local modes of production.

In the invention of tradition debate, Pacific Island destiny was related to economic and cultural responses to colonization. Colonization was seen as the inevitable incursion of capital and consequent overturning of local modes of economic and, further, cultural production.

Political economy denied nonhuman sources of knowledge. It constructed knowledge as ideological, emerging from the human practice of material acquisition.

The invention of tradition debate reconfigured contemporary indigenous knowledge as ideological. Claims about ancestry or bloodline as the core of identity were Western-derived responses to colonization. Stories that tell us that the cosmos manifests emotion, intent, and purpose were not given a full reading. Storytelling was reconfigured as representation.

The kupuna *knows the answers. He has given me a* kaona, *a phrase with multiple meanings. I open the door and (he) . . . is there, still sending thoughts. He is a small man, old, with deep-set eyes. He does not speak to me, but we are still conversing. He tells me that we can talk-story, or I can sleep while we travel to the . . .* heiau/marae.

It is at the confluence of two different tide systems (where) important practices related to atonement take place. I am aware that the stones, left by the people to show others the way and to make offering, will look like part of the landscape. I am fumbling to lock the door. The kupuna *says to me, again, "What is the ancestry of experience?"*

He pauses, then says, "You do not have to lock the door; nobody will want those things. The way to this place of sacrifice is flat. There are no hills. The ride is easy."

(We are) going to a place like Waipi'o on the Big Island, Hawai'i, where there is a confluence, the great falls of Hi'ilawe, the birthplace of Kamehameha. I'm still trying to lock the door. "It is just such a place of confluence. It is a place of importance to you," he says, looking through me. As I wake up his voice says to me, "First, you must make your claims. Stake your ground then, and dig our voices up. We will manifest." (JOURNAL: 1994)

I had this dream before a meeting to evaluate my dissertation proposal:

Ivan and I are watching a salmon run, standing above a cement wall lining a flowing stream. At the end of the wall are smaller cement paths through which they are supposed to go, and on these paths stand game wardens, assigned to protect the

The invention of tradition debate surfaced and flowed in scholarly circles throughout the Pacific and ultimately played out. The speed with which it traveled and changed and the new formulations it fed call up the image of a wave.

The academic genealogies of the early writers I have mentioned are varied. However, one epistemological ancestor, political economy, offered a unifying primordial cosmology, which was woven into the fabric of much of their work.[12]

Robillard (1992, 22) discusses how Polynesian and scholarly discourses of social change incorporate languages that sustain their particular worlds. He concludes that the anthropocentric language of political economy used to describe Pacific Island social change marginalizes the supernatural.

He echoes Povinelli's (1995, 505–506) suggestion that political economy has not been interrogated because it has become invisible, widely accepted as part of a "neutral" or "objective" paradigm. This cosmology, for the most part invisible and unexamined, excises ancestry from experience and Earth from identity.

I believe that the cosmology of political economy is not only at the root of other academic conversations such as the invention of tradition debate, it is also embodied in many academic environments.

Orr (1992) notes that in such environments scholars have little or no relationship to Earth, the land that surrounds them. Architecture, landscaping, and the design of work spaces routinely separate humans from Nature.

salmon. We are there to witness the salmon run. They are running up from where we stand, on the wall, through these cement "gateways."

But something is wrong. A lot of them are turning back. Being surrounded by cement has made them lose their way. We keep putting our hands in the water, so that as they turn back, the salmon will gently bump into our hands. This some of them do, and then they turn, to run upriver where they will spawn, going past the game wardens, on their cement "pathways." There is a sense that this is a life and death struggle.

One very large salmon that seems to be green (rather than pink) is in trouble down the way. He is actually jumping out of the water, trying to land on the cement, pounding himself against the wall.

Ivan gets a hook and line and hooks the salmon from the mouth, and we hurriedly carry it over to where the game wardens are, hoping to put it back in the water where it will be saved and go upstream. We realize it is bigger than a salmon, and its greenish tint marks it as something else, which still needs to be saved, needs to run upriver to spawn.

As we get to the game wardens, one of them, a woman, begins to yell at us for having hooked the fish. There is little time to respond and we merely say, "Hurry, this fish was trying to jump on land. We need to save it so it can go upriver." She seems to immediately understand our intention, and we bend down to help unhook this huge fish. Nobody questions its size or its need to be saved and move upriver.

Ivan goes to pull the hook out, and the woman and I realize that the fish's eye is somehow damaged by the hook, which has gone through the roof of his

There may be no sense that we are sustained by the land.

In such environments, capital, in the form of funding, animates practice. From within this scarcity paradigm, one's destiny is seen to proceed from one's ability to produce and appropriate knowledge. Among colleagues, this conditions competition for scarce resources.

Sources of knowledge that are nonhuman or require patience may be denied. A need to be in Nature and reflect may be subsumed by a feverish work schedule. An attitude of *ha'aha'a* (humility) may be viewed as inappropriate. One's family may be seen as peripheral or as an obstacle to "student success." Ancestral knowledge sources may be walled off from classroom dialogues.

These environments embody an inverted "other" of Hawaiian cosmology from which the ancestry and experience of Hawaiians (and other indigenous peoples) may be evaluated. Yet they may appear to be "neutral," escaping examination and interrogation.

When scholars interpret texts or discuss people's practices, the anthropocentric language of political economy is often the voice they choose to make their claims. The disconnect evidenced in this cosmology, separating ancestry from experience and Earth from identity, makes it easy to routinely erase the subjectivity of land. What are potential consequences of that erasure for everyday people, or for scholars?

The invention of tradition debate probably did not directly affect many of the subjects under discussion. *Kūpuna, kumu hula, hālau hula* members, canoe paddlers, political activists, parents who put their kids into Hawaiian language immersion programs—everyday people who make change—do not necessarily look to

mouth. The fish will lose his eye. Ivan nevertheless pulls the hook out and the eye does not seem damaged. I say to the woman and Ivan, "I don't know why this has happened—why is this one so dislocated?" We turn him over and in his stomach are pounded two very large nails, more like stakes. The tines of a fork also protrude from his stomach.

I hold the fish while the woman and Ivan pull out these things in his belly. We are all crying. There is no blood, and he seems fine and flops back over on his belly. I am wishing there were a way to say goodbye, when he rises up on the water, on his tail. Then he grasps my head, sort of caressing my head, and shaking my hair through his fingers. I am shocked to realize he has a hand, and fingers.

He says, "Go up that hill and through the trees, and then look down at this place. You will see something very different. It is important to you." He repeats this claim, and I realize he is mahimahi *(dolphin fish). He joins the salmon and moves upstream.*

I look up at this misty hill (like British Columbia or Moloka'i overlooking Kalaupapa). Through the distance I see the trees he is telling me to stand among when I look down on this place. I realize that he is telling me to look here, where we "are" from this ancestral place.

I had this dream while working on the comprehensive examination:

I am wandering around somewhere that sort of looks like Kaua'i. I know I am going to a sacred place, but I can't find my way; the landscape is covered with mist. The mist begins to rise. I have no feelings

the academy for validation. The voices and actions of everyday people were contained, but only within a limited academic discussion—not where the everyday struggle lived.

For those in the academy, within which abstractions and formulations gain a life of their own, did this discussion have consequences?

Because the invention of tradition work wrote over the voice of the Earth, it was easy to contain the voices of present-day indigenous scholars who made claims about land.[13] For indigenous scholars, though debilitating, this is not new or surprising. Nor does it eclipse the importance of everyday struggles outside the academy that inform the work of many indigenous scholars. It is simply part of a larger engagement that requires tenacity and courage.

The scholars with stakes in this discussion may have experienced heated, even unfriendly interactions. Yet this is not new or surprising either. Possibly the only consequence is to academic knowledge-making itself; the emptiness of the same story, the same cosmology re-packaged, retold, and endlessly re-validated.

Long after the invention of tradition debate has been forgotten, the cosmology of political economy that it reproduced will seep into new academic discourses. Images, stories, and ideas—artifacts of this cosmology—will seep into new claims and debates, reproducing the same sort of discursive terrain.

because I am a part of what is happening: I am just a person watching the mist rise. When I wake up I am grinding my teeth and moaning. Ivan is telling me, "You're having a nightmare." This is strange because there was no emotion as the mist rose in the dream—I wouldn't have typified it as a nightmare.

Of all the dreams I had, this was hardest to understand. It seemed to be a dream about knowing, or about finding out. I had the feeling that something was about to be revealed to me when I woke up. Why was I grinding my teeth?

I remember getting up and going to the window after that dream. It was that peculiar moment between night and dawn when the land, lake, and sky would melt into one another in various hues of gray.

I felt that if I had just held on to my dream a figure would have walked toward me in the mist. Then I would have known. Who was grinding my teeth?

I looked out the window at seemingly tiny whitecaps—silver tribes of foam on the lake. They were processing in rows, barely brushing against one another—telegraphing deeper shifts below the surface.

These texts, political economy and the invention of tradition debate, contain stories about Earth, ancestry, and experience that trace the contours of their own discursive worlds. These are the discursive worlds visited by the Hawaiian literature and its inheritors. These are the discursive worlds that will receive their stories.

We occupy the confluence of these texts, the Hawaiian literature, the literature of political economy, and the invention of tradition debate. They each use a particular language to sustain a particular commonsense worldview. Like wave systems, they each create unforeseen phenomena—backwash, undertow, artifacts washed ashore.

We need to remember that in that confluence we are provided with various ancestries of experience. We are provided with various ways to talk about who we are, what we learn, who we want to be, and how we want to structure our practices and lives. Choices emerge. Deep below the movements of these wave systems, on the ocean floor, the sand shifts, imperceptibly. It may be that as we occupy this confluence, deep inside us, structures of intention shift, imperceptibly.

3 Dig Up Our Voices

Kalo and Her 'Ohana

Shortly after my dream about the mist rising, I began to prepare to do preliminary field work on O'ahu. Initially I planned to observe, record, and transcribe Hawaiian cultural events. I also planned to tape and transcribe interviews with participants in cultural production—particularly *kūpuna* active as teachers, and young people. After this preliminary work I planned additional field research either on- or off-island, depending on the nature of the preliminary fieldwork, and suggestions for comparative work.

Most of the field research and interviews were to take place on O'ahu, mostly in and around Honolulu. Much political activity on the part of sovereignty and activity in cultural production was taking place in urban areas in Hawai'i. Pedagogies of cultural production in an urban setting seemed a fitting subject for my dissertation in the sociology of education.

I planned to take field notes on the events I attended and interview people involved in those events. Even though I was adhering to the proper research protocols, somehow it felt as if I would be "using people."[1]

Ethnomethodology, as a way of doing research, allows us to receive people's stories that might provide a contrast to *political economy* and *the invention of tradition debate*. Ethnomethodology privileges the role of the "talk" people use, as it evinces how they construct their own realities.[2] There is no privileged discourse, no "one true reality." However, we can ask: "How is the 'real' socially constructed as real?" Rather than directly producing a theory about how people create knowledge, ethnomethodology asks how people construct knowledge.

In everyday situations as they interact, people "do knowledge" in a particular way, creating meaning as an ongoing enterprise Through the sequencing of acts and talk, people organize their interaction, construct meaning, and accomplish knowledge (Heap, 1990). Not only do they constitute individual selves through their narratives, they also shape collective selves.

We can assume that the people who are interviewed will not only say what they know and mean but they'll also, perhaps unconsciously, show how they produce knowledge and meaning in their talk. Through the content, form, and sequencing of their talk, people will accomplish "social

I felt caught between my Hawaiian-style ideas of learning and my University-style ideas of research. In my own experience in the Hawaiian community, there was an aversion to being intrusive and overly curious. It was extremely impolite to "take control" of interaction with someone who was teaching you or telling your something. On the other hand, at University, community people were "informants," and I was encouraged to focus on "getting data" that would be relevant to a pre-formulated research question.

As I was working through these issues, I decided to call Kalo, my friend who had been involved closely with me in the Hawaiian Club in San Diego. After she had moved back to Hawai'i, I had visited her and kept in touch with her. When I had last visited Kalo on O'ahu, she was involved in a self-determination organization. She knew of my attempts to find out my ancestry and had helped me with that project in Hawai'i.

However, many moves and changes in the last eight years or so had separated us. I had not spoken to Kalo in a while. When I called her, heard her voice, and we began to share our news, those years seemed to fall away. Kalo told me she was a public school administrator and was involved in a Hawaiian women's civic club that supports Hawaiian culture and communities, helps its members, and which is an auxiliary to a men's civic organization.

Kalo offered to help with my fieldwork and suggested we *holoholo* (travel around). We could attend some events and interview *kūpuna* whom Kalo knew through the civic club. Some

structure" as they see, describe, and propose a definition of a situation.

We can also assume that the interviewer's words will tell us her feelings about the interview, her relationship to the *kūpuna* she interviews, her take on Hawaiian identity, and her personal agendas. The interviewer will not just be "asking questions"; she will be actively guiding the production of knowledge.

Certainly political and economic forces have shaped social structure and social change in Hawai'i. Perhaps less noticeable is everyday talk that people creatively produce. Hawaiian identity is embedded in Hawaiian common sense notions and approaches that come into the language in the form of stories, music, or everyday conversation. The late Edith Kanaka'ole, noted *kumu hula*, spoke of the way language contains common sense knowledge:

As soon as one of the *kupuna* felt the urge to chant, they would chant. All the children were made welcome, were invited to come and hear. The ones who were most interested would listen and learn. You learned all at once about your homeland, your *'ohana* (family), the flow of life, your language—and the names—all the understanding you should have. You learned the relationships in back of a word. You learned life, flowing like water, the flow moving from generation on to generation. (Hess 1979, 3)

Hawaiian ideas about land, ancestry, and identity can be located in practical, familiar, everyday language. Commonplace ways of talking about things reveal the ways people construct their worlds and themselves. In everyday

of them were in the "Kupuna in the Schools Program," a publicly sponsored program in which *kūpuna* are hired to teach Hawaiiana in the schools. The *kūpuna* we would interview were well known and involved in teaching and community work on O'ahu. I was amazed at her generosity and excited about the prospect of being able to spend some time with her again. Toward the end of our conversation, Kalo also asked if I was going to continue my "search" and I said, "No. There's really no need." The idea of having to revisit this issue was troubling and I felt that a search for my ancestry would distract me from my fieldwork goals.

After I spoke to Kalo I revised my plans and rethought this preliminary trip. I asked Kalo to conduct the interviews and positioned myself as a listener, since I felt the knowledge of *kūpuna* to be constructed in relation to others, and having lived off-island for so long, I had no deep relationships with *kūpuna* in Hawaii.[3] I felt that in a formal interview, *kūpuna* would have no space, or relationship, within which to truly share their knowledge with me. I was also aware that I could not at that point incorporate both my role as an "interviewer" and my role as a learner. I needed to dispose of the role of "interviewer" in order to be able to listen to *kūpuna*. I knew that although Kalo would conduct "interviews," her relationship as a learner would prevail.

I also felt that the sorts of information yielded in an interview between Kalo and *kūpuna* she was close to would be deeper than for the people I had planned to interview, because of the closeness of the relationship. This was what was most compelling about Kalo's offer. I believed

talk identity is (re)created, discourses are opened and sustained, and society is transformed.

In Hawai'i, there is a strong tradition of "talk story," or participating in everyday conversation. Talk story is a form of everyday talk, consisting of conversation about family, friends, everyday happenings, or gossip. People also might talk about the plots of movies, TV shows, or books. People often bring up stories having to do with the past.

The object of talk story is to tell a good story and not to "give information." People don't usually interrupt such stories—that would be considered rude. Ito (1985, 304) notes that although it is permissible to exclaim in wonderment or indicate interest, questions that break the story's flow are not considered polite. Through talk story, people "pass the time of day" and connect in a casual context. Ito (1999) suggests that through everyday activities and "talk story" urban Hawaiians who are not necessarily connected to the land or do not have a "conscious phenomenological understanding of Hawaiian culture" nevertheless express shared patterned ideas conveying Hawaiian culture (148).

We can theorize "talk story" as a specialized sort of talk. We can also think of the interview as a specialized sort of talk. Talk story seems like insiders' talk, where speakers cocreate their own process of knowing and are

that what might become central was not the information they gave but how they structured knowledge in relation to Kalo.

I felt that there was the possibility that the interview would begin to resemble talk story, and there would be a space, in that case, for the *kūpuna* to truly share their knowledge with Kalo. Although I could not account for this feeling, I had a strong sense that interview occasions demanded my silence.

Before speaking to Kalo I had expected to interview people to whom I wasn't connected, and therefore to get fairly terse answers to my questions. I had formulated my list of questions in my research proposal without taking into account the opportunity to have a person related to those interviewed conducting the interviews. I had felt a great sense of insecurity about this—there was something about it that seemed such a deep departure from the ways that I had learned from others in our community in the past.

Kalo was giving me a great gift. I felt a deep sense of relief at my newfound silent role. Kalo had freed me from any sense of my own intrusion or inappropriate curiosity in the context of an interview. Hopefully, Kalo and her "interviewees" would feel empowered to "invent" their own theoretical frameworks and enact their own intentions.

Since I wanted the *kūpuna* to be much freer to talk, I revised my interview questions, cutting them down to only five that Kalo could reformat, resequence, use as a guide, or dump entirely, as she wished. I wanted Kalo and her *kūpuna* to have more space to talk story.[4]

not interrupted by outside protocols. In contrast, an interview may often involve the interviewee performing knowledge for the interviewer. Interview protocols, questions, or realizations that the interviewer is an outsider may alter the interviewee's performance. My suspicion is that when an interview becomes more like talk story, people are more likely to be saying what they really mean.

The ethnomethodological approach suppresses the researchers' drive to theorize or to come into research with a preconceived set of assumptions or agendas. Usually researchers are empowered to textually "invent" the culture they believe themselves to be studying (Wagner 1981). In this context field notes become extensions of the ways that field experience transformed the writer's own notions and culture (ibid., 12).

Data reformulated into ethnographic writing "enacts a specific strategy of authority" and erases the talk and action of informants (Clifford 1988, 25). These partial "ethnographic truths," now textualized, lose their connection to the practices of specific actors (Clifford 1986; 1988).

In such accounts the "describer" (or writer) voices all knowledge as a monologue. In some ways the power to articulate meaning is taken from those who are "described." The researcher has appropriated words, adapting them to her own intentions or theoretical frameworks.

My questions were:

1. How did you come to be involved in teaching others about Hawaiian culture? Why do you do it?
2. What do you feel is important to pass down to the younger generation?
3. What dangers are Hawaiians facing today, and what strengths do Hawaiians have in facing those dangers?
4. What is the role of Hawaiian spirituality and Hawaiian knowledge about the land as we move into the future?
5. A lot is happening right now—are you hopeful for the future?

Much later, when I began to transcribe the interviews, the cadence of Kalo's voice and the other voices I taped was missing. While I heard their repeated words or phrases as emphasis, on the printed page they looked redundant. While I heard their pauses as an invitation to reflect, their silences looked awkward on the page. I decided to try to write their words as the poetry I heard.

I also felt that encasing shortened excerpts of their talk in my own descriptive narratives seemed to obscure their practices. For me, their words constituted a narrative, an experience, and could "stand alone." In contrast, my comments were academic formulations, whose existence relied on the voices of the *kūpuna*. I decided to include my thoughts and comments in the columns alongside their words. Following are their words and my thoughts.

Some ethnographers attempt to reinsert the describer in the described, in order to make transparent the conditions of the production of their own knowledge (Borofsky 1994). They may write reflexively, describing their own process of knowledge production.

Other researchers may find ways to do more dialogic work in the field, collaborating more closely with those who are the subjects of their research. This approach suggests that meaning always partly belongs to another person, who is part of the interplay of talk (S. Hall 1997).

Ethnomethodological approaches may help researchers to stay inside the dialogic nature of talk. In doing so, perhaps it is more likely that the "other person," who is part of the enterprise of creating meaning, may not be closeted away.

It is probably the closeting away of "subjects of research" that most unfairly empowers us when we write about others. Ethnomethodological approaches may to a certain extent destabilize the power that we hold when we do research.

Kalo took me to interview her 'ohana during a holiday gathering. We met at the home of Kalo's sister (Mom) and her husband, Kalo's brother-in-law (Dad). They live in a Hawaiian Homelands area. Kalo's two nieces (Big Sis and L'il Sis), and Kalo's nephew (Junior) were there. Kalo's mom (Grama) was also present. I've used pseudonyms here that refer to their relationship to one another. A few other family members sat nearby in the kitchen, listening and commenting. Smaller children came in and out of the room, and family members held a baby in turn. I added a few questions of my own at the very end of the interview, because I knew Kalo's family members.

'OHANA

Mom: We can't even buy our land.

Big Sis: No. It's sad.

[Silence, Baby vocalizing.]

Dad: So, why SHOULD we buy the land, when we OWNED the land? When was OUR land? Suddenly there is this man, he tells you you cannot go onto the land. Now it's "private property."

Big Sis: Because when they got you running, running back and forth you ain't gonna achieve anything, nothing will be achieved. Then you still, by the time you ready for die, you STILL fighting over that piece of land. Buy 'em back from the white man. You like the land back?

MY THOUGHTS

The issue of land pervaded the interview. Here, Mom is talking about the land Hawaiians once lived on.

Dad refers here to the *haole*.

Big Sis is referring to the process of trying to get one's family plots back by legal means, using reparation monies to purchase land. Her voice, as she enters into a debate about how to reclaim the land, is filled with frustration and outrage. There is a sense that she is saying: "Just do what it takes!"

Buy 'em back, all the money they giving us!
Buy the land back!

L'il Sis: The land is not the key! The water is the key! You got the water; you got the white man!

Mom: But the water is on the land.

Big Sis: Buy the land back. The water comes with the land.

L'il Sis: The water is everything. The water is our life.
('OHANA: 659–723)

At this point Big Sis is yelling and she has shifted the discussion back onto the economic dominance of the *haole*. All voices are raised.

L'il Sis's thoughts about the water, unlike prior comments, remind me of the notion of water as the essence of life in *The Kumulipo*. It seems that she has somehow reframed the discussion. Her voice is trembling. In this section, the topic of water/land shifts from buying them back, to their relatedness to one another, to the idea that it is "our life." It flows from a focus on dispossession to a statement that sounds grounded in spirituality rather than materiality.

Dad: I'd rather live in the *lo'i* and live on the land.

Mom: No, I don't think in your condition you can handle the *lo'i*.

[Others: laughter]

Here Dad discusses the land by referring to the *lo'i*, the *kalo* (taro) patch. Dad says he would like to go back to old ways of farming. Mom brings up his inability to engage in those practices due to his present physical condition.

Big Sis: See? See? You know that's the same stuff that keeps pushing the Hawaiians back. When the Hawaiians say, "I, I like do this." "No, I don't think you can do THAT." No. I don't think that's right.

[Others: laughter]

Big Sis does not make it obvious as to who has a part in formulating or circulating notions that disable Hawaiians. She focuses instead on the consequences of those notions.

Mom: No, you gotta be realistic.

Big Sis: No, no. You saw that. You put your mind to it, you can do it.

The discussion becomes a debate on the topic of impracticality of engaging in subsistence practices on the land.

Junior: Yeah.

Mom: That's what I say, we lost the land, where we going go? We cannot go back to our culture. Unrealistic. That's not for us already.

Big Sis: So what we do, we, we get the land back, right?
('OHANA: 801–831)

Kalo: How do you feel about the land, the issues about the land? Part of the Hawaiian Homelands, the Five-F, the Ceded Lands, the Crown Lands?

Mom: Any land in Hawai'i should have never been sold to outsiders.

Junior: Should be written.

Mom: The land should have stayed with . . .

Big Sis: That's it, return 'em. Any land that wasn't supposed to be sold should be returned. That's it. Period. I don't care what's on it, who on 'em, return 'em. No belong to the person who sold it to them, if the person who bought 'em. "Sorry, you take it up with the person who sold 'em to you," and so forth. Cause this land was not supposed to be sold. From the beginning. Return it. *Jus' li'dat.* Simple. No gotta sit down and, "No, but I paid fifteen million for this, yaaaaa." (Voice rises.) "Oh, that's YOUR problem, *brah.* You go take 'em up with the guy you paid that fifteen million."
('OHANA: 1072–1098)

Mom's statement presupposes that culture emanates from practices "on the land" and that therefore culture is not within reach. Big Sis completes the circle linking culture to land, by suggesting that the land, and thus the culture, can be reclaimed.

Kalo modifies the original question about land, speaking of different types of land in relation to current legal and political realities. She invites a debate about the present. Mom discusses all land, regardless of Kalo's distinctions, and moves immediately into issues about loss of land in the past.

I think that Junior is saying that it should be enacted into law.

Big Sis interrupts, asserting the importance of Hawaiians having been forced to give up land over the problem of how to deal with the buying and selling that went on. The history of dispossession haunts the family and enters this discussion in emotional ways. The land is tied to issues around loss rather than past experiences of abundance. *Jus' li'dat* means just like that. Big Sis takes up a complaining tone especially when she gets to "yaaaaa." *Brah* means brother. Big Sis is alluding to the commercial or wealthy interests that presently possess much land in Hawai'i.

Mom: . . . of all the Hawaiians in the island, to vote, "yes, we sell it" not one body making the decision to sell.

Big Sis: Right.

Mom: It's wrong. But that's what happened.

Big Sis: No, but they, they say: "You sell your land, or you die."

Mom: Right! But they're . . .

Big Sis: Right! The Bayonet Constitution. Either you GIVE ME THE LAND you, for this fifty cents piece, or I going kill you! Take 'em. No. What you going do? You fight 'em, they kill you, they get it FOR FREE!

[Silence.]

Big Sis: How you gonna act?

[Silence.]
('OHANA: 1622–1650)

Dad: Because, before the people of Hawai'i was farming for the *kalo,* was farming for survive.

Big Sis: To live, yeah.

Dad: Now, everything's you get money. Yeah?

Grama: Yeah, it started out way, it happened way back. When the Hawaiians were pro-

Mom voices deep anguish connected with loss of the land, and notably talks about "not one body" here. As I reflect on the term "nobody" I get a visual image of absence. "Not one body" conjures up a line of people waiting, waiting for their objections to be heard. This drives me deeper into her anguish.

Although "they" is a designation that shifts during this interview, "they" is often used to designate *haole* interests. Discussion of the past centers on loss. The lines between Hawaiians and non-Hawaiians are clearly drawn when it comes to historic or present-day dispossession.

The force of this statement and the silences surrounding it convey intense hopelessness and rage. Big Sis's use of the term "you" grounds this historical process in the present, as does her question: "How you gonna act?" This phrase merges Hawaiians in the past and present, rather than separating them by asking, "What could our ancestors have done?" The *'ohana* weaves a narrative of dispossession that alternates with a debate about present-day ways to find the way back to land and culture. In this debate, past and present inhabit the same space.

The discussion about land also shifts back and forth between loss of land and loss of culture and language.

The story quickly moves from the past to the present, and money is constructed as the key to this historical shift.

hibited to speak Hawaiian. That's why they keep the, the grandchildren couldn't speak Hawaiian.

Mom: Besides, our culture was a trading culture. We never sold anything.

Grama: They weren't allowed; they were PUN-ISHED if they spoke their own Hawaiian language.

Mom: We were, we traded off the ocean to the mountain, and the mountain to the sea. And that was our survival.

Grama: *Haole*s from the mainland came here, the missionaries. That's what happened to our culture.

[Baby intervenes, vocalizing, gurgling.]

Dad: That's why we gotta get that back into the educational system . . .
('OHANA: 529–567)

Big Sis: Cause I'm proud of Hawai'i, Hawaiian where I come from. So I get involved, like that. I'm considered an activist because I like to get involved. In things that I believe in. I believe many of the Hawaiian people got ripped off. Right?

[Others: Ssshh! Ssshh! Laughter.]
('OHANA: 126–134)

Dad: Ninety-six years. Ninety-six years. The *haole* right. Tell the Hawaiians: get on the stage

The story shifts back to the past when Grama focuses on loss of language and culture.

Mom discusses subsistence strategies on the land and the change to a cash economy.

Grama, referring to the 1896 ban on the Hawaiian language (H. Trask 2000a) links language to subsistence strategies on the land. Listening to this discussion, I did not get the sense that it was about two different topics. Rather I felt that Mom and Grama were merely telling two different sides of the same story: how displacement by another culture led to historic subsistence practices vanishing, as well as the parallel silencing of the Hawaiian language.[5] "We" and "they" both describe Hawaiians in history. When Mom says "we," Hawaiians appear as a collectivity and history is brought into the present.

Dad moves us from the missionaries directly into present-day solutions. The educational system is perceived as part of the solution. There is often, for me, a fluid sense of traveling in time during this interview.

When Kalo brings up the issue of culture, Big Sis responds with a proud, activist stance that is still related to losses suffered in terms of land. Others in the *'ohana* "shush" her, perhaps feeling this interview should not be about dispossession. As an adoptee, listening to the interview, I find myself reading "Hawaiian" (Hawaiian ancestry) as a site—almost as a geographic location.

and dance. Show these other *haole*s what we dancing about. And I give you money. You like one damn fool. Yeah, okay. Instead of you go dance yourself, and you collect the money, and the Hawaiian, you collect the money, no! You let the *haole* guy collect the money, he put plenty in his pocket and he give you little bit. And he: "Come on, girls, get out on the stage and you dance. You show 'em your culture." Ah? When you can do 'em yourself, and you tell the *haole*, "Eh, pay me for dancing. I show you my culture." Right?
('OHANA: 836–855)

Dad talks about the tourist industry in relation to culture. His repeating of "ninety-six years" lends an anguished undertone to the story about Hawaiians allowing themselves to be victimized and exploited. Dad's story intensifies in its forcefulness. This story seems to be about humiliation, appropriation, and material loss, although not about loss of culture. The phrase "show 'em your culture" almost seems like a double entendre; it reminds me of people showing their bodies. Dad's assertion: "Right?" adds force to his claims.

Dad: The Hawaiians own the hotel. The Hawaiian gets their own Hawaiian dancers, right? And all the money stays in the Hawaiian.
('OHANA: 886–889)

As Dad presents an alternative, he constructs Hawaiians not as individuals, but as a whole, a body: "All the money stays in the Hawaiian."

L'il Sis: I believe the Hawaiians have gotta get off their butts . . .

L'il Sis constructs the issue as having to do with Hawaiian agency and right action.

Big Sis: Oh, too heavy!

Although Big Sis teases L'il Sis, she asserts her claim.

L'il Sis: . . . and start going after what they want. But you can't just sit down and say "Grumble, grumble, grumble," and then . . .

Mom: No, but the Western culture *wen'* teach *us* that we should rely on somebody else to do the job and when we do that, we get . . .

Wen' teach means "taught." Mom focuses on learned dependency. Dad inserts the consequence of that learning, and Mom agrees. They chain, cooperatively completing one another's sentences.[6]

Dad: Ripped off.

Mom: Ripped off.
('OHANA: 1284–1301)

Mom: Who's gonna be, who's gonna be the chief? I'm the last, oh, I'm the bloodline, and blah blah this, blah blah that. What have they done for us? That generation? That's a good example. What has that generation done for us Hawaiians?

('OHANA: 1866–1872)

Mom: Mr. ----!

Dad: What?!

Mom: Say something about your heritage.

Junior: Yeah. I said something!

Dad: Eh. I'm a *haole* underneath here, yeah? [Laughter from others.]

Kalo: A Hawaiian at heart.

Dad: Only part-Hawaiian. Yeah? No?

Mom: Huh? How much you need to be a Hawaiian? Huh?

Dad: Quarter maybe . . .

('OHANA: 136–155)

Kalo: How do we, how, how do we, we, we teach our culture? And why do we do it?

Discussions about culture and values leads to a discussion about leadership and service to the Hawaiian people. Mom interrogates the idea of chiefly bloodline. Mom's derision towards those who argue their chiefly bloodline intensifies as she says "blah blah this, blah blah that." She suggests that their arguments are trivial and questions their inaction on behalf of Hawaiians. After a discussion of *haole* thievery, Mom's discussion of Hawaiian perpetrators struck me as a message about the messiness of history.

Mom addresses Dad by their last name, teasingly. At this point Dad has not yet said much.

Junior teases his dad as well.

Dad starts talking about his "*haole* blood" and jokingly challenges the notion of blood quantum (amount of Hawaiian blood), a notion sometimes used to classify (and declassify) people as indigenous Hawaiian. Kalo is (perhaps teasingly) using the often-used phrase "Hawaiian at heart." This phrase, often used to give non-Hawaiians "insider" (or "honorary Hawaiian") status, has the potential for serious or comedic overtones depending on the context, and relationships of the speakers.[7] I felt at this point that *'ohana* members were acknowledging and perhaps trivializing the issue of blood quantum. Mom's question and Dad's answer had a casual and almost humorous tone that seemed to open up a space to interrogate the idea of blood quantum.

Talk of culture merges into talk of identity when Kalo asks how culture is taught.

Mom: By sitting down and talking, by having family gatherings. And that's how we share a lot of things. I mean, we share our, our, by sharing the information with one another. By having family discussions.
('OHANA: 11–19)

Kalo: But even more so, why do we have to pass it down to the next generation? Why does (Junior) have to know what it is to be a Hawaiian? Or who it is to be a Hawaiian?

Junior: I'm Hawaiian.

Kalo: And what's so important about it?

Big Sis: Cause it's our culture. It's the culture we come from.

Big Sis: It's where we come from, and it . . .

Mom: And it should be handed down. So that all the generations that follow know what the Hawaiian culture is all about. Their values is all about.

Big Sis: Because, it's not so much our culture and values; it's who you are! As, as a person, as the blood that runs through your veins. You one Hawaiian, you should know where you come from. What your people was like. To live. Shouldn't be stopping us from learning. Who we are. But because that's what they did, now we get hard time tracing ourselves back. To our identity, ourselves.

[Others: Silence.]

Mom formulates family as a source of knowledge, nesting the process of teaching culture in everyday talk. She links culture, history, and identity and doesn't mention why they teach Hawaiian culture.

Kalo's critical questions seem to challenge the 'ohana, and to structure their discussion as a debate with lots of "give and take." It seems that she wants them to explore the complicated layers of history and identity. They are more than willing to engage in this debate, cocreating a process of knowing. Junior asserts his background in a proud way, and Kalo responds quickly with a challenging question, trying (I think) to tease out a deeper formulation. L'il Sis answers for Junior, constructing Hawaiianness almost as if it is a place, a construction Big Sis echoes.

As family members further their ideas, they sometimes first confirm the claims of the previous speaker. Here, L'il Sis, Big Sis, and Mom all "chain," creating a complete and seamless formulation.

Here Hawaiianness emerges as a genetic link connected to the need to know one's roots. This is knowledge needed for survival. The formulation of "tracing ourselves back" is an important one: identity is something to which we must return. This contrasts with the offhand way in which the 'ohana approaches issues of blood quantum. Identity in this case represents a loss, and "they" seem to represent

Big Sis: Right?

[Others: Silence.]

Big Sis: We get hard time. I get hard time *erry* time I still think about *da kine*.
('OHANA: 290–329)

Dad: Ah. Hawaiian is what the *haole* gave. (Voice rises.) Us *kanaka*s. Not Hawaiians. They named us Hawaiians like they could. Over here was Hawai'i, right? They thought over here was Hawai'i. See? Same like Samoan, they call Samoa, Samoa. They CALLING them Samoans. They not Samoan. We not Hawaiians. (Baby cries in background.) We *kanaka maoli!* The *haole* gave us that name: "The Hawaiians." Because we from Hawai'i. And then they stop us from using our own language, our own stories.

[Voices from kitchen yelling: "Hawaiians, Unite!"]

Dad: The Western way.

Big Sis: Oh, you gotta do that, the Western way or fucking die. We do their way or, or die. Learn how to live like the *haole*s, or die. It's all wrong. They took everything from us. We had everything going.

Mom: They changed our values. That's how they did.

Big Sis: No.

haole. (*Erry* means every. *Da kine* means these things.) When Big Sis says, "To our identity, ourselves," the silence that follows reminds me of the silence that follows the thud of a heavy object dropping to the ground. In my memory, it seems Big Sis looked around at other *'ohana* members at that point. Her last statement seemed reflective, rather than directed at family members, or anybody in particular.

This notion of having one's identity structured by others and of being divested of language crops up everywhere in the *'ohana*'s interview. *Kanaka maoli* can be translated as indigenous, genuine, or true Hawaiian.[8]

Dad sequences directly into "stories" from "language."

Big Sis contrasts a time of abundance ("We had everything going") with a terrible narrative of dispossession ("They took everything from us").

Mom: And our history.

Big Sis: You get 'em inside. Nobody can change 'em. Just be little more careful; cause now we gotta relate like we live the white man world, we gotta try, try BE like the white man. For come and react him. In his face kinda thing.
('OHANA: 334–376)

Big Sis: Hawaiian values. Of *aloha, kōkua.* Helping each other. It's the only way we going to survive . . . sharing . . . what we have. . . . That's how we going survive. Cause people take advantage of us.
('OHANA: 163–179)

Dad: Went 7–Eleven, eh, this guy, he just went inside. He opened the hot dog and put everything on it. You know, he get Coke . . . and he, he walk out.

[Others: laughter.]

Big Sis: He walk right out!

Dad: They said, "Eh! You gonna pay for your hot dog?" And he told them, "Eh, my hot dog is sort of down (motions to stomach), down in here."

[Others: laughter.]

L'il Sis: Right.

[Others: laughter.]

Mom feels at this point that "our history," along with "our values," has been transformed. As in other places in this discussion, the word "our" drew me into a sense of collectivity. Big Sis here describes values (and possibly history) as internal, unchangeable, and enduring. They are a part of one's identity. She asserts that being like the "white man" will not result in actually changing one's true identity.

Big Sis speaks of Hawaiian values, which she feels are central. *Aloha,* mentioned first, can be described as "love, affection, compassion, mercy, sympathy, pity, kindness, sentiment, grace, and charity" (Pukui and Elbert 1986, 21). *Kōkua* can be described as "help, aid, assistance, relief . . ." (ibid., 162). Big Sis associates these values with survival in the face of loss. Identity is linked to survival.

Issues about the land filter into issues about culture in a number of ways. Dad tells this story just after the family has talked about *haole* illegally taking the land. He is laughing as he tells his story.

As he opens up into the story, even though it is funny, its message is about how the islands were taken from Hawaiians, without "permission." Also, this story can be taken as a metaphor for the way that the land has been "eaten up."

L'il Sis: Was YOU, Dad?

[Others: laughter.]

Dad: No [laughs].

Big Sis: *Portagee* guy.

Mom: He was hungry, and it was Christmas. If I was the store manager, I let 'em have 'em.

Big Sis: Yeah.

Junior: [laughs]

L'il Sis: See? That's why the Hawaiians don't make anything. We give everything away free, that's all. We plenty heart.
('OHANA: 908–944)

L'il Sis participates in the telling of the story, which for her offers an opportunity to tease her Dad.

Portagee means of Portuguese background.

Mom gets involved with the story as a discussion about the value of sharing, and how she herself would share.

L'il Sis then adds her own moral about sharing to Mom's take on the story. Although the story begins as a metaphor for dispossession, it becomes a humorous tale, then a lesson about how Hawaiian values are implicated in the loss. Sharing becomes linked to dispossession rather than abundance. Interestingly, L'il Sis, in saying "We plenty heart," sounds approving. Values are constructed as a series of choices here, and it appears that the ethical choices are made: to give everything away. There is neither a sense that Hawaiians are hapless victims, nor do these things "by accident."

Later, Dad takes up the issue of implication of Hawaiian values in loss, in a different way, saying, "No more hospitality. The more hospitality the Hawaiian give, the more the *haole*s take 'em, and they keep 'em, they put 'em in their pocket" ('Ohana: 967–970).

L'il Sis: (Yelling) They help every Hawaiian they going be broke, the Hawaiians ripping off the Hawaiians.

Mom: That's what it is.

L'il Sis speaks about the idea that not all Hawaiians share. The question of how to adhere to Hawaiian values and still "make it" emerges. L'il Sis calls into question the notion of Hawaiians helping others, this time in terms of helping other Hawaiians.

Big Sis: Exactly what it is. Why? Because the, the one Hawaiian that ripping everybody off, *wen'* learn the white man way!

L'il Sis: That's the way that, that's the way we living now.

Mom: And that's the way we gotta get it done, the white man's way. We gotta get educated (voice rises), get out there.

Big Sis: Ah, but you looking for the change, you *wen'* go making money, you change.

Mom: Of course, money change, and that's what I said! Money is power!

Big Sis: Corruption. We changing. Come different. *Pilau* that. Yeah, I rather NOT.
('OHANA: 1339–1365)

Dad: You know one example is, this guy he used to have all the soda machines in the airport. So he's surviving, you know. Every year, Christmas day, he buy the Christmas tree, and all that, decorate 'em. Plus, donate hundred dollars every year, and somebody going turn him in. All the soda machines. Because he's making all this money. And now, every year they get nothing. That was, was one Hawaiian that, that you know, he, he was enterprising. He, he brought in his, his soda machines, whatever, but he was giving his share, yeah he was sharing, yeah, he was sharing with his Hawaiian people. Everybody. But they turned him in to the state. Yeah.

Big Sis traces the idea of Hawaiians ripping off one another to the *haole*.

As in other parts of the interview, in relation to values a debate emerges. The practicing of Hawaiian values may at times seem to present a dead end, yet the changes to do with taking up "*haole* values" are treated as highly problematic. This section is emblematic of the intense debate over values that threads through the *'ohana*'s talk. The use of the term "we" also threads through their talk. When they use the term "we" instead of "some Hawaiians" or "they," family members ground choices and responsibilities as their own, or ground ancestral history as personal history.

Here, Big Sis resists the discussion of money as power, constructing the changes in values that money would bring. *Pilau* is a word meaning "rot, stench, rottenness; to stink; putrid, spoiled, rotten, foul, decomposed" (Pukui and Elbert 1986, 329). This term adds force to Big Sis's claims. Later, Dad opens up into a story about a Hawaiian who shares and is punished for it. Although this person was apparently making an illegal profit, he shared his profit. Dad feels that by the letter of the law, this person was punished by the state for sharing with "his" Hawaiian people. By using the term "his," Dad connects this person more closely to the collectivity.

Mom: Even Hawaiians who make the climb and stay up there. All the Hawaiians will always *kōkua*.
('OHANA: 2158–2187)

Mom: That's what the white man *wen'* teach us, how to be aggressive. If you not aggressive, you get nothing. If you gotta step on ten people, so be it! You step on ten.

L'il Sis: That's not our culture.
('OHANA: 2228–2234)

Mom: Feeling bad means you never lose, lose your, your, your Hawaiian-ness. Your feelings as a Hawaiian.

Grama: Proud to be a Hawaiian.

Dad: Finished. That's all. It was there for you.

Mom's notion that Hawaiians will always help one another appears throughout the interviews. The values of *aloha*, *kōkua*, and sharing pervade the interview. Stories and strategies often reference Hawaiian values. Speakers sometimes appear to take a position counter to one they took earlier on. One position is that Hawaiian values may lead to further dispossession, so Hawaiians should take up *haole* values to survive. The other is that Hawaiian values are essential to identity, immutable and ethically righteous. Family members cocreate a tension between these positions in their talk, challenging one another's (and sometimes their own) claims.

During the interview L'il Sis discusses how she has recently been able to accomplish something ahead of her peers because of an opportunity open to her. Some of her friends felt this was unfair. Although this did not involve cheating others, it involved obtaining something that others didn't have, much sooner than she normally would have obtained it. Mom responds to L'il Sis's quandary by citing "white" cultural attitudes as necessary. L'il Sis's self-examination is not included here, since it is perhaps too personal to share. Her continued self-examination was relentless despite her parents' attempts to bring her to closure.

L'il Sis rejects Mom's claim.

Mom finds a way out for L'il Sis, by giving her permission to feel bad, as confirmation of her Hawaiian identity. Mom infers that L'il Sis's feelings reflect her values.

Dad preempts further discussion.

Mom: And anybody else who had the money.

[Others: Silence.]
('OHANA: 2340–2349)

Mom depersonalizes the issue, removing it from the context of Hawaiian values. L'il Sis never indicates whether or not she has come to terms with this dilemma. In another context, explaining why she took this opportunity could be easy, automatic, and possibly even unnecessary. Here, it is a question of ethics. I felt here that the silence was once again reflective. It also felt related to Dad's statement: "Finished." There was a sense, for me, that he was setting limits to the discussion.

Leilani: You teach other people about your Hawaiian culture?

Junior: No.

Mom: Why is that? Cause you don't know, right?

Junior: Yeah.

Mom: They don't teach you that in school?

Junior: Oh, they teach ME, but . . .

Leilani: What do they teach you in school?

Junior: All kind stuff.

Leilani: Like what?

Junior: Like *da kine*.

Dad: How to eat *poi, li'dat*.

Junior: Yeah! YEAH! They going teach us about . . .

Discussions about teaching and learning come up in the interview. Toward the end of the interview, I broke my silence and asked Junior a question about teaching his culture, focusing the discussion on him. I spoke to him at this juncture because I knew Kalo's family from before the interviews, and felt comfortable with the way that older family members sometimes question younger members.

Later, listening to this tape I wondered what Junior's knowledge base might be like if he had a *kupuna* close to him, living nearby or in the same house, or even just seeing him often, in a teaching role. I also began to wonder how different the interview and everyday family talk might have been as well.

I got a sense here that "what they teach" was just what *da kine* means—a collection of various things.

Junior does not confirm L'il Sis's statement that he learns about values. Rather, Junior seems to suggest that stu-

L'il Sis: Values

Junior: Then they have us do stuff, you know. [Voice rises.]

Mom: Don't they teach you about our land, and our, our history, of our King, and our Queen and our overthrow, oh . . .

Junior: No matter what teacher you get, my teachers really, aw . . .

Mom: Why is that?

Junior: I dunno.

Mom: So what you are saying is that the teachers are at the wrong thing?

Junior: They don't teach.
('OHANA: 42–98)

Kalo: What do you want to learn from Grandma? From Papa and Grandma? About you being Hawaiian?

Junior: Um, I . . .

Kalo: What you learn from your Grandma where you live?

Junior: They don't tell us about *da kine*. I don't KNOW.

Big Sis: Everything all hush-hush.

Junior: Yeah!

dents engage in various cultural practices like making crafts.

Mom talks about "our history of our King and our Queen, and our overthrow." At such junctures identity seems to *infuse* past, present, and future. I think it is her use of the word "our" here that pulls me into synchronic time. There is also a fusion of monarchy and overthrow—a sad sense of rupture. For me, this accomplishes a deeply collective sense of identity.

Mom seems to be asking about the curriculum; however, Junior's response seems to be that no actual teaching goes on. At this point Junior has raised his voice and is clearly frustrated.

Kalo asks Junior a question, again focusing attention on him, and talking about learning in the context of family.

Kalo clarifies that she's not asking about Grama (on Junior's mother's side), but about Junior's Grandmother on his dad's side, who lives nearby (Grandma). Junior makes it clear that his *kūpuna* are not really a source of knowledge for him.

Big Sis confirms this, referring to the silence of the *kūpuna*.

Big Sis: Because we don't know. And when you ask, they tell, "Ne'mind, not your, not your *kuleana*. No. Nah." The older people, they no like talk to us younger generation. We irritate 'em. Because we more inquisitive. Like know. More. "Why? How come? How come *li'dis*? How come *li'dat?*" They get all *pressure-out.*

Junior: That's right, yeah.

Big Sis: *Pau.* Stay mum.

L'il Sis: That's why. They didn't talk out loud about . . .

Dad: That's why, that's why I say, go school! Learn!

Mom: They not teaching that in school!

Junior: Yeah they do, they do!

Dad: Lotta, lotta things is common sense. You just gotta get your . . .

Mom: There's nothing common sense about our history.

"They" refers to *kūpuna. Kuleana* refers to right, privilege, property, concern, or interest (Pukui and Elbert 1986, 179).

"Li'dis" means like this. *"Li'dat"* means like that. *Pressure-out* means to be stressed. It almost seems here that Big Sis is getting Junior "off the hook" in terms of analyzing why he's not learning from *kūpuna.* It also seems that this has been her experience. *Pau* means finished.

L'il Sis relates the reticence of *kūpuna* to the idea that they were silenced in the past.

Dad shifts the responsibility to schooling. Mom revisits the frustrating notion that the schools are not succeeding, suggesting that schools don't teach what the *kūpuna* might have to impart.

At this point Junior seems confused. Now he is saying that the teachers do teach, when earlier he said that they don't. Perhaps he is saying that there is a Hawaiiana curriculum, while before he was saying that (for him) it doesn't work. This part of the interview moved me because Junior was obviously trying to articulate a deep sense of frustration and disconnection he experiences in the schools, despite a curriculum that includes Hawaiiana and Hawaiian history.

Dad seems to be saying that a lot of things about Hawaiian culture are easily learned, or understood, or everyday sorts of knowledge, while Mom seems to be tackling the issue of history not being common sense. I wasn't sure how to take this—whether it meant that it didn't make sense or it was not easily learned and taught.

Big Sis: You never know, you gotta ask, you know you gotta go find out. RESEARCH.

Dad: Yeah, you know if you don't plant the seed that thing not going grow . . .

Mom: Well, who's planting the seed?! Surely not the teachers in school!

Junior: Cause they don't know! They don't know!
('OHANA: 190–249)

Big Sis: You, you gotta teach 'em when they get the negative, when they give you a negative, you turn 'em into a positive. When they tell you, "Hawaiian, you no can do that," turn 'em around and throw 'em in their face and show 'em what you CAN do. Teach the babies what we can.

Mom: We need to turn the past philosophy about Hawaiians around.

Big Sis: Teach the babies what we can. You know . . .

Mom: and make . . .

Big Sis: the stereotypes . . .

Mom: and turn everything that was negative into a positive.

Big Sis: Got to teach them.

My thought was that what happened—the dispossession that she has spoken of—was in essence "senseless."

The fact that for family members *kūpuna* are not always available to teach and the schools are not always able to teach constitutes a crisis in learning for Junior. His talk evinces more and more frustration. I felt that Junior was trying to say there is a Hawaiian curriculum in the schools but the teachers can't really "pass down knowledge." We could say that he is saying they just aren't familiar with it. Or we could say that he is saying it isn't their own (or his own) family knowledge. Maybe he is saying that the *kūpuna* know but (in his case) aren't available to teach, while in the schools they teach what they do not actually know—have not actually experienced.

Big Sis links learning to a sense of possibility and agency that she feels children sorely need.

Mom and Big Sis collaborate on this formulation, creating, between the two of them, a poetic chain of related assertions.

Mom: The process that we have to go through now, in, in the white man's culture, is what . . .

Big Sis: you gotta teach the children . . .

Mom: what keeps a lot of us from moving ahead.

Big Sis: That's right, we gotta teach the children how to live the white man culture but no forget who they are inside. No forget where they come from. That's right, they can beat the white man, and they can be on the top or whatever, telling the white man what to do instead of the white man telling *us* what for do. And teach our babies that we gotta try for—you know, the white man telling you, knock you down and say you no CAN. No! Keep going! Forward! Don't let nobody tell you you canNOT. Because that what they told our, our ancestors. That we canNOT. We couldn't do this, and we couldn't do that. We gotta teach our babies no shame talk.

[Baby crying in the background.]
('OHANA: 402–450)

Big Sis: Gotta teach.

Dad: And language, and everything. All that they pulled away from us.

Mom: Honey, the language is gone. We cannot come bring the Hawaiian language anymore. It's too late for me.

Dad: You gotta. For the kids.

Mom inserts the idea that dealing with "white" cultural practices and structures immobilizes Hawaiians. Despite this shift, Big Sis asserts repeatedly her side of this formulation: teaching the children.

Big Sis then moves directly into positive talk about negotiating cultural values in a way that Hawaiians can navigate dominant culture, yet retain core values and identity. Again, she creates a profound connection between culture and "place."

Big Sis achieves a dramatic shift starting with her phrase "and say you no CAN." She delivers her claims with force, attaching them to historic attempts to silence Hawaiian people. Except for the baby crying in the background, there is a pause—the speakers are silent.

Big Sis reasserts her claims about teaching, and Dad chains into Big Sis's formulations. Mom redirects the 'ohana into a debate about language.

Mom: So there's nothing on language I can pass on to the next generation. I can pass down the values, the Hawaiian values, and our Hawaiian history. Only what I know, but other than that? I have nothing more to give. And that's because I wasn't taught. I lost out.

Big Sis: You pass 'em down. You gotta make sure the babies get educated. That's how you pass 'em down. Because you don't know the knowledge. Somebody else knows. I think that's how. The white man knows, pay that white man, teach you. And then you know.

Junior: I'm not gonna PAY the *haole*.

Big Sis: 'Cause the *kupuna*s they no more the patience for sit down with us.

Mom: We still lost because we have a hard time accepting other people teaching us our language, and that, that sets up another barrier.

Dad: What you mean when you say people?

Mom, Big Sis, Junior: The white people!

Dad: You talkin' about me, half-and-half!

Junior: (laughs)

Mom: How many half-and-half teaching us our language?

Big Sis: Not too many, not too many. These are all people like Gard went to college.

Mom is identifying herself as the weak (or missing) link in the chain of knowledge that passes from generation to generation in her family. The sentence "I have nothing to give," followed by "I lost out," holds much sadness, but roots the sadness in a loss for the next generation, rather than a personal, individual loss for Mom.

Big Sis posits schooling as a solution. She asserts that the knowledge can be passed down, even by strangers, or *haole*.

For Junior, the idea of paying *haole* to teach the Hawaiian language is problematic, while Big Sis indicates that the loss of knowledge from the *kūpuna* leaves no choice.

Dad challenges notions of difference and *haole-ness*. Throughout the interview it seemed to me that when the idea of *haole*-ness (or blood quantum) was raised, he resisted or ruptured it.[9]

Mom seems to know the answer to her own question. She is talking about *haole* who may be outside the community, not people like her husband. Big Sis confirms this by saying the teachers are like Gard, Kalo's husband, who is *haole*. Big Sis is also complicating the story further by citing a *haole* who is a family member.

Mom: The people like the white people are more susceptible to accepting the language than WE are! And that's sad. See, if I could teach my daughter, my daughter would comprehend more than if somebody else wants to teach my daughter. Somebody outside of our culture. You cannot teach the language and not speak it twenty-four hours a day. You gonna lose it. So if our kids was to pick up the language, we cannot converse with them, cause we don't know the language. And because we caught up in this white man's . . . way of living, lifestyle, and everything, go out, make money, and support, we don't have the time to, to share with one another. We busy out there trying to survive.
('OHANA: 473–626)

In Mom's assessment, the genealogical link is broken. She talks about the role of money and stress in her life—the ways that it fragments her connections and the practices of passing down knowledge in families.

Mom: Yeah? And we cannot teach the kids. It's gotta be the whole, the whole foundation, needs to know the language. In order for us . . . and then we need to have a cultural center, where people going come from the outside, TO US. Bring them to us, and we'll teach 'em what Hawai'i's all about. Being a Hawaiian is all about. From the culture, from the language, right down to everything . . .
('OHANA: 1442–1452)

In talking of teaching and learning Mom deals with the crisis in learning by offering a new idea—that of a cultural center, where learning can take place for all generations.

Leilani: What's the future of the Hawaiian people?

Junior: Nothing! It's so screwed up! [Voice rises.] Yeah!

Kalo: So, if it's screwed up and you could fix it, how would you fix it?

At the end of the interview I ask Junior about the future. It is the only other time I break my silence, because I feel that he is the youngest and at that point has offered no thoughts on the future. I also feel that family members will "pick up the ball" and address Junior on the topic. When he gives his answer, he seems frustrated and angry.

Junior: I don't know. [Silence.]

Aunty: Think!

Junior: I thinking, I thinking. Everybody says, think, think. Help me think! Help me think!
('OHANA: 2398–2419)

I feel that when Junior is saying "Help me think," he is asking for the verbal collaboration that will help him to work through the question. At other points in the interview one of his sisters also seemed to speak up for him. His nods or completion of their sentences seemed (to me) to indicate that their responses worked for him. I also felt somehow that he was alone. His was the generation experiencing the "cultural renaissance" in the school curriculum, yet he seemed to be saying it wasn't really working for him.

The interviews brought up issues about ancestry for me. Although Kalo told me, "This is an important time for all of us. You should be here. This is where you belong," I continued to struggle with the fact that I had no genealogy:

And yet . . . there is such a thing as birthright here . . . so the emotionality of it is draining. Who is your family? Who is your family? Who is your family? (MANA'O: 1368–1397)

Sometimes seemingly insignificant events or encounters seemed to hold a code, that although unknown to me, opened a door within me. I did not know the language of that code or what lay beyond that door.

Just as Ivan and I turn to leave from Nu'uanu Pali, two men in lavalava *(a kind of sarong) come up. The wind gusts their long hair crazily. Their hands*

In this 'ohana speakers work in concert to produce ideas: they "chain" ideas, completing one another's thoughts. They also reveal paradoxes, tensions, and contradictions around the issue of land. When they voice pre-Contact views on land, those views emerge in a debate about how the land might be retrieved. Historic loss of land provides a relentless theme in the stories they tell, and emerges as part of their everyday lived experience.

Money is discussed as a source of power, particularly in retrieving land, fighting for self-determination, and reappropriating culture. Money is also described as disabling, leading to greed and the loss of core Hawaiian values. L'il Sis lives the contradictions between her values and the structures in place that invite her to "get ahead" in ways that compromise her values.

Values are seen as sustaining and essential to survival. At other junctures values are described as leading to vulnerability and victimization. However, it is not assumed that values should be changed in order to avoid victimization and vulnerability.

are united, four very large hands. They are very big men. Hands—cupped around something. "What is it?" Ivan asks. One looks up and says, voice quiet, "Pueo." Then he takes a closer look at Ivan. His voice changes, taking on a more matter of fact tone, gets louder. "Hawaiian owl." We lean over and one hand is uncupped to show us the owl. They think his wing is injured.

He is quietly sitting in their hands, not fluttering about, not trying to leave. He observes us. They are going to feed him coconut, then take him to the Humane Society. . . . They are deliberately and gracefully, in concert, moving down towards a panel truck with the pueo. (MANA'O: 1439–1474)

Culture involves not only sharing but also appropriation and humiliation. At some points identity is seen as immutable; at others it is seen as susceptible to threat. Transmission of culture is seen as rooted in connection, and in everyday talk as well as other forms of learning. Discussions about culture or identity shift into discussions or debates about land. Culture and identity are formulated as tied to 'āina.

Although Kalo had deep and abiding ties to her family, it was clear to me that *kūpuna* in the community were a central force for change in her life. Kalo did not get knowledge just from her family, but from these other *kūpuna* as well:

Kalo calls to tell me that Aunty Aho and Aunty Hala (members of her civic club) are on TV. They spoke at a Woman's Conference in Hawai'i, now being aired on a local station. We speak for fifteen minutes or half an hour while this show plays. Kalo is near tears. She tells me that shortly after the conference, Aunty Hala died.

"Every time a kupuna *dies," she says, "I feel the knife cut into me." I write this phrase down. It circles and circles in my head, drops down and circles and circles in my guts. I am reminded of the wounded* pueo, *circling, circling, circling down, falling from the sky. The eyes of the* pueo. (MANA'O: 1498–1516)

A crisis in language and knowledge emerges in this interview. The knowledge of *kūpuna* is constructed as essential, yet the *kūpuna* don't always feel comfortable in sharing their knowledge and lose patience with questioning of younger generations. It seems to me that some family members, particularly Big Sis and Junior, feel a loss around the fact that their grandparents don't speak to them about the past. Mom regrets her inability to pass knowledge down.

Schooling is seen as responsible for the crisis in language and knowledge, and also seen as a potential solution to the problem. At this point in time schooling is seen as failing to solve this crisis in language and knowledge.

I found that in my role as a listener, during the interviews, I was often filled with strong emotions. Hope and anguish were those I felt the most.

During the interviews, I was not taking down information, writing on my pad. I was not evaluating the relevancy of answers to my research topic. I was not focusing on the next question, or wondering how I could shift the direction of the process. I was just sitting, listening as deeply as I could; often marveling at the directions that people took in their talk.

Although after interviews, Kalo and I often drove around, stopping to do errands or have a bite to eat, I still had trouble letting go of the emotions generated during interviews. It seemed that the words, once uttered, didn't leave me.

Somehow, issues about knowledge of my ancestry were surfacing. I could not shake the sense that, at any given moment, some relative or some important knowledge related to my ancestry was just within reach. Oddly, while in Toronto or San Diego I felt strongly that I simply did not know; somehow in Hawai'i it always seemed like I was "about to know." It was almost a physical sensation.

Was this only natural since the topic of my research was about knowledge? Was it that discussions with people seemed to end up on the subject of my ancestry? Or was this just a message I was getting—and where was that message coming from?

In their interview, the 'ohana share the ways that they cocreate and continually interrogate knowledge. There is intensive sharing of core values and beliefs and a rich sharing of the tensions, contradictions, and paradoxes that are part of the daily lives of 'ohana members. It also seems to me that sharing comes about through patterned, habitual strategic moves, which family members make in their talk. People habitually chain, tapping into sources of shared, common knowing. This process is also one of contestation; they good-naturedly and relentlessly rupture one another's constructions.

Dad's stories are utilized by others to create their own conclusions or moral imperatives. Mom and Big Sis contradict each other about how to situate core Hawaiian values. Family members seamlessly chain narratives about loss of land and values. Junior asks for (and often receives) help in "thinking."

I felt that in this debate I was positioned as the learner while Kalo consistently challenged the 'ohana to address the overlapping political, cultural, and spiritual discourses that complicate their lives. Relentlessly, the family interrogated their own, and one another's formulations, choices, and motives. Above all, they worked in concert to reveal the problematic discursive space that "Hawaiianness" occupies.

I decided to also ask Kalo to answer the five questions. Rather than interviewing her, I gave her the list so she could take them up in her own sequence and her own time frame while I sat silently. After a civic club event where members sold food items, talked story, and made *lei*, we sat together in a historic churchyard. As she spoke into the tape recorder, I was aware of the rustling leaves of the *hala* and the wordless graves sitting nearby. Breezes ruffled our hair and nearby birds chirped.

KALO

"What do you feel is important
to pass down to the younger generation?"

Hopefully, everything we do today is . . .
is preparation or planning,
or a legacy per se
that we can leave to the younger generation.
Everything we do now,
hopefully is in preparation for our youngsters,
or people who come after us.

Whether it be the environment,
or whether it be our Hawaiian values
and concepts that we pass on
to the next generation.
And a positive wellness,
wholeness, of,
of who we are as Hawaiians.
And leaving a legacy of positiveness
of strength, of courage, of energy.

All the things that are, that are positive
in the Hawaiian . . .

MY THOUGHTS

I felt drawn into a sense of responsibility by the repeated use of "we" and "us" and "our" that started here and continued throughout.

The first thing to pass on is land.
Values and wellness or wholeness follow.

As Kalo repeated these words, pausing, I was deeply aware of the place we occupied—particularly the graveyard nearby.

the Hawaiian culture,
in the Hawaiian culture.
The Hawaiian values
that are being passed down to us,
through our *kūpuna*.

And then through us as *mākua*,
and then to the next *'ōpio* generation.

'Cause Hawaiians don't separate
they don't separate
themselves from the environment.
We are one, one and the same,
and we need each other,
and depend on each other,
and have this interrelationship with our
environment.
And that's why the land is so important.
Because without the land there would be no
life.

If we reflect on the story of Hāloa and Kalo
the story of how
how the Hawaiians got *kalo*, which is taro,
which is the Hawaiian staple,
from which we make *poi*,
and which is at every
every Hawaiian meal . . .

and that the story of Hāloa teaches us
that if it was not for the premature birth
of the firstborn of Wākea and, and Papa,
that this firstborn that was deformed
was planted in the earth,
and from that Kalo grew,
and then the next child,
which was Hāloa and perfect form

The *kūpuna* are holders or "vessels" of knowledge that comes through them to us.

In this phrase, knowledge feels like energy flowing through the bodies of successive generations. *Mākua* means "parent, any relative of the parents' generation" (Pukui and Elbert 1986, 230). *'Ōpio* means "youth, juvenile; youngster; young, junior" (ibid., 292).

For me, this sequence first ties knowledge to connectedness to land. Connection to land sequences to connection to others, then back to connection to land, which completes the circle of life.

Kalo shifts from land to a reflection on ancient cosmology from *The Kumulipo*.

Kalo anchors this reflection in the act of eating *poi*. I don't think she is saying *poi* is eaten at every meal; rather, it is eaten at every/any traditional Hawaiian meal.

Kalo shifts from the traditional Hawaiian meal to *The Kumulipo*, and where humans come from.
Wākea is the sky (father), and Papa is the earth (mother).

which became the grandfather for
ALL Hawaiians to come afterwards.

You . . . you need *kalo* first
in order to FEED your people,
and that's why *poi* is so important.
If you make that kind of connection
with the earth,
and with God, in
in one
in ONE being.

That Hawaiians are so connected
to the heavens, to the earth,
to themselves
and the *ipu* is very important.
This is another symbol that the Hawaiians use,
that the vine that connects us is really the
umbilical cord
that connects us from one generation to the
next,
as well as that connection to the earth,
and that connection to the gods or god,
or whatever spiritual being that you might
believe in.

It's your connectedness.
And in that connectedness
we get strength.

So it doesn't matter where Hawaiians live.
They can live all over the world,
it doesn't matter,
when you say that you are Hawaiian,
we never say well, you know,
how much Hawaiian do you have?

The story of creation connects us genealogically to *kalo*, and to abundance. Here eating *poi* becomes a reenactment of cosmology. Kalo expresses a phenomenology where subjects do not exist separately from one another or from the universe itself. There is no boundary between subjects and objects of experience. As she repeats and emphasizes "in one," she pulls me into reflection on this phrase.

The *ipu* is a gourd that grows on a vine, is used to carry food or water, is used as a percussion instrument, and is also used for healing purposes. Pukui and Elbert (1986, 103) note in their definition of *ipu* that in the phrase *"Ka ipu o ka 'ike"* a container of knowledge refers to a learned person.

There was a pause before these sentences and after them as well. These sentences seemed to me to come out as a sigh.

Here Kalo negates blood quantum. I also felt a personal layer of meaning, as if Kalo was alluding to my connection to her. I felt as if she was speaking to and for me.

Which is a total,
a, a total
ALIEN concept.

But the fact that you ARE Hawaiian
and you ARE 'ohana
and that we eat out of the same *poi* bowl.
And that we come from the same roots.
And that's the connectedness that people don't
understand,
that brings all Hawaiians together,
no matter how much Hawaiian they have by
blood quantum.

'Ohana means family, relatives, or kin group. The 'ohā is the taro corm that grows from the older root of the *kalo*. Kalo structures a compelling inclusiveness where Hawaiians are all one 'ohana. She again negates "blood quantum" and utilizes metaphor to poetically construct a compelling sense of inclusion.[10]

Wherever they live,
if you are Hawaiian, you are Hawaiian.
And you are accepted into the 'ohana.
Unconditionally.
There are no, no restrictions,
no limitations, no obstacles, no barriers.
The fact that you are Hawaiian,
you're part of the 'ohana.

Here I again felt that on some level this interview was for me.

Kalo's poetic and forceful restatement of unconditional acceptance came up into my chest, then into my throat from my *na'au* (my guts), at this point. I remember sighing, the release of my breath.

And then Hawaiians continue to say after an
introduction of you know, I am Hawaiian,
What is your name, you know,
and who is your family?

Often Kalo saw my discomfort at being asked about my family. Here I felt that she was somehow reframing these encounters.

Those are the two key most important things
that Hawaiians want to know.
And that connects us to each other.
And that is very important.
That's why our genealogy is so important
and that genealogy connection to our,
of course, to our *ali'i,*
and then, of course, because the *ali'i*
to the gods themselves

Knowledge here is structured around connection.

Kalo's repeated use of the word "our" reinforces this sense of connection among the people, the land, the *ali'i*, and the gods.

And again,
back to the land,
so it's very
it's
it's a
it's a CIRCLE.

It's a circle of love
And that's why the *lei* in the Hawaiian culture
is so important, because when you give
someone a *lei* it's an enclosure.

The *lei* is always closed, never open,
because it's an encircling of . . .
of that connectedness within the Hawaiian
'ohana, within the Hawaiian society,
and within the Hawaiian culture and values.
Um, I think I kind of rambled on . . .
I'm thinking about um, question two.
(KALO: 3–131)

During my fieldwork, besides interviewing
Kalo, her *'ohana,* and *kūpuna,* I met with Kalo
at length almost every day. Because of the location of Kalo's house in relation to where I was
staying, almost every day we were traveling
past the burial place at Nu'uanu.

I would look past the iron fence, through
the car window, and privately wonder whether
the lady I had met there was still living on the
grounds. Despite (or perhaps because of) feelings of closeness I had towards Kalo, I had
never told her about that meeting.

One day, while we were driving past the
burial place, I suddenly turned around in the
passenger seat and said to Kalo, "You know, I
met the woman who lives there. She was very

Kalo really slowed down here. I felt she was not only creating a circle of relationships in the cosmos, but that she
was pausing, circling around, leading me to an important
claim.

Kalo had given me a *lei* on my arrival, and had introduced
me to others as her sister. Here, her talk about the *lei* as a
symbol of love burst in me.

Kalo did not say, "You're part of my *'ohana;* that's why I
gave you the *lei."* Yet I felt that between the lines, she was
telling me that. I remember that at this point, having been
deeply moved by Kalo's monologue, I was surprised to
hear her describe herself as having "rambled on."

In contrast to the *'ohana,* Kalo spontaneously formulated a
richly layered cosmology in answer to only one question:

- legacy: responding to the question
- lineage: people as containers of knowledge
- knowledge about connection to the land
- land: as life giving, and connected
- *poi:* symbolic of connection to land
- *ipu:* symbolic of connection
- *ali'i:* connecting us to the gods
- *'ohana:* unconditional inclusion
- *lei:* as a circle of love and enclosure
- legacy: return to *'ohana,* culture, and values

nice to me. I talked to her about the whole adoption thing." Kalo voiced surprise at this, and asked me if I wanted to stop by and see her. I said yes, and Kalo quickly pulled into the driveway on the grounds.

Kalo and her mom and I got out of the car and walked among the graves. The house where that woman from ten years or so ago lived was still there. Kalo and her mom said they'd wait in the car, and walked back to where it was parked.

I walked up to the house and knocked on the door. I could see through the screen that the place still looked the same. The woman I had met so many years ago was seated at the kitchen table, with three men. I could hear a low murmur of voices. I heard her raise her voice and say, "Who is it?" Realizing that she had guests, I contemplated leaving but she had already come to the door and was opening it.

As she opened the door I said, "I was here years ago and talked to you and I just wanted to thank you." She said, "Come in! Come in!" I took my shoes off and walked into the room, while she sat down in her chair. Although it seemed that she was older, she still looked much the same as when I had first met her. I was unsure as to whether or not she remembered me, and assumed that she wouldn't. She reached out from her chair and took my hand.

Then she said to the three men: "This is the one I was just talking to you about!" They nodded, saying "Oh, yes." She pulled me toward the table by my hand until I was up just next to her. They all looked at me, nodding up and down.

Kalo's answer contains the seeds of many thoughts she later took up, sequenced here in a pattern of interconnection. She voices no paradoxes, tensions, or contradictions in relation to land, which she discusses in relation to abundance. She creates a seamless flow of metaphors that visually renders the cosmology of the Hawaiian literature.

Nor do values, which are seen as sustaining, hold any contradictions in Kalo's talk. For Kalo, knowledge is based on land, and passed down through lineage. She does not construct losses or crises to do with knowledge, but depicts knowledge as continuing to be passed down.

The 'ohana and Kalo voice cosmologies that inscribe beliefs about the nature of *earth*, *practice*, *destiny*, and *knowledge*.

Both Kalo and her 'ohana talk about the land with great emotion. The 'ohana talks about the rupture of life on the land and debates how to reverse that rupture. They debate about the extent to which capital should condition their values. In contrast, Kalo constructs Hawaiians as genealogically connected to Earth and Sky.

Both Kalo and her 'ohana privilege traditional Hawaiian *practices*. The 'ohana debates whether or not Hawaiian practices should change in the struggle for scarce resources. In contrast, Kalo connects current practices to essential immutable values.

She said again that they had just been talking about me. They looked only mildly surprised to see me. I had never met any of the men before in my life. I was almost dizzy with a sense of confused unreality.

Although she introduced me to the men, who were all older and seemed to be prominent in the Hawaiian community, I later forgot what she had said about them. One of them said something to the effect that "there are so many Hawaiians living on the mainland who are looking for their people." They asked what I knew, so far, about my ancestry, and asked me about details about my life. I told them what I had been told about my ancestry, and told them about my life.

I mentioned that I had dreams, and they asked me to tell them what the dreams were about. I told them about the woman and the man and the fish who entered my dreams. A man who looked like he was the oldest among them said, "Oh, they have been trying to contact you." The woman said, "Yes, it's coming on time that you will know who your people are."

I was surprised to discover that there were tears rolling down my face. I was still standing there by the table. I was not at the moment aware of any great sadness or happiness. But my emotions must have been of sufficient intensity for tears to be rolling down my face.

There was a brief silence. They sat, looking at me, nodding. I said goodbye to them and they murmured phrases of good luck and support to me. She took my hand as I turned to go and said, "Come here again and pray on it. Pray. I am sure you will find your people. It's time." (Taken from: Mana'o: 2374–2493)

For both Kalo and the 'ohana, *destiny*, or social change is contingent on the choices Hawaiians make. The 'ohana see Hawaiians as destined to struggle against the effects of colonization and the incursion of capital.[11] Kalo views destiny as related to sustaining cosmic connections that enfold Hawaiians.

Both Kalo and the 'ohana use strategic moves and sequences to create *knowledge*. 'Ohana members struggle to retain Hawaiian knowledge forms as their material existence is transformed. Kalo places lineage at the core of Hawaiian identity knowledge-making.

The differences between the two interviews seem to hinge on the relationships therein, and the strategic moves made by participants in order to meet particular pedagogical goals.

Kalo's interview with her 'ohana teased out disconnections and debates within the contested terrain they occupy. In terms of learning, they created a critical and challenging dialogue. It felt like an oft-engaged in internal debate, enabled by Kalo and with me (the audience) in mind. The learning task seemed to be to define "right action" in the midst of a complicated struggle for survival.

Kalo's interview seemed more personally directed toward me and offered a timeless cosmology through connection. It incorporated the knowledge she gets not only from family, but also from *kūpuna* outside her family. In terms of learning, she nested her claims within a deeply coded set of symbols that awoke in me a sense of acceptance. The learning task seemed to be to anchor in me knowledge about the nature of the universe and our place in it, as Hawaiians.

4   We Will Manifest   Aunty Limu and Aunty Lau

Usually when I went to Hawai'i, I would contact Aunty Limu, a *kupuna* who had taught me
language, *'ukulele*, and *lauhala* in San Diego,
and who was now living on O'ahu. When I got
in touch with her this time, I also asked for an
interview. This would be the only interview
where I would be both interviewer and learner.
Aunty Limu denied me the interview. What
follows are my written journal entries (*mana'o*)
from that time. I offer my thoughts (on the right
side) as well.

*I ask if I can interview her. "What about?" she
says quickly. About what she does and how she
feels about it. Yes, there will be a tape recorder, or I
will have to take notes. Yes, she will have to sign a
release, but I will not use her name. A long pause.
She looks at me, a worried look. I can see that she is
uncomfortable and (not like her) at a loss for words.
I interpret it almost as a trapped look. I say I want
to understand how she feels about what she does.*

She says she is so sorry, but no. She is not angry, but seems regretful. She goes on to talk about how Hawaiians don't DO Hawaiian culture like they should. She talks about how Hawaiians are too lazy to do their own stuff—they try to buy the lauhala *and not to make it. She tells the story about some Hawaiian woman who is very interested in* lauhala *so she wants to buy it off of Aunty Limu. When Aunty Limu tells her the price, this woman is not at all willing to pay what the* lauhala *Aunty Limu created is really worth. Aunty Limu feels very hurt and insulted by this. Hawaiians must be too lazy to do their own work. The* haole *are more interested in making these things. So now the* kūpuna *are dying and information will be forever lost, Aunty Limu says. Who will teach how to make* lauhala *when the* kūpuna *are gone?* (MANA'O: 630–682)

She shifts the subject and talks about a Hawaiian Homes Commission meeting where she spoke up. They were talking about building some structure, on Hawaiian Homes Land, which would be like an old-style Hawaiian house, and which would function as a meeting place. She said to these people that this house wasn't important. Hawaiian house-making was not such a great thing, not such a big deal. It was living on the land, planting and fishing, that was important. These ancient people were planting, were cultivating the taro every day. They were catching fish, collecting limu *(seaweed) every day. They used to live on the land. Some building will not make any difference. This is how people used to live. So why in hell (Aunty said) were they trying to spend all that money to build one damn building?* (MANA'O: 707–728)

MY THOUGHTS

Aunty Limu is telling me exactly why she will not give me this information without implicating me in her story.[1] I need to listen to the story, place myself in it, and look at the moral of the story, then look at what it means about me.

Here I remembered guiltily that I was a clumsy, lazy, impatient, and fairly uninterested student of *lauhala*.[2] I had quit lessons with Aunty Limu early on. I take it that taping her voice for a University project is wrong—that it puts her knowledge in the marketplace without respect for her needs and goals as a teacher (or *kumu*).

Aunty Limu grounds Hawaiian identity (in this case) in practices on the land rather than in artifacts or structures. This story can also be taken as instructive about why Aunty does not grant me the interview. It is everyday practices on the land, not a symbol, that shapes Hawaiian identity.[3]

Aunty Limu says, "Isn't that funny that we were
just talking about you? You should call Aunty
Rita." She goes on to say that she was at an event
where there were many kūpuna, and she was sit-
ting near to a certain kupuna who Aunty Rita
believes is actually my birth mother! Aunty Limu
said to this woman, "Eh, I have a friend who knows
a girl, and she thinks this girl is your daughter, out
of wedlock." The woman said, "How DARE you
speak to me like that?" Aunty Limu said, "I can
speak to you any way I want. You don't have to get
so offended." "She really got insulted with me," says
Aunty Limu."Oh well, maybe you'll find out later.
No use pushing it. Maybe Rita has the wrong idea."
(MANA'O: 884–898)

Later that night I wrote:

. . . . I think, specifically, much fondness as she dem-
onstrates she feels for me . . . Aunty Limu does not
want to make little pieces of her knowledge, part of
a project I have in mind; she does not want selected
stuff about what she does to be used by me in what I
do. She knows I go "to school." She knows, I believe,
what that means about how her knowledge, her feel-
ings, her words, will be used. As a sociology student
I worry about what my supervisor and advisors will
have to say if I don't "get data," and yet I know I am
learning things on a much deeper level. As a person
who has known Aunty Limu and who learned under
her for about five years, I feel very, very wrong
asking her for this interview. And yet I know that
she, by her story of "other Hawaiians," has avoided
directly speaking to me about my role.
(MANA'O: 682–705)

Here I felt that Aunty Limu was telling me that she felt connected to me and would speak up for me, despite the fact that she was declining to be interviewed. And through Aunty Rita (who teaches me on the mainland) we would remain connected. It's interesting that she also shifted to my origin story. It also felt like a message about the search that Aunty Limu thinks is important—a search for gene-alogy rather than a search for an academic degree.[4]

I contacted Kalo about this:

I said, "I just don't know how I feel about this. I just don't want to intrude." Her statement was, "Just remember. You have a right to be here. You deserve to be here. You're Hawaiian. You're not intruding. What you're doing is good." (MANA'O: 1274–1280)

. . . Underneath this all, though, still, is the awareness that I have two selves: one who is a part-Hawaiian sociology student, one who is a part-Hawaiian woman with connections here in the islands. These two people battle one another in my sleep, and in my waking hours seem to betray and shock one another. Both parts want to believe Kalo, but feel a wrenching in the gut remembering the discomfort of Aunty Limu when she said, "No," and her story about her assertion of my "roots" to another kupuna, *told so quickly after her "no." Others have stolen knowledge from our ancestors in order to provide data, fodder for their theoretical formulations. What makes me any different?* (MANA'O: 1290–1317)

As always, Ivan and I spent time with Aunty Limu visiting her apartment, visiting her *lauhala* classroom, driving her on errands, and going out to eat. She spent much time with me "talking story" and introducing me back into her life. Although I was no longer intending to formally interview her, I taped and wrote copious field notes after every encounter with her. I felt that the things she was saying to me were very meaningful. I didn't solicit her comments but listened to her "talk story" as I had when I knew her on the mainland.

Saying this, I felt as if my body, an off-island body, was colonized. As an off-island Hawaiian I felt as if my body had been stolen from the land. I felt, from deep within my guts, that I was to blame for that theft. I also felt myself to be speaking as a visitor to a colony, albeit a colony in the painful throes of decolonization. Kalo's heartfelt answer did not remove this perplexing mixture of loss and self-blame. I thought: "If our bodies are history, in my body, the history of the 'āina is scratched out."

I am told, by indigenous scholars and people who are *kūpuna* to me, that there *is* a difference. Yet, often the answer to this question that I carry within myself is that there is no difference.[5]

Picked up Aunty Limu and took her to the ----
Senior Citizens Center, a large, rambling two-floor
building where she teaches lauhala. . . . *Aunty*
Limu was wearing one of her homemade lauhala
and lei hulu *hats, a* mu'umu'u, *and carrying a*
huge cloth bag full of lauhala, *scissors, and other*
tools, cloths, etc. In addition, she was carrying her
large handbag. She didn't allow Ivan to carry her
bags, and when he tried to help her to set up the
chairs by offering to take the chair she was holding,
Aunty Limu told him, "I can do it myself." She
moves like a teenager. Finally, as he insisted on put-
ting chairs at the table she had set up, she said, "Oh
well, go ahead, Tarzan, suit yourself."

This refers to a hat woven of *lauhala*, and decorated around the brim with *lei hulu*, or feather *lei*.

Just minutes after Aunty Limu arrives, and the
three of us are seated around the table, another
woman arrives. She asks if I am Aunty Limu's
daughter or niece, and Aunty Limu says she knows
me from the hui *in California. She asks me how long*
I will be in Hawai'i, and if I'm staying with Aunty
Limu. . . . Then she asks me my whole name. When
I give it, she says, "What is your maiden name?"
Aunty Limu interjects, saying, "She was adopted."
"Oh, you're hānai. *What family?" the woman*
says. . . . Aunty Limu interjects again, saying, "No,
she was adopted. They didn't tell her who her family
was." "Adopted?" the woman asks, "By Hawai-
ians?" "No, by haoles," *I say.*

Often when I was with Kalo or Aunty Limu, people engaged me about my birth story. Sometimes Kalo or Aunty Limu ended up "moderating" a discussion about my birth story.

Hānai is a traditional form of informal adoption within the Hawaiian community, occurring most often within extended family. In the *hānai* system, children usually remain connected to their genealogies and their biological parents.[6]

"She's here to find out who her family is," Aunty
Limu says, surprising me. "Who do you think they
are?" says the woman with a note in her voice.
Aunty Limu tells the story about Aunty Rita and
the ---- family name, and her altercation with ----.
The woman murmurs at its end, "Well, I know

Although Aunty Limu knew I was in Hawai'i to do research, she invariably told people that I was trying to find my family. I am still not sure what that "note" was in the woman's voice, but I do know that the concern people showed over this situation unsettled me.

you'll find out when it's time for you to find out." It seems that my story has a note of sadness for her. Then she and Aunty Limu start talking about how young people can't buy homes and how people are losing their land. What they are building . . . is for outsiders, for tourists. Aunty Limu nudges me and says, "Are you keeping track of this? You'll learn a lot today." (Mana'o: 917–1010)

Aunty Limu suggested we stop for lunch at ----'s where there is great dim sum. It is a very well-known and somewhat ritzy place. . . . Aunty Limu had obviously been there before; the personnel knew her. We sat and she began ordering dim sum, lots of it. Ivan and I glanced at each other, wondering if we had the funds to pay.

    Aunty Limu begins talking about her trip to the doctor, (who) told her to stop eating pork, fatty fishes, fat, and salt. She told him, "I'm Hawaiian. I have to eat my Hawaiian food." The nurse told Aunty Limu she was "prediabetic." Aunty Limu said, "I'm Hawaiian. I have to eat my 'ahi, 'opelu, aku (yellowfin tuna, mackerel, scad, bonito). . . ." Aunty Limu goes on for some time just naming fish to us. It's like an incantation. It reminds me of the naming in The Kumulipo. *Aunty Limu talks about how whenever she has money she has to take her friends or her relatives out and go to a nice restaurant. She likes to buy people food. "How can you be Hawaiian and not eat?" she asks. She talks about how her friends mean the most to her, more than any possession.*

    I feel sick doing all this. There is something wrong with it. It's wrenching my stomach. I wish I knew the right thing to do. Something in my blood

Her thought that when it was time I would find out was commonly voiced, especially among *kūpuna*. I felt it to be the opposite of statements like "Good luck in your search," which made me feel as if I were searching through the forest for knowledge. In contrast, statements such as hers made me feel as if I were standing in the clearing, waiting for knowledge to come to me. Also, this shift of subject to the inability of Hawaiians to get a place to live seemed to occur often, right after talk of my situation. It was as if, for Aunty Limu (and in my experience, others of her generation), my situation was linked to homelessness or dispossession.

Although I usually leave out material that is too personal or potentially embarrassing for people who were part of my field work or interviewees, I have to suppress the urge to delete this. This is not because it embarrasses Aunty Limu, but because it embarrasses me, the cheapskate. My budgeting of money for field materials, books, and cassette tapes flew in the face of Aunty Limu's sense of abundance and largesse. This happened time after time for me with *kūpuna*.

Aunty Limu didn't say "Hawaiian food" but said "my Hawaiian food," constructing a relationship. For me there was something really funny about Aunty Limu's response to the diagnostic label prediabetic with her identity. It was as if she were trumping a clinical identity with an indigenous identity.

cries out. 'Ahi, 'opelu, aku. . . . Aunty Limu is so old. I don't know if she'll be here next time I come here. Who will recite to me the names of these fish? Who will remind me that food is sacred, and that money is just for spending on people?

After lunch Aunty Limu motions to her suit-case-like plastic purse. "Give me that, please," she says with authority to Ivan. She pulls out a hundred dollar bill and pays for lunch with it. Her change from the waitress is minimal, and gets taken up again as a tip, by the smiling waitress. Ivan has taken out his wallet and she has slapped his hand saying, "Put that thing away." (Mana'o: 1084–1140)

Aunty Limu's reminiscences, as always, were accompanied by a deep undertext. Once Aunty Limu mentioned songs we had sung together which reminded her of me. I mentioned a song called "Hanauma Bay," which reminded me of Aunty Limu, and she started talking about her childhood there, and how the place had changed. As she sequenced into memory after memory, she spiraled me down into a sense of place, a love for the land. She would point out places as we drove on errands:

We drive Aunty Limu to Ala Moana Center so she can do some business at the post office. We are driving through Waikīkī. As we hit a main drag she points out where her relatives used to fish. A deep, deep pond. The water was so deep black-blue. She will never forget it. It's a parking lot now. "Those haole *contaminated the islands," she says. "They contaminated every place they went." She talks bit-*

I initially left this statement of mine out, because it felt extraneous; but going back to it, it feels important. I can't say why Aunty Limu always brought me to these sorts of conclusions about life, but she did. Regardless of the impression she had on me, it is somehow typical of my background in schooling/research that I didn't say, "Who will teach me *lauhala?*" That would be a question more in keeping with Aunty Limu's "knowledge agenda." In spite of my doubts about my own "knowledge agenda," I was still not going to follow hers. If the goal was getting a cosmological clue, Aunty would want me to get it by learning to weave *lauhala*, and I'd rather search for it in her talk.

*terly about how the missionaries came and took
everything, brought diseases, took over the government. "Every place they go, these* haoles, *they
contaminate," she says.*

Aunty Limu met this thin haole *girl on the
bus in Waikīkī. This girl was wearing a scant
bikini. Aunty Limu said to her, "Look at you!
Shame! All your ancestors, those missionaries
came and took us, we were naked, and made us
wear long dresses. And now you come here dressed
in nothing. Shame on you!". . .*

*Aunty Limu changes the subject to something
else that outraged her because we are just now on
the street where it happened (a side street in Waikiki). She says, "See there? I'll tell you something
that happened right there"! There were these two
real big Hawaiian guys on the street who, Aunty
Limu says, were getting ready to beat up these
two little skinny* haole *guys. Aunty Limu told
the big Hawaiian guys, "You make me shame to be
Hawaiian. Go home. Why you guys going beat up
these little skinny* haole *guys"? Aunty Limu says
they went home.* (MANA 'O: 1142–1203)

*Aunty Limu points out the fishpond she played
at and mentions how the water was so blue,
blue-black. She talks about how she and her kid
brother went down to this pond and fished and
gathered. . . . The pond had everything in it.
They didn't take too much; there was plenty for
everyone. "Get plenty to eat there." "Plenty" is
one of the most prominent words in Aunty Limu's
vocabulary.*

*Then she points out the place where a stream
flowed. When she was a child she caught* 'ōpae

Aunty Limu pretty much seemed to lay things at the feet
of the missionaries, a formulation that could certainly be
accused of being technically incorrect. Yet, I can't explain
why, but in her story it always felt right to me. It was as if
she collapsed post-Contact history into a few blurbs, and
as if clothing were the metaphor for all forms of domination. Aunty Limu often moved into a bikini story of some
sort: from contamination, to missionaries, to disease, to
government, to a woman in a bikini. Aunty has described
more than one public bikini confrontation. Therefore,
descriptions of the women, and the ensuing confronta-
tions, vary in graphic intensity. I feel that for Aunty Limu,
the *haole* woman in a bikini was a powerful (and unavoid-
able) image standing in for Hawaiian history.[7]

Aunty Limu often alternated between joyous abundance
and the obliteration of that abundance. All that history
seemed contained in her body, in her presence, in the
back seat of the car, pointing out the window.

(shrimp) in that stream. . . . The stream where she caught 'ōpae is covered by a road. This conversation has taken place while we are stopped at a red light. The light changes. (MANA'O: 1618–1652)

Aunty Limu told us she was leaving in a few days to go to Vegas to help her "dream niece" to move. When Aunty Limu was much younger, she was living near Waikīkī. She slept in the sleeping room with her brother, she says. Her sister lived somewhere else, I think she says on the Big Island (I'm not sure). Aunty Limu dreamed that she was in heaven . . . (and) her dead aunt came up to her. She was so excited, and said, "Where's Mama, where's Mama"? Her dead mother came up to her and hugged her, holding her and rubbing her arms. When she awoke from her dream her arms still tingled. She could still feel her mother's touch on her arms. She knew then that her sister was going to have a baby, a baby girl. . . . So when her sister told her she was pregnant, she said, "I know. You are going to have my dream niece." And she has been very, very close to this niece ever since. This niece is leaving her husband, and Aunty Limu is going to Las Vegas to gamble, and then help her niece to get settled in a new place. She is taking her niece some money, using other money for her plane ticket, and using a bit of money to gamble and have fun in Vegas.

Like many of Aunty Limu's stories, this for me was a story about the deep connection that family members have, a connection that transcends space and time. Often in her stories there was a description like this one about being hugged, then having her arms tingle, that operated like a mnemonic device for me. I would remember a look, a feeling, a bodily position, or a sensation she had described, and the entire story would materialize.

Aunty Limu laughs with delight and tells us the story about how she got the money to do this. There is no way with social assistance and with her job she could afford this trip. So she went to the bank. At the bank, according to Aunty Limu, there was this real nice Pākē *guy, maybe part-Hawaiian. He was "just starting out, just learning the ropes." He had graduated from college very recently, and this was his first job. It was in the loan department. She told him she wanted this money to go visit her niece and help her find and pay for an apartment to live in, away from her husband. He asked her about her source of support and she told him. He was a "very, very nice boy," Aunty Limu says. She thinks he will be very good, he will do a very good job, but now he's just learning. He gave her forms to fill out.*

She met another nice woman at the bank. This woman has been there longer. This woman was taking the forms Aunty Limu filled out and said, "Good luck." Aunty Limu describes this woman as a girl who was in an office beside the boy who helped her. Aunty Limu came home with a very good feeling and prayed for money to help her niece. Two days later the girl called her. When Aunty Limu knew it was the girl from the bank she yelled, "Did I get it"? The girl said, "Yes"! (Here Aunty Limu laughs quite a bit.) Aunty Limu said, "I'll be right down." She hung up and took the bus there and signed the forms, and got the money. (Mana'o 751–829)

There was no doubt, from the way Aunty Limu talked about the search for my genealogy as my purpose, that for her, my genealogy constituted the real "knowledge agenda." Although I felt that the "search" was uncomfortable and unnecessary, it seemed as if genealogical issues were always surfacing. Kalo took me to a local *hālau hula* performance. There, she hoped to introduce me to Wayne Keona Davis, a *kupuna*

Pākē is a word used to describe people who are Chinese in origin. The people in the bank aren't gatekeepers whom Aunty is asking for money. They are just nice young people who are in their own trajectories in terms of learning and knowing. She ponders how they are doing. Although the word *need* would be more suited to a request for a loan, Aunty Limu just tells them she *wants* the money. Aunty Limu's use of the term *want* reflects a different vantage point.

From an outsider's vantage point this should be a story about submitting a loan application to a bank. But Aunty Limu's story is about these nice young people she met. Later, Aunty Limu prays for money, not for herself but to help her niece.

So Aunty could be just another nice *elderly lady* trying to get a loan and laughing with delight. Or we could weave a story about how capital and its effects are constantly (although perhaps not consciously) subverted in her talk.[8]

Aunty Limu constructs stories about the land, that celebrate abundance and often end in a brief description of its historic loss. From missionary history on is collapsed while her stories of abundance seem timeless.

Aunty Limu constructs money as a manifestation of abundance, to be used to help her connect with others. Prayer emerges in relation to the abundance she experiences—in relation to what she wishes for her niece, not

she wished for me to interview. He was a genealogist and member of the Royal Order of Kamehameha I. Kalo spotted him making his way across the room, a distinguished gentleman with an imposing presence, gray hair, and gentle eyes. They hugged and Kalo introduced me to him, stating that we wanted to sit down with him and talk story, and that she was working with me to interview *kūpuna* for my dissertation.

He sort of raised his eyebrows and said something to the effect that, "I don't know if I qualify as *kupuna*." He wrote his name and phone number for me, and we discussed when we could call him. Then we drifted to our separate seats for the concert.

Although Kalo still seemed to feel that it was important for me to meet with Wayne (as well as other *kūpuna*), she later became quite ill. We never found a time that would work to interview him. I was relieved. Kalo's life was very stressful, and I felt I was contributing to her ongoing state of exhaustion. Also, another *kupuna* had told me that the Royal Order of Kamehameha I had historically met up at the Mausoleum at Nu'uanu. Although I wondered if this was the group that was part of my origin myth, I also felt that interviewing a genealogist would only remind me that I might never know the names of my ancestors.

for herself. In her talk, Aunty Limu doesn't lend agency to capital but to her values, which obviously sustain her.

Aunty Limu does not construct her own survival, or that of her values, as a struggle. In fact, she constructs herself as singularly invulnerable, while those who anger her seem to shrink down to dots on the landscape.

Aunty Limu shares her culture, but only under conditions that don't involve appropriation. She often constructs what could be called her identity in terms tied to 'āina. Her talk, at a stoplight, is filled with *aloha 'āina*. Her discussion with her nurse becomes a reminder of the gifts of the sea, and a reminder of who (and what) Aunty Limu is.

Aunty Limu constructs her knowledge as essential, yet doesn't share her knowledge if the terms of sharing are not her own. In her talk, through (perhaps unintentional) habitual strategic moves, she constructs the connections that shape her life.

Aunty Lau was a *kupuna* who agreed to be interviewed by Kalo for my research, although, like the other *kūpuna* Kalo interviewed, Aunty Lau did not know me. Kalo and I dropped by Aunty Lau's place to interview her. We brought along some food, and Aunty Lau welcomed us into her front room, which is full of her accomplished *lauhala* weaving. Kalo had already arranged the interview with her by phone. After we talked story for about a half hour, Kalo told Aunty Lau about my schoolwork and about the interview, detailing the information on the release form, which Aunty Lau signed. Here, Aunty Lau talks about teaching Hawaiian culture in the schools.

AUNTY LAU

I learned a lot in the Hawaiian
in the classroom.
And being in a district that
there is other cultures too,
it was hard to have, most of all,
the teachers to accept my culture.

And I saw their,
you know, their feelings,
cause they have so much to teach
and here I come with my Hawaiian culture.
So I thought to myself, I came home,
and I asked the Lord to help me,
to show them that I
should not be a threat to them.

But I'm teaching part of my culture,
cause WE LIVE HERE IN HAWAI'I.

MY THOUGHTS

Aunty Lau's first response to resistance is empathy, followed by prayer. She asks for help not in overcoming resistance, but in reassuring those who feel threatened. Like Aunty Limu, she is asking for help for others, not for herself.

Her voice becomes raspy,
shakes.

And in my time,
we couldn't even speak Hawaiian in school.
And I could see that our language
was getting lost already.

And this
I'm trying to teach in school
it's not the language
because we have all different cultures there,
but a little of our language.
And it worked really well.
Really well.
(AUNTY LAU: 106–127)

And he
he introduced his name to me.
So I said, "Oh yes," so
his grandchild came
RUNNING up to him,
hugging me, saying
you know . . .

[Yeah, "Kupuna, kupuna."]

And I said,
"Oh, this is your grandson, oh yeah."
And he said he,
he does not want for me
to teach Hawaiian to his grandson.
So I said, "Why?"
and he said, "Well, I'm Filipino,
and he's Filipino first."
So I said, "That's true. That's true."
I said, "But if I know Filipino
I will teach in Filipino.
But I don't know Filipino,

Her voice continues to shake, yet her tone takes on force and emotionality as she talks about "her time" (rather than a constructed "past").

The phrase "it worked really well" seems to refer to a compromise to teach just a little Hawaiian language, but could also refer to having empathy for others and engaging in prayer.

Aunty Lau tells a story about learning and connection concerning a Filipino grandparent who did not want his grandchild to learn about Hawaiian culture.

Kalo inserts what she feels is said to Aunty Lau in the story. Aunty Lau nods and continues her story.

Aunty Lau speaks to this grandfather not as a teacher might to a child's caretaker, but as one elder to another, in agreement about preserving both of their cultures. Her approach is inclusive and accepting.

and he must learn English, right?"
So I said,
"You teach him Filipino when he go home.
As soon as he knock the door
and walk in, you talk Filipino to him."
I said,
"Then you will teach him Filipino,
I will teach him little bit of Hawaiian,
and ---- will teach him English."
You know.
"Look at me," I said, "No be like me."
You know.
"They stand up to speak Hawaiian.
Now my children have to go University
to learn Hawaiian."
I said,
"You don't teach Filipino;
then they have to go over there to learn, right?"
He said, "Ohhhh, you right!"

[Kalo chuckles.]

So after that, he would send the little boy
with things Filipino.
(AUNTY LAU: 148–168)

[What limitations or what barriers
that you think that the Hawaiians
with our culture and with our background
having to live in both the *haole* culture,
as well as our Hawaiian.
How do you see us, as today?]

To me
I see we cannot live back the way we lived.

Aunty Lau is referring to the child's teacher at school.

Her next claim is perhaps unintentionally disarming. She connects with the grandfather about the importance of his teaching role as an elder. After her earlier discussion about not being permitted to speak Hawaiian, "They stand up to speak Hawaiian," is a powerful image. It seems that now the grandfather is in relation to Aunty Lau as one elder to another. She accepts and enfolds resistance in an apt understanding of their shared concerns about loss of culture. Later in the interview she describes the Filipino food that the grandfather sent to her through the child.

Kalo constructs the question to Aunty Lau in accord with the idea that Aunty Lau earlier shared about not being able to speak Hawaiian at school.

While Kalo constructs her question in terms of *haole* cultural dominance, Aunty responds by addressing the past, and Kalo agrees.

[Yeah. Yeah. Cannot go back.]

Way back.
No way can we go back and live that way.
And we
we must make the best of it.
And to me
I'm proud to be an American.
I'm proud to be an American.
I have to accept it.
My mom did too.

The whole trouble with our Hawaiians
they're not educated enough
they don't want to be educated enough,
and that.
And my mom wasn't educated.
I mean she knew lots to know
there's respect for others too.

And she always used to say,
"Read the culture. Read the culture."

She said,
"Royalty wasn't good to their people."
You know, I believed my mom.
I believed my mom, and that.
And she said,
"It takes royalty that took us down the drain."

She said, "They didn't care for their people."
And she told me
even my aunt, my last aunt
she said

Aunty Lau enfolded these two contradictory ideas: that of being proud to be an American and having to accept/make the best of it. At that moment I felt that Aunty Lau was able to enfold any set of contradictory situations/constructions that could exist.

I don't think Aunty Lau is speaking solely about reading. Perhaps she is also talking about learning, researching, discerning, and coming into deeper understandings of the culture.

Aunty Lau refers here to the complicity and misdeeds of the *ali'i*, alleging that they didn't always act in the best interests of the common people. I felt at this point that instead of the *haole* being the more powerful dominant group, Aunty Lau formulated a different power relationship—between *ali'i* and commoner Hawaiians. It seems that there is a deeper moral to this story, perhaps about victimization and complicity. This is amplified when Aunty says "because of the way they feel." She is alluding to long-standing feelings of betrayal and distrust.

"Hawaiians will never get their way,
because of the way they feel."
And I see it.

No Hawaiian organization will ever. . . .
You see, when they start one organization
another one will fight it.
You start another one
another one will fight it.

So, until they learn how to love. . . .
And I think that's what's wrong with our
Hawaiian people.

Ah, a lot of it is jealousy too.
Yeah.
Instead of helping, yeah?
Coming together.
Like they say, *lōkahi*.
Be together, all in one.
They're not doing it.
They're talking about it.
But they're not practicing it.
(AUNTY LAU: 251–316)

[What are our, what are our strong points?
What are our strengths? In the Hawaiian culture?]

What do you mean?

[We know that our culture is valuable.]

Mmm hmm.

[The fact that we were here first.]

Aunty Lau is referring to Hawaiians getting self-determination. By saying "you see," Aunty Lau pulls us into the point
she is making.

Inner spiritual integrity and ethical actions are essential to
a Hawaiian future. Causes for social change emerge from
right action, rather than external socio-political or economic forces. Aunty has shifted the possible barrier from
being *haole* culture to an inability on the part of Hawaiians
to learn how to love.

Lōkahi means unity, agreement, accord, or harmony.

When Aunty Lau attempts to understand the question,
Kalo talks about what she views as strengths, shifting into
the issue of her relationship with Aunty Lau. This process
of connecting seems to move Aunty Lau more deeply into
the question and into her own thoughts and perceptions.
Aunty Lau's affirmations begin to overlap Kalo's claims.

Right.

[And we just look at the quality of your *lauhala*.
The best, I mean, you know,
you're a master weaver. And I'm . . .
both Leilani and I are just proud, you know,
to know somebody—]

They were very smart people.

I think Aunty Lau is shifting Kalo's statements about her skills onto those who wove *lauhala* in the past—people from ancient times.

[And that you would give us your time,
your precious time, you know,
away from your family,
and even the things that you have,
to share a part of that with us.
You know, that's, that's a gift that,
that Leilani and I,
that I've always cherished.
So, those for me are the strengths
or the positive
aspects of our culture
that I just cling to.

Then Kalo speaks emotionally for some time of her feelings about Aunty Lau and her knowledge. As Kalo spoke, Aunty Lau looked at her with what I felt was an intense gaze. Here Kalo has positioned me as a learner, in relation to Kalo, rather than an interviewer.

Because the life that you've lived,
I will never experience that.
I'll read about it, and we can sit down
and we can *kūkākūkā* about it.
But I only can live through you
and what you've shared.
So, for me, those are the real
powerful kinds of stuff.]

Kūkākūkā means to consult, confer, or deliberate, and implies that two or more people are in a discussion. Kalo has moved away from a focus on the interview question to the idea of passing down knowledge. She claims Aunty Lau as the conveyor of a deeply shared, and therefore lived, experience.

OK.

Uh, let me share something with you.
And I told you, Kalo, way back,

When Aunty says "OK," she completes the shift in tone that Kalo has introduced. There is a pause. Aunty Lau seems to be setting the stage to tell Kalo something important. Aunty Lau then "fixes" Kalo in relationship with

I think you're related to my mom, them.
So let me share something with you,
from what my *kupuna* had shared with me.
My *kupuna* said
when the first Hawaiians came on their canoes
there were people here already.
There were people.
And the people were small.
They were small.

And when those people CAME,
they overtook these people,
that they had to hide in caves.
And they took these people as slaves.

So I told her, I said,
"Are they the ones that they call the *menehune?*"
She said "No. *'A'ole.*"
She said "What they used to call them was
the *ko'i mū.*

Cause they used to hide in caves."

I remember my grandma,
when we used to play outside,
she said, in Hawaiian,
"Stay out there later so the *mū* boy,
the *mū* come and get you."

We used to run and we used to say,
"Who?
Who are these people?"

So she said,
"They were the first people here."
And she said,

Aunty Lau's own mother. Then she tells Kalo that this knowledge is directly passed down. This preamble seems to place the knowledge squarely in the context of the relationship between Kalo and Aunty Lau (and their families). It grounds knowledge in ancestry.

'A'ole means no. The *menehune* are the race of "little people" said to inhabit Hawai'i before the arrival of people later referred to as Native Hawaiians. Pukui and Elbert (1986) say that they worked at night building fish ponds, roads, and temples. One of the many definitions for *mū* is "a legendary people of Lā'au-haele-mai, Kaua'i, often called *Mū-'ai-mai'a*, banana-eating *Mū*" (ibid., 255). Pukui and Elbert also defined *mū* as "public executioner; he procured victims for sacrifice and executed taboo breakers; children were frightened by being told that the *mū* would get them" (ibid.). Pukui and Elbert define *ko'i* as "axe, adze, adzelike, sharp, projecting, as a forehead" (ibid., 160).

"The Hawaiians
those tall ones came on the canoes
they didn't do these people justice."
"That's why."
She said . . .
"The Hawaiians will NEVER
will never be happy,
until they undo what they did
to the first people here."

And you know, I SAT,
I LOOKED at her,
and, you know,
she's old,
but my mother's last sister.
And she put her head down,
she said, "I'm telling you that."
And it does
to me it makes sense in a way!
She said,
"They even used them as slaves
and they used them when they built their *heiaus*,
they used them as sacrifices."
You know.

And she said
"Until they undo what they did
to these people that were formerly here,"
she said,
"they'll never be happy."
She said,
"You see how they *hukihuki*?
Hukihuki."
She said "They'll never."
She told me
"You teach your children that.
So they know what love is."

Aunty Lau constructs a cycle of atonement suggesting that Hawaiians look at their own behavior, question their own ethics, and undo their own bad practices. She puts forward the issue of a long-forgotten injustice for which accounting and restitution must be made. We get a sense of a need for atonement here, a sense that reparation must be made for a wrong committed.

Aunty Lau has distinct memories not only of what was said, but also of her reactions, and especially how her *kupuna* reacted. She puts this Aunty's words into a powerful context by describing the moment so vividly. Aunty Lau's phrase "it makes sense in a way!" seems to assume that we might think this story farfetched.

Hukihuki means split apart, pull in different directions. Here Aunty Lau might mean that Hawaiians will never be happy, or will never come together, or she might be alluding to self-determination. Aunty constructs the central lesson as having to do with love. It is notable that Kalo thanks her just now, since Aunty Lau has just said that this message is for Kalo's own children.

[Thank you for sharing that.]

Yeah, and I told my children, I said,
"You don't have to tell this to anybody,"
I said.

"But you look at it, you look at it.
And you READ the culture from way back,"
I said,
"They never did justice to the people."

I said,
"Look at the *Makahiki*.
They would come and take the BEST.
And look at trading with the sandalwood,
how people would
leave their farming."
(AUNTY LAU: 328–446)

Actually nobody OWNS the land.
God owns the land.
And how it was done,
it was how the *ali'i* did.
They gave;
they GAVE.
They never educated their people.
There were some people in the wilderness
that did not know
they had to pay their taxes
to maintain their land.
So, didn't care.
And you know, whenever,
whenever,
when I was a child,
because I was able to understand Hawaiian
I used to HEAR the old folks talk about that.

Aunty Lau indicates that this story can be private, and may be suggesting that at moments this reading of history could be disbelieved.

I think that as before, when she says "read the culture," Aunty Lau is speaking about a practice of research, learning, and discerning. She refers here to the misdeeds of the *ali'i*, saying that they demanded the best that the commoners had during the *Makahiki*. This ancient festival began when the Pleiades appeared on the horizon at sunset and its sequences were based on the Hawaiian lunar calendar. During the *Makahiki*, which lasted about four months from around mid-October, commoners from each district gave offerings. Aunty Lau is asserting that the *ali'i* took too much from the commoners. She brings up the complicity of the people in deforesting Hawai'i in order to trade with foreigners. She resists the *haole* vs. Hawaiian dichotomy, then the *ali'i* vs. commoner dichotomy.

Here Aunty Lau is talking about how the *ali'i* gave land and resources to the *haole*.

I think she means the *ali'i* didn't care about the common people, and ultimately confiscated their lands.

When they talked about *ali'i*,
they didn't speak very well of them.
(AUNTY LAU: 466–482)

And that's why when they say,
"Oh, I belong to *ali'i* line,"
she used to say,
"How can they belong to *ali'i* line
when they all came on the same canoe?"
[Laughs]
"They MADE themselves *ali'i*."

This refers to Aunty Lau's aunt. Her words caused me to think about what "having royal blood" means, especially given the part of my "origin myth" about "royal blood." It seemed that it would confer a sense of responsibility rather than entitlement.

So I said, I used to argue back to her,
I said, "How do you know?"
She said, "My *kupuna* told me,
and I'm telling you."
And, you know,
this is only what I believe, you know,
because that was handed down.
(AUNTY LAU: 488–499)

Aunty Lau discusses how she argued with her aunt, and describes how her aunt validated her own knowledge: As Aunty Lau says "I'm telling you," her words take on a different sort of weight as they are passed through her line to Kalo.

I would share with him,
so one evening he said
he had an argument with his girlfriend's
grandmother,
not an argument,
but just telling her what he believed in.
And she argued back with him,
and so he said he went to school,
he got the book,
that Kamakau book.

Aunty Lau then opens up into a story of how she would share with her grandson, and how he disagreed with another *kupuna*.

[Uhmhmm.]

Took it back to her and showed her.
And he said because she said,

Aunty Lau is referring to one of Kamakau's books. Her grandson does not use the text as a source; rather he uses it as a verifier for his source, his *kupuna*, Aunty Lau.

she asked him,
"Who did you hear it from?"
He said,
"My grandma."
She said,
"Oh well, your grandma didn't learn it right."
So he brought that book,
he brought the Kamakau and showed her.
And she said
she really didn't know
it was like that.
So I said,
"You know, don't argue.
Just say, 'This is the way I was taught,
and this is the way I have to go research on it.'"
I said,
"And if they argue, don't argue.
If they think differently,
then you respect what they say."
Yeah. I said,
"You don't argue with older people especially."
He said,
 "But, Grandma, I had to show them
that I knew what I was talking about.
I may be younger than them,
but I knew what I was talking about."
He said,
"Because, Grandma, when you told me,
I took it up to Kamehameha
to our Hawaiian teacher. . . ."
(AUNTY LAU: 549–588)

The future.
Aaahh.
If we are more humble people,
our future will be beautiful.

Aunty Lau infers that this other *kupuna* acknowledges the validity of Aunty Lau's information.

Aunty Lau's wish is not that her grandson validate her teachings, but that he practice respect for the words of other *kūpuna*.

Aunty Lau is suggesting that knowledge is not simply about truth-value but based on different knowledges handed down through families, through genealogical connection.

Aunty Lau's grandson explains that because they are *her* words, which he has had validated by his teacher, he felt the need to assert to others that this knowledge was valid.

Aunty Lau responds to a question about the future by immediately talking about humility.

But if we have Hawaiians,
our Hawaiians,
think that they're better than the next person,
instead of learning from one another
then we not,
we not going to,
we going have,
our future going to be
the SAME WAY,
SAME WAY,
from one generation to the next.
That's the way I feel.
But if we show respect for one another . . .
(Aunty Lau: 612–625)

You know Michael?

[Hmmhmm.]

He learned from his grandfather
on Moloka'i.
And when we became *kūpuna* in the school
he was one of the youngest.
But his grandmother,
and he used to come and help his grandmother.
So he shared something with all of us,
you know.
And ---- argued with him.
And I guess he was taught not to argue
cause it's the oldest of all of us, yeah?
And he just clamped up and
I KNEW HE WAS HURT.
And this one boy is very smart.
Aahh.
So when it came to me
he never answered, he never said anything.

Aunty Lau asserts that a lack of humility prevents us from learning from others and leads to stasis; the future does not improve.

Here Aunty Lau's voice became more forceful. She got a bit louder the second time she said "same way." Her repeated and emphasized phrases evoke a sense of frustration and desolation.

Aunty Lau begins a story that emerges as an example of her point about humility and learning. I think it's important that she's chosen someone whom Kalo knows as the central character of her story.

Aunty Lau is referring to another *kupuna*, who was the eldest of all those present at the meeting.
This *kupuna* is also someone whom Kalo knows and respects.[9] Aunty's voice began to shake a bit here, and I felt she was remembering this incident, feeling bad all over again for this boy (who is really a middle-aged man). That Michael was taught not to argue is important—it marks him as one who was brought up well. It is apparent that Aunty Lau is quite disturbed that Michael has been silenced by the older *kupuna*.

He sat in his corner.
And when the subject was over
our resource teacher said,
"Oh, can we share?"

So she went around,
the *mana'o*, the thoughts
and all of—you know,
when came to me I said that
we sometimes have to accept
our younger generation
cause they also learned from THEIR *kūpuna*
and not two *kupuna*s alike.
Like when we come from a different district,
we learn different.
So I said, "Sometimes we must accept our
younger generation.
Because they also have learned
from their *kūpuna*
which was taught a little different."

And you know,
---- knew that I was talking to her.
This was the subject, yeah?
And she finally caught herself, yeah.
Apologized.
Which was SO NICE.
She apologized to Michael.

And we went on a field trip to Moloka'i
and this boy knew.
He knew the story from his grandfather.
So you see sometimes we have to listen
to the young generation too.
And that's what's wrong with us.
You know.

Aunty Lau is referring to a process where the group leader went around the room so that each person could share all his or her thoughts, concerns, and feelings about the material they had shared.

The local dictates of the *'āina* structure the knowledge of *kūpuna* in Aunty Lau's story. Knowledge comes from the practices of families on the land. She is speaking indirectly to the older *kupuna* and is addressing the issue of respect for the younger *kupuna*'s knowledge.

Aunty is referring again to this older *kupuna* who had dismissed the knowledge shared by Michael, the younger man. Aunty Lau now credits the older *kupuna* with "catching" herself and apologizing. The care Aunty has taken about the feelings of all those involved is notable here.

Now Aunty Lau confirms Michael's knowledge because it was passed down to him. With "So you see," Aunty constructs the message of her story, which is about listening to the younger generation and to other people in general.

There are some that:
"We were taught this way."
No.
Hawaiians say *pa'akikī*.
They so hardheaded.
You know.
But I say,
"Listen to other people too,
cause they learned their way too."
(Aunty Lau: 631–689)

Pa'akikī means stubborn or obstinate.

Throughout the interview Aunty Lau also shared stories that were much more personal in nature. These stories had to do with situations where she was offered money but decided not to take it, for reasons that (I think) have to do with her own sense of integrity. An example is one story where she was called by one site *to* *"help out down there. And it was minimum wage but IT DIDN'T MATTER!"* (Aunty Lau: 49–51). When she's at this site she's approached by someone whom she knows personally, and who is responsible for another site. This acquaintance offers Aunty Lau more money if she will go to the other site, to teach. It will involve quitting the job at her first site:

I said "OK." But when I went to sleep that night, I couldn't, I couldn't WAIT for the next morning to come. And so I called her early in the morning. I refused her. . . . She: "I'll give you more money than them." I said, "They helped me when I really needed help!" (Aunty Lau: 66–74)

In this story, Aunty Lau did not want to leave her first site because they had given her a job when she needed the money. We do not know this until she talks about how they helped her. Although she can make even more money by quitting this site, they have helped her and she doesn't want to leave them without a teacher. In this story and others like it, abundance tended to come to Aunty Lau

This other person keeps offering Aunty Lau more and more money, but Aunty Lau still says no. Later another extra job comes up for Aunty Lau, which will enable her to make extra money but still stay at her original site. She accepts that job.

When Aunty Lau's stories became more personal and more talk-story, Kalo quickly said *"Pau."* Aunty Lau said *"Pau?"* Kalo said "Yeah, *Pau,"* and I turned off the tape recorder. Then Aunty Lau just kept talking for another half-hour to hour or so. I am only including my own description of one of the stories she told here. My tape of my own *mana'o* offers a sense of how I took up Aunty Lau's knowledge.

And that was really an intense interview, uhm, after the interview when we turned it (the tape recorder) off, she started telling a couple of stories. So I want to go back and try to remember the stories. The first story that she told was about her grandparents who had lived on the lo'i. *You know, had lived on the land, and, she started talking about how she was at this (pause) event where she was with some other* kūpuna *and they'd all brought their* poi *pounders and they had all, they were all getting ready to make* poi.

And she talked about the whole process of, you know, peeling it, and . . . cooking it, and cleaning it. . . . And, what really moved me was that as she was talking about this she became emotional. Her voice started getting shaky, and her eyes started getting full of tears.

after she made such decisions. Right action, and putting integrity first, resulted in abundance. Money appears to be tempting in this story, but it is clearly not useful as a means to an end. Still it comes to her, after she has kept her integrity.

It happened here as in other junctures, that when stories became personal, the tape recorder was turned off, then stories became more and more personal, emotional, and full of laughter. In this case, the story felt like another example of an earlier message, except that there was much attention to the details of *poi*-making.

Typically, I forgot the process of making *poi*, yet remembered the emotionality of her talk. I'm sure I got the details of *poi*-making wrong, and I can't say that I want to learn more about them. But I do want to learn more about how Aunty Lau so deftly pulled me into such a deep place with her talk. I also remember that as Aunty Lau spoke of the process, her voice carried a kind of repetitive lilt, as if she was lightly singing through a list.

And the story was about how this other aunty, an older aunty, her family lived where they did DRY kalo *farming. And, uhm, Aunty Lau's family, like many other families lived where they had WET* kalo *farming. And so they learned different ways of making (laughs) the* poi, *and what, what the essence of it is, is that this other woman was upset because they kept peeling parts of it, of the skin off the* kalo, *to, to, to let the pigs and dogs eat.*

And, I think the essence of it was that she (the other aunty) had said this was wasteful, but the reason that Aunty Lau—them (and the others) did this is that they wet-farmed. They came from valleys where kalo *was wet-farmed . . . and so in between the leaves and the body, the corm of the* kalo, *you know even if you clean it, there's still, what she said, stuff, mud and stuff inside the* pukas *(holes). . . . And so there is a disagreement about that and (laughs) what was meaningful to me was that she went through the whole process of explaining how this was done. And, took some time to explain it.*

And, the moral, for her, of the story was . . . that everybody is in a position where they have to learn from each other. And different people learned it different ways from different kūpuna *. . . different families, different* kūpuna *who taught. And different people learned different ways and we have to be patient with each other.* (Mana'o 193–276)

Aunty Lau's description of the land that her family farmed, along with the catches in her voice, filled me with the practice of *kalo* farming, and in some ways the presence of the land. As I listened to her, there was no way I would stop her to write down the exact nature of the process, or to repeat it so I could remember it. I didn't really want to take my eyes off her. Aunty Lau's story took us from a vivid and emotional description of her childhood *kalo* farming to her adult participation in a group of *kūpuna* disagreeing about preparing *kalo*. The context smoothly changed back and forth from wistful to comical.

I laughed here because Aunty Lau's description of how she offended the others with her behavior was so humorous. At some point I remember her saying something like "Oh! The LOOKS they gave me!" and laughing. As Kalo and I became an audience, witnessing Aunty Lau being chastised, she positioned us in close relation with her, and with her message, which arrived at the end of her story. Aunty Lau conceptualizes knowledge as fluid, context-dependent and perhaps *'āina*-dependent. And most of all she grounds knowledge in respect for the conditions that structure knowing in the life of all the participants. She has respect for these other "knowers" and validates their knowledge, because it comes from their particular relationships to the land.[10]

After the interview was over, Aunty Lau gave us *lauhala* (woven) fans she had made, and I commented on this in my *mana'o*:

The other thing that I thought was really—well, I guess it was notable—was that she had made a lauhala *fan with a pattern on it that was beautiful. It's, you know, I, I had been looking at it, sort of intermittently through the interview or, you know, through our talk to her. She . . . gave us each a fan and she gave me the one that I had been looking at. I guess it's one of those coincidental things (sighs). It was a very touching interview (voice lowers). I think Kalo and I were both sort of tired after it because the interviews—it's so clear that they're (sighs) they are truly sharing. And it's so clear that work has been done that hasn't, hasn't been OK. Still (voice shakes) about sharing with Kalo and with me, that's a real gift.* (FN1: 382–408)

When we got up to leave, uhm (sighs) (pause). (Voice shakes) well, before we got up to leave, Aunty Lau started lecturing Kalo about how she couldn't do it all at once, couldn't do the haole *thing, and the Hawaiian thing. . . .* (MANA'O 374–381)

Clearly, the sighs and pauses betray that on some level I was questioning my "place" in interviewing people.

After Aunty Lau gave us the fans, and we were about to leave, she gave a very short but intense bit of advice to Kalo, telling her not to extend herself. Her last few stories had been very personal stories, having to do with saying no when there is too much going on. This advice addressed how Kalo was trying to balance her work, pursuing a degree, "taking care of her family," and activism in the Hawaiian community. It also addressed the fact that Kalo was not well, and was still quite busy working on behalf of others. Aunty Lau divided the work into "*haole* stuff" and "Hawaiian stuff." This advice also seemed (somehow) to simply flow out of the stories Aunty Lau told at the very end of our time together. My telling of the stories betrays, in the pauses and sighs, much emotionality to do with Aunty Lau's gift, Kalo's well-being, and my roles as a learner and interviewer.

After our time with Aunty Lau, we sat outside at a small park, and I asked Kalo about the interview. Kalo was making decisions about her community involvement and her career, which were pulling her in different directions. She was also feeling ill. One story Aunty Lau told was about agreeing to do something and later realizing it would not be right to do it:

KALO ON AUNTY LAU

MY THOUGHTS

[Would you tell me what you think she was saying?]

She,
it was a warning for me.
That I need to be more cautious
as to what I do when it concerns our culture.
And that I need to be at least prepared
or at least have an understanding,
have a deeper,
a deeper understanding about,
about,
about what it is that I do
having to do with our culture,
that I need to be more,
more aware that it's on a deeper level
that I,
that the work that I do,
that it's not just superficial.
And it's not just trying to survive in,
in both worlds.

It seemed to me that she was also,
that she was saying that
even though she had sealed it by saying
she would make this basket,

After I ask Kalo what Aunty Lau was saying, Kalo moves directly into the personal messages that she received.

Kalo looks deeply into the ethical lessons that emerge from Aunty Lau's talk and examines her own life. Kalo seems to be talking about surviving in the *haole* versus Hawaiian worlds, and referring to the deeper moral imperatives Aunty Lau was teaching her. These moral imperatives seemed to eclipse the "*haole* versus Hawaiian" construction, and Kalo seems deeply aware of that.

Here I am still referring to a story Aunty Lau told Kalo about promising to do something that later turned out to be the wrong thing to do. I think at this moment I also wondered if the burden of helping me with my research

that on a really deep level it wasn't right for her.
For her on some, like
a spiritual level.
She knew that it wasn't right.
That it's heavy and
she can't get released from it.

Yeah
and that because we are Hawaiian,
the answers that we give to each other,
it,
it's so much more meaningful.

[Unh hmnn.]

You know,
they're not just,
just surface level.
Because when we do things
in the name of our culture
or the fact that we are Hawaiian,
it's,
it's not just us that we speak.
You know,
we speak for our family,
you know, we speak for
those who came before us
and those that
that will come after.

But I also know that my spirituality is,
there's, there's no dichotomy.
You know, my spirituality is my belief.
And my belief is not
to the ancient Hawaiian gods.
I have great respect,
and I don't like the,
the respect

was too heavy for Kalo, especially given that she was not feeling well.

It felt to me here that Kalo was referring to the layers and layers of meaning that can be sedimented in a talk like the one we had just had with Aunty Lau. On another level I felt that Kalo was saying that these interviews were not just a superficial process of finding out about "Hawaiian culture."[11]

Kalo moves into the notion of connection between the generations, and seems to imply that great care must be taken in what is said.

She also revisits what she has said in my earlier interview with her about our connection to the gods. She is saying that she respects the Hawaiian gods, and that they are important to her identity, but she might also be alluding to

to be misconstrued as this is what I worship.
And it's my culture
and I have great respect for it because
it's my identity,
who I am.
And from that identity I draw strength.

But
"At what price?"
was what I kept hearing her say.
And if the people who say
that they care about us, that they love us,
don't understand a "No,"
then you know what?
It's not your problem.
It's their problem.

But you gotta be true to yourself.
You gotta be true.

If you say you are Hawaiian,
you better listen to the words of *kūpuna*.
If you say that *kūpuna*
are the source of our culture,
that they are the source,
that they know, then we better listen.
And the message to me was very clear.
That I gotta make a decision.
And I think I have.
Cause she's,
she's made it for me.
For me to decide. (KALO: 69–108)

She also said,
she also said, that
you cannot be *po'o pa'akikī* either,
you cannot be hardheaded.
You cannot be stubborn.

the fact that she is a Christian. I think she is referring to the idea that some might construct a dichotomy between her respect for Hawaiian gods and her Christianity. Kalo does not want to "buy into" that dichotomy.

Here, Kalo took up the messages in the interview with Aunty Lau as moving her into being more self-protective. Here I also felt that I should not mention visiting/interviewing *kūpuna* for a while. We had quite a few more planned, but I felt that interviewing was adding stress to Kalo's life and exacerbating her issues about being self-protective.

Kalo locates the *kūpuna* as "the source of our culture," and an undisputed source of knowledge.

Clearly, the thought of "weighing" Aunty Lau's words is not an option. I did not know which element of her life Kalo had decided about: the choices between career and community, the question of keeping particular promises exacted by other *kupuna* (whom Aunty Lau also knows), or whether Kalo should continue to help me with my research.

Po'o means head. *Po'o pa'akikī*, a variant on *pa'akikī*, means hardheaded and stubborn.

And you, and you better listen.
She kept telling me.
You do too much,
you do too much.
You're not well.
And you need to make sure
that what you do is what,
what you,
what you should be doing.
That's why I got the message
loud and clear. (KALO: 171–200)

I felt that this interview is for me.
The visit today is for me. I don't know why
I didn't see.
I see it now,
I see it now.
I didn't see it four hours ago. (KALO: 227–231)

Aunty Lau may have chosen stories and metaphors that apply to Kalo. Aunty Lau made it clear she was sharing knowledge with Kalo because they are related. Kalo almost seemed to be talking to herself here.

"I felt that this interview is for me. The visit today is for me. . . . I see it now." These statements by Kalo about her interview with Aunty Lau resonated for me. Even though I was in Hawai'i to do research, it seemed as if people, often strangers, were involved in discussions that "were for me." These were not discussions that I invited; rather, they just seemed to happen. All too often, the topics were "roots" and my genealogy.

Sometimes our schedule of errands, events, and meetings seemed to result in an exponential growth of such occasions. A chance meeting with a *kupuna* or a conversation with people preparing food for an event could result in an emotional discussion about my genealogy. I often felt emotionally drained after these discussions. The sense of being cared for, coupled

Aunty Lau constructs stories about teaching and learning that begin with the historic silencing of language and loss of culture. These stories often end in a reversal of those silences, and in connections made, whether in the classroom, with her *mo'opuna* (grandchildren), or even with those who disagree with her.

Aunty Lau constructs her life as abundant, as a result of right action. Money appears in her talk as a peripheral, problematic consideration, rather than a cause of abundance. She speaks of the *'āina* as owned by nobody but God, and speaks unhappily of those (Hawaiian and *haole*) who, she feels, have abused the land.

Aunty Lau complicates readings of history to do with victimization or complicity, collapsing them into lessons about spiritual and ethical integrity. She constructs the future as contingent on the timeless Hawaiian qualities of spiritual integrity and right action. Issues of responsi-

with a feeling of loss, was overpowering. I also felt drained because I found myself constantly wondering if I was talking to someone who was part of my biological family—my *'ohana*. Often other people would wonder out loud—or say I looked familiar to them.

One occasion in particular had an effect on me. I remember it in part because it involved my decision to avoid such discussions by heading for a place that expressly catered to tourists:

. . . Ivan and I decide to go to a restaurant and bar on the beach. I am tired of all this serious talk about my "roots." This restaurant has a Hawaiian feeling, but is usually full of tourist-regulars. There's a band . . . that plays Hawaiian and easy-listening kinds of tunes. The "bouncers" are Hawaiian guys; the waitresses are mostly haole *young women; there's a* lei *stand in the back of the restaurant, adjacent to the bar, and the bar seems to be packed with milling, standing, and sitting people. . . .*

A tourist gives me a flower lei. *I thank him and notice a flower I can't identify on the* lei, *so I go back to the* lei *stand to ask the woman stringing* leis *what flower it is. She is busy, so I ask a very large Hawaiian man if he can tell me what flower it is. He does, and as I say "Thank you" and start to leave, he stops me. He looks deep into my eyes and asks me if I am Hawaiian. I say: "Yes, but not from here now, living in Canada."*

He asks me my last name, and I give it, then he asks for the maiden name. I say that I was adopted and he says, "Oh, hanai.*" I say, "No, it was a formal adoption. I was adopted by* haoles *and lived on the*

bility and atonement arrive in her talk; these formulations empower her listeners and Hawaiian people in general.

Aunty Lau shares her knowledge freely with others. She accepts and enfolds resistance by validating the knowledge and the position of others. Aunty Lau constructs her knowledge as coexisting with the knowledge of others. Prayer, reflection, and respect are key components of her practice.

In her talk, through (perhaps unintentional) habitual strategic moves, Aunty Lau constructs knowledge as context-dependent and sometimes *'āina*-dependent. Through patterned ways of interacting with Kalo, she passes knowledge down through genealogical (ancestral) connection. Aunty Lau's descriptions of knowledge shared through connection are imbued with imagery that activates it easily in the memory of the listener. She endows knowledge from her *kūpuna* with the weight of those *kūpuna*.

Kalo receives knowledge not only from Aunty Lau's direct advice but also from the personal messages that seem to underlie Aunty Lau's stories. Kalo experiences Aunty Lau's knowledge as personal counsel passed down directly. Kalo accepts the challenges proffered by Aunty Lau, even though they may result in difficult decisions.

Aunty Limu and Aunty Lau voice cosmologies inscribing beliefs about the nature of *earth*, *practice*, *destiny*, and *knowledge*.

mainland." He motions to a bench at the back of the restaurant and says, "Sit down; we have to sit and talk about this." I am surprised at this and say, "Oh, OK."

The man, whose name is Kimo, asks me what I know about my birth. I tell him what I know. He asks me if my ancestors ever come to me. I tell him about my dreams—the larger woman, the small man, the mahimahi. *He becomes somewhat teary-eyed and tells me: "It's your ancestors. They are trying to communicate with you."*

He says, "You must meet my wife (Aunty Kimo)." It turns out she is the one working at the lei *stand, stringing* lei *with a younger Hawaiian guy. I meet her, and Kimo retells my birth story. She says, "Oh, it is so important to know where you came from, who your people are."*

Then she tells me a long and interesting story about how she was able to meet her half-sister, quite by chance. She says, "My half-sister and I are still so close," mentioning a few more details about her half-sister. I say to her, "Is your half-sister So-and-So?" She is amazed. I know her half-sister. I heard the mirror-image of this story from her half-sister, more than fifteen years ago. Aunty Kimo grabs my hand and kisses me, saying, "We're 'ohana!"

Kimo and Aunty Kimo introduce me to the other lei-*maker, a man a bit younger than me, who talks at length of his own origin-myth. He, like me, was formally adopted and needs to find his family. . . . We talk about people we know in common on the mainland, and about Aunty Kimo's half-sister. . . . When we're ready to leave, I go back to the* lei *stand and kiss Kimo and Aunty Kimo goodbye . . . a sense of strangeness and intensity, and of emotional exhaustion.* (MANA'O: 2578–2749)

Both Aunty Limu and Aunty Lau talk about the *earth* with great emotion, constructing an abundance paradigm that excludes notions of scarcity. They both seem to use money only in service of their values. Aunty Limu talks about abundance of life on the land and compresses the narrative of the loss of that abundance. Aunty Lau talks about losses related to land, laying blame at the feet of both *haole* and Hawaiians.

Both Aunty Limu and Aunty Lau seem to take Hawaiian values as a given to be lived. They tell stories where outcomes are based solely on integrity and right action. Aunty Limu constructs knowledge as emanating from physical *practice*, whether making *lauhala* or living on the land. Aunty Lau tells stories where it is practice on the land that activates different knowledges, which may all co-exist.

For Aunty Limu, who was not asked questions about *destiny*, the future doesn't arrive in her talk. We do know that she successfully plants her feet in the present that surrounds her, and directly challenges aspects of modern Hawai'i that disturb her. For Aunty Lau, social change is contingent on the choices Hawaiians make. She constructs destiny as related to spiritual integrity and right action.

Both Aunty Limu and Aunty Lau use strategic moves and sequences to create *knowledge*. In their talk, they maintain and privilege Hawaiian knowledge forms. The effects of colonization do not arrive in their talk as much as the agency and responsibility that accrues to Hawaiians. They place lineage at the core of Hawaiian identity and knowledge-making. Aunty Lau's knowledge is given to Kalo in a spirit of complete, unconditional acceptance. Kalo reflectively uses this knowledge to interrogate her own practices.

5 Place of Confluence

Tūtū 'Ōhi'a and the Kā'ai

Another *kupuna* who shared her knowledge with Kalo in a spirit of complete, unconditional acceptance was Tūtū 'Ōhi'a. Kalo interviewed Tūtū 'Ōhi'a (*tūtū* means grandparent) in the front room of her home, where she was surrounded by Hawaiian books and Hawaiian artifacts. Kalo's mom, Kalo, and I brought her a fruit basket and talked story, without mentioning the "purpose" of our visit:

After about 45 minutes of talking story, there is a pause and Kalo says, "So, Tūtū, we want to ask you some questions about Hawaiian culture." Tūtū, unsurprised, shifts in her seat and says gently, "Yes." Kalo says that I am going to school on the mainland and I am interviewing kupuna *about their experiences and feelings. She describes to her everything on my release form, saying, "So, is that OK, Tūtū?" Tūtū says yes; and we give her a pen, and she signs the sheet.* (MANA'O: 1999–2012)

Excerpts from her interview follow:

Hawaiian family is a,
is a family that is shall I say, closed.
Father, mother, children, aunts, uncles,
there is a strong connection
and they have support of the *'ohana.*
More during our times than these times I think.
I don't know.
But during our time,
if one *kupuna* was sick or gone
the others would come and take care.
And we lived like one family in those old days.
And,
And in that way we were able to survive.

Talking about "our times" as compared to "these times" seemed to pull me more into Tūtū 'Ōhi'a's memories than another sort of construction might. Survival is connected to family, to taking care of others.

As I have said we were poor in money.
Grampa didn't work.

Tūtū 'Ōhi'a qualifies poor as attached to the idea *only* of not having money.

He raised taro, potatoes, cane, chickens, pigs
for us to eat.
And we always had plenty to eat!
But when it came to money
we didn't have any unless one other
gave us some money.

Tūtū 'Ōhi'a names the things her grandfather grew rather than saying (for instance) that he grew vegetables and raised livestock.

[Laughter]

Do you think I'm heading up on our strengths?

Tūtū 'Ōhi'a's response to a question about the dangers facing Hawaiians and their strengths sequences from traditional family, to getting food (or "subsistence activities"), to abundance. The idea of food and cultivation shifts into the idea of plenty, and the idea that money was not needed. She talks about living on the land, the abundance that ensues, and the peripheral nature of money within that abundance.[1]

[Yes! Yes!]
(TŪTŪ 'ŌHI'A: 35–60)

More support, and put the welfare
of the child first.
Some parents I think,

some of our Hawaiian people
they spend all of their money foolishly.
I don't know if they still do it.
But in the days when I was growing up
there were families like that.
They always looked poor.
They looked as though they
didn't have enough of anything.
Because that's the way they spent their money.

But my grandmother and grandfather
always had everything we wanted to do.
And we lived the Hawaiian way.
We . . . we cooked outside, you know.
Everything was cooked outside.
But in spite of that the food was
good and simple food like
taro tops,
taro stalks,
the taro in the *poi,*
the sugar cane for us to chew and
EVERY *māhealani,*
māhealani is the full moon,
we'd all plant.
Yeah.
Our bananas.

But, you know, my brother and sisters
and my sisters and I
would go up there and mine would just grow
up like a puny tree!

[Laughter]

And nothing would come out of there.
My sister had a good hand!

When Tūtū uses the phrase "our Hawaiian people," I am pulled into her talk not as a researcher, collecting her stories, but as a person younger than she, listening to and learning from her assessment of "us."

Tūtū 'Ōhi'a moves quickly from the idea of abundance into Hawaiian practices by saying "we wanted to do" and "cooking outside." Then she moves into a naming of food, particularly the taro *(kalo)*. The repeated word taro pulls me back into its symbolic significance.

The phrase "for us to chew" again seems to reference a sense of plenty. Tūtū says "every *māhealani*" while looking around at us—there is a sense that something very important is being said. Tūtū 'Ōhi'a slows down here, and what is again evoked is a sense of abundance. Tūtū introduces planting in the context of her family relationships.

Here I felt pulled back into Tūtū's life as a child as she entered into this description of her sister. She seemed to be remembering her childhood. Tūtū created a circle from the idea of putting the child first, to abundance, to a childhood story of her sister, described from what seemed to be the viewpoint of Tūtū 'Ōhi'a as a child.

Whenever she started planting anything,
as soon as that thing started growing,
the flowers came out!
The leaf . . . very good!
But yeah, she had
a good planting hand as we call it.
[Chuckles]
(TŪTŪ 'ŌHI'A: 62–94)

[What is . . . what is the role, Tūtū,
of Hawaiian spirituality
and Hawaiian knowledge about the *'āina*
as we move towards tomorrow; as we move
towards the future?
The role of spirituality and our land.]

Kalo alters my original question, which was written: "What is the role of Hawaiian spirituality and Hawaiian knowledge about the land as we move into the future?" She also asks the question as someone who is related to Tūtū.

I think at this time . . .
You see, the early days
when people had big tracts of land,
they took care of their land.
They took care of the water!
Everything came that way because
that's the way we did.
We had the land and we had the water.
Nobody went into the pool where the water was
because our water came from the river.
And many pools would dry out before ours.
And when summer came and we had
a long drying, dry period,
the water was all practically evaporated.
And that's when Grandpa would clean
all of that pool; leaves and rocks
and things that have come from *ma uka*.

Tūtū shifts quickly from the present into recalling (and re-calling) her early days, in answer to a question about the future. She draws us once again into the past and connects abundance directly to *mālama 'āina*. She answers a question about spirituality by talking about the land and *mālama 'āina*. As I read her description of abundance as "everything came that way," I have a sense of abundance as manifestation, related to what "we did"—the practices of *mālama 'āina* that people enacted.

Ma uka means mountains. Tūtū is speaking of debris that came down from the mountains.

And so we always had clean water.
And people would come to our water that way.

OK.
Today
when we say take care of the land
I don't think many Hawaiians have that, really.
Cause they live in cities, towns, and they live,
some of them
live in apartments.
No yard;
some of them have a yard,
oh that's all right
but still . . . there's very little of that.

The only way they can get it is by us.
Us telling them.
Take care.
Take care of the land.
You know the land feeds us, you know.
And the rivers give us water.
(Tūtū 'Ōhi'a: 126–161)

Now I was reading in the paper . . .
Am I going away from myself?

[It's all right, Tūtū; it's OK.]

Now I was reading in the paper
just this afternoon.
They're taking the water so that
windward houses
can have more water than they've ever had. . . .
But this story that I read said
they came to ask this man
to buy the land and he said "NO.
I don't want anyone to buy my land."
Because the water went through.
And they said, "The water is going to be
used for the plantation."

Tūtū's shift ("OK") seemed to create a link between the past and a powerful statement about its relevance to the present. First she talks about our everyday talk of *mālama 'āina;* then she says that Hawaiians of today don't have that. It seems to me that she softens the discussion about "they" by saying "that's all right," yet her point, that we don't practice this value, is powerful to me. Tūtū uses the term "we" in describing her *'ohana* and describes Hawaiians who live in apartments as "they." She is talking to us (Hawaiians who live under the conditions she describes), but she uses the term "they." "Us" in this statement refers to the *kūpuna,* who are the only source for modern-day Hawaiians. Then she constructs "us" as "all of us." In telling this story, her definitions of "they" and "us" have been fluid but at the end consolidate as "we." Again, land and rivers have agency and intent, related to abundance. There is a very strong sense again of *mālama 'āina.*

Tūtū 'Ōhi'a asks for confirmation of a direction she is taking. I wondered if she was reminded that this was an interview and wanted to make sure that, nevertheless, it was OK to go into another story to make her point.

She is now referring to a story about the past.
"They" in this case are outsiders, non-Hawaiians.

But he said, "No.
I still want to have my,
my taro patch filled with water."

So they started building a dam.
These people who were taking the water.
And no water came down.
So this man said,
"Oh, I didn't even give them permission,
I didn't sell them the rights
but here they took it away from me."
So he went up and he,
he destroyed the dam
and the water came flowing down his place.
Back again.
But the wife was different.
SHE wanted to come to Honolulu!
So she could have a satin *holokū*.
So she could have this and this of the,
of the American. She wanted to be
like the Americans dressed and everything else.

But the water came through again.
And they never . . . the plantation
didn't bother him any more.
The water always came through his place.
And so he said, *"I don't need that money*!
If I can get money, it's not going to feed me!
I need the water, so my plants will grow.
My food plants will grow, and I can live."
So he was wise.
More more wiser than his wife.
(TŪTŪ 'ŌHI'A: 161–208)

You know, I read someplace
that the Hawaiian spirit was the *hā*.
It was their breath. Yeah. It was the breath.

At this point in the story Tūtū became an impassioned storyteller. Tūtū 'Ōhi'a talks about water as an actor in this story. Tūtū's description of the man's destroying the dam culminates in the water coming to him. She doesn't say (for example) "so he had the water back." When she emphasized the word "flowing" and at "back again," I sensed laughter behind her words. "Back again" almost seemed like Tūtū was explaining the return of an old friend. In Tūtū's story, there seems to be a relationship among the intent of the taro farmer, the intent of the plantation owners, the intent of his wife, and the intent of the water. A *holokū* is a loose-seamed dress, fancier than "everyday" clothing. "Like the Americans did and everything else" somehow keeps us on the "surface" of American "culture." Tūtū continues calling people running the plantation "they"; then she constructs an impersonal entity: "the plantation." Notably, the result is that there is no real "they" by the end of this story.

In this story, it is the man and the water who are in a relationship, with the purpose being to grow his taro. Money is peripheral to real abundance; it is the water that brings abundance.

Tūtū answers a question about spirituality by calling up the idea of *hā*. As she told us of her reaction to *hā* as related to her daughter, Aunty Jane,

I was SO surprised to see that, you know.
And I thought,
"Oh my! that's where Jane has been."
Jane has gone way down into the culture;
Many of us are only on the surface.
You know all these surface things.
But going down, yeah.
Spirituality. That's a hard topic to discuss.
It really is.

[I feel, Tūtū, for me . . . the fact that,
that our people believe in the power of prayer.]

That's right.

[And . . . everything we believe is spirit.]

That's right.

[And that's why the power of prayer and that
whatever we did was always preceded
with a prayer.]

That's right.

[And Aunty Jane, of course, has reinforced that
constantly. At all of our meetings.]

That's right.

[All of our gatherings.]

That's right.

Now you see when the Hawaiians went to plant
they used the plants around them.
When they went to gather

I felt pulled further into her story. Her daughter, Aunty Jane, is very active as an educator and leader in the community. Tūtū's description of where her daughter has been locates spirituality and culture as a place, deep beneath the surface, a place we journey to. I feel that she is also saying that it's hard to discuss *because* it is so deep. I felt at this point that she was saying that as a topic, spirituality was too deep for words, or that she had reached an impasse in talking about it.

Kalo responds to Tūtū's pause and possible puzzlement as to "where to go" with the topic of her feelings about prayer, rather than trying to elicit more information from Tūtū 'Ōhi'a. This statement that "everything we believe is spirit" is not the same as saying everything is "infused with" spirit. Rather it collapses materiality into spirit. During this interchange (and as I played the tape back) I felt very moved, as if I were listening to only one voice. Tūtū's affirmations came as exclamations, and she nodded her head. Her answers to Kalo sometimes overlapped slightly with Kalo's claims. And, as Kalo brought us back to Aunty Jane, Tūtū's affirmation was more like an exclamation. I felt again as if I were being brought back full circle, to Tūtū's claims about *hā*. I felt, as I looked from Kalo to Tūtū 'Ōhi'a, who was nodding at Kalo, that they were constructing a connection and agreement. Immediately after the last "that's right," Tūtū moved into an exposition on subsistence and *mālama 'āina*. It was as if Kalo had created (with Tūtū) a momentum for that transition connecting breath (*hā*) to prayer, to planting, and finally to *mālama 'āina*.

Although she does not mention the word *mālama 'āina*, Tūtū constructs a forceful reference to the practices of *mālama 'āina* after listening to and affirming Kalo.

these plants for medicine
they asked the plant.
They didn't just go and pick
whatever they wanted and destroy.

When they went to the beach, you know,
they were very careful.
They didn't ill-use the beach
like clean their fish and shells
and leave them there like
some of our young people have done in the past.

And it's because they don't understand.
They have not had it.

So they, they didn't have that feeling
that there is this thing that
God has given us
for us to use
but at the same time take care of it.
(TŪTŪ 'ŌHI'A: 211–284)

I'm thinking of one incident
that happened to me.
When I was helping at the Queen's Hospital
they have a little room in there
where they display things, yeah, things,
pictures of Queen Emma and the King,
and of plants, and anything.
And the leader there asked me if
I could pick some 'ohuloa[2]
And I said yeah, I could.
And I went down to Mokuaiea, to my daughter,
and on the way home just as I was
coming into Mililani,
I saw this 'ohuloa plant on the side of a hill.
And I got out of my car and hurried,

Tūtū 'Ōhi'a ties abundance to practice, a particular way of having (not owning) and caring for the land and the water. Her talk moves us from the land to the beach/sea.

This constitutes a response of *mālama 'āina* to a question about spirituality. Instead of comparing Hawaiians to non-Hawaiians, Tūtū thinks in terms of younger generations of Hawaiians. She looks inward at her community, and "they" become the "younger generation." Perhaps for me, this way of talking makes her words a lesson for those younger than she. I wonder if, in other types of talk, "they" is such a fluctuating, or fluid term. Again Tūtū describes those who do not live on the land as not having "had it," then grounds "it" in the realm of feeling, the feeling of having been "given this thing."

Tūtū again moves us into a story. It seemed to me that each successive story uncovered another layer of knowledge and led the way to a yet stronger claim about *mālama 'āina.* It is notable that she says "helping" at the hospital. We are not told whether this was a job or volunteer work. Her work is described as an act of helping rather than a status.

went in, pulled the thing
and you know I felt as though
somebody had taken me and *threw me down!*
And my arm began to hurt.
So I came home driving.

I was all alone with the *'ohuloa.*

And when I got home I said to my husband,
"Take me to the doctor, I think I broke my
arm."
He said, "How?"
I said, "I felt I was thrown down on these rocks.
I was pulling the *'ohuloa* plant."
He said, "You didn't ask for it. You just took it."
"You had no business to just take it
without asking for it."

So I went to the doctor, they x-rayed it,
it was OK."
But eight months later,
this arm began to hurt me.
So I went back to the doctor. I said,
"This thing is hurting me.
I injured my arm
about eight months ago," and he said,
"Seems like you have really broken it!"
I said, "Oh. And I used it all these months."
So when he took the X-ray
it showed the break right here. . . .
And so I asked him,
"How am I going to do things?"
He said, "You just have to let it heal by itself."

And it did.

In this phrase Tūtū creates a sense that the plant has consciousness and intent. She says "threw me down!" as an exclamation.

I felt that Tūtū 'Ōhi'a here amplified a sense of the plant as a presence, as a being with consciousness.

This is an interesting development in the story that could be taken in a number of ways. Did the first X-ray get fouled up? Did the break "grow" over a matter of time? And what would it mean if that were the case? Despite this ending (which I think resists interpretation), I remember this story as the one where the plant threw Tūtū onto the rocks and then sat with her in accusatory silence as she drove home.

You see.

So we believe that things
didn't belong to us.
They belong to God.
But if you want to use it, ask.

And then they respected that so much.
They respected so much.
They respected land,
respected the trees.
They respected the air.
Everything.
Water.
Everything that gave life to them.

And to me, I lived that life as a child.

And I didn't appreciate it.
Because I was aiming to be American.

And you know,
to do things like an American.
Because we were going to school then.

You see.
And it took many many years
for me to realize
that I had
the BEST of,
of the,
of the culture, with my grandparents.
(TŪTŪ 'ŌHI'A: 284–341)

So you see, simple life, simple food,
simple doings but a
GREAT TRUST in God.

Tūtū paused here and began to slow down. With "you see," Tūtū constructs the instructional nature of her story.

The word "respected," as it was repeated, lent increasing emotion to each phrase for me. She paused here and again seemed to look at each of us as she spoke.

There is a pause, then Tūtū 'Ōhi'a places herself back in the story. Her voice shakes a bit and from here till the end of her story there are many pauses. Tūtū is sharing with us (I feel) a strongly held claim, but she is doing so by telling us about her story and her lack of knowledge, rather than focusing on others. Again, Americans are peripheral, and Tūtū constructs a notion of imitating their surface behaviors, learned through schooling.[3]

Tūtū 'Ōhi'a's voice shakes here. Knowledge flows from the story, not as a "moral," but rather as an emotional sharing. I am reminded of the way Kalo seemed to pause, to repeat, in part, the words "Hawaiian culture" in her interview.

Again, using the words "so, you see," Tūtū 'Ōhi'a draws us into the moral of her story. She ties her powerful Christian beliefs and practices to a disciplined but happy upbringing.

On Sunday when we got up in the morning
Grandma cooked enough food for supper.
We ate our breakfast before church.
And church lasted till about two o'clock.
From ten o'clock till two o'clock.
No lunch.
But we would just go home
and eat the food cold
because they had learned
that Sunday was a day of rest.
And it belonged to God
And it didn't belong to us.
And we were happy.

Our children of today would not like it.
We used to say in church,
Here the old folks are having their lessons
and they're preaching back and forth
and here we were
only seven, eight, nine years of age
sitting there quietly
with our teacher back of us;
if we wiggled or,
you know,
got a little shaky around the place,
they would—he would tap us
and we would sit down there.

And I have always wondered what—
why I never hated church.
I grew up, I became a church person,
taught Sunday school
and went to church
with my children.
But now you find that less and less.
Churchgoing.
You don't have to go really, but it's gone.

"So you see" constructs the lesson—and the repeated word "simple" builds up to her exclamation about trust in God.

In Western (non-Hawaiian) culture, it might be somewhat paradoxical, that "it didn't belong to us and we were happy." Our understanding that not having something might *not* be construed as a state of happiness outside Hawaiian culture, amplifies the power of this statement.

Again, I felt drawn into Tūtū's childhood, and there seemed to be a smile, or laughter, behind her story. "We" are "us kids."

Tūtū again softens her statements about others (this time non-church-goers) by saying, "You don't have to go, really." Yet she ends this on a sad note.

Everything was, we asked God.
Everything.
When we were short of this,
oh we, we asked God.
To help us.
And we always had it.
(Tūtū 'Ōhi'a: 342–372)

Now when my son and my daughter
were going to school
I wanted them to have
the best education we could afford.
So my daughter went to Kamehameha
and my son went to Punahou.

And you know there were times
when it was hard to pay the tuition.
The tuition time came around very quickly!

And we would talk,
my husband and I,
we would talk and we would pray:
"God, show us a way that we can get
this couple hundred dollars that we have to
send,
and we have to pay for school."

And we'd pray.
My goodness! In a few days we had it!
I don't know how!
You know, the thought . . .
the good do this, and the good get it.

When you pray,
Here's another thing I say about prayer.
When you pray, and it doesn't come out,
that's your answer!

Tūtū's strong belief in God is again tied to abundance. Abundance is connected to spirituality.

Interestingly, Tūtū then turns to education in relation to what was asked for.

The wonderment Tūtū 'Ōhi'a feels about this abundance is evident in her exclamations. Her story is about how *pono* (or right action) is linked to abundance.

Tūtū brackets her claims by saying, "Here's another thing I say." It seems as if she is inserting a mnemonic device into her talk.

A "no" is an answer.
A "yes" is an answer.
But most people think:
"Oh, I want it. I want it."

God will say "yes" or "no."
If it's good for you he'll say "yes."
If it's not, it's "no."
I always say that to people.
I believe in that!
(TŪTŪ 'ŌHI'A: 372–400)

Tūtū amplifies her claims by asserting, "I believe in that!"

To have the good spirit
you have to be
kind and obedient.
Respect.
All those things come with spirituality . . .
that's why the Hawaiians always say,

In her discussion of spirituality, Tūtū 'Ōhi'a moves from claims about spirituality to tie together prayer and abundance.

Tūtū ties spirituality concretely to practice, to practicing humility.

*"Pōmaika'i ka po'e ha'aha'a
o ka na'au no ka mea no lākou ke aupuni o ka lani."*

Blessed are the humble,
for the kingdom of heaven shall be theirs.
See?

And that,
that comes from the Bible!
And that's true!

If you *ha'aha'a,* if you humble,
there are times
when you are going to be in trouble,
there are people who will help.
But if you,
you think you are too good
and look down on people. . . .

Tūtū connects humility directly to the idea that it enables a sort of reciprocity. Humility helps us to be connected in a reciprocal way. It readies us to accept help from others, and readies others to help us.

You're going to be in trouble
when you need help.
And they'll say,
"Oh! Times when she was good she fly up,
but now she comes to us for help."
(Tūtū 'Ōhi'a: 481–505)

Many Hawaiians,
many Hawaiians, and still some today
have a second sense of
this thing that we call spirituality.
There's somehow you can see
that trouble is coming.
That's given to you by God!
My grandmother used to be that way.
And she used to say, "This, this, and this,"
and I would just look at her and half-believe
her.
But I was a child.

But, when she was ready to die,
a week before she was ready to die,
she said to me,
"Oh, I'm going to die next week.
Because they're coming for me.
They're over there by the door.
They won't let anybody come to help me.
I'm going to leave you folks."
And I said,
"Oh no, you're not going to leave us."
Sure enough, the next week, she died.
See?

And she had this sense of helping people.
Now that's another thing, helping people.
Like she would have dreams
and the dreams

When Tūtū says "this thing we call spirituality," I begin to see why the question did not lead directly to an answer on her part. "Spirituality" is either a gloss for all sorts of experience (as Kalo says: "Everything we believe is spirit"), or it's a word that stands for nothing and takes us nowhere. Kalo's response to Tūtū earlier opened up a "reading" of the word that allowed Tūtū to discuss all sorts of knowledge that brings us into helping/caring relationships with others and with the land. I realized later that my original question set up a "dead end" for Tūtū 'Ōhi'a.

"They" are the dead, active in the lives of the living. They come for the living, occupy the space of the living, and prevent others from extending the life of one whom they wish to take.

Tūtū ties helping people directly to spirituality in the context of dreams. Knowledge comes to Tūtū's grandmother in dreams. Significantly, it is knowledge that will allow her grandmother to help another *kupuna*.

would say this and this and this to her.
So she'd get up in the morning,
it was Saturday . . .
I'm home.
And she'd say,
"We're going over there, to that house,
to see that *kupuna*. She's not well."
And I said,
"How do you know?"
And she'd say,
"Because I had a dream last night."
So sure enough,
when we get to that place
this *kupuna* is in bed.

So my grandmother would go and sit down,
talk with her, and,
and then my grandmother would say to her,
"You are the cause of your own trouble.
You, your mouth has said this,
but you didn't carry it out.
You just went back on what you said.
You said that your daughter,
who is now going with a certain man,
you will not allow them to sleep in your house.
She can go wherever she wants to go
but not in your house.
But you have allowed that.
And see?
You have gone back on your word.
And so the only way you can clear this illness
is we pray and ask forgiveness,
because God is a forgiving god.

So they would pray,
and all of a sudden this woman gets up,
walking around the house, well.

Tūtū seems to be reliving a particular visit her grand-mother took her on, but also she could be (and seems to be) collapsing many visits into one.

Tūtū suggests that one's words are more than a symbolic code. Utterances stand for actions and create conse-quences. Promises made and not kept result in negative consequences. The idea of forgiveness as healing is a powerful part of Tūtū's story.[4]

This is another instance where Tūtū 'Ōhi'a shifts into describing how as a child she didn't understand the posi-tive value of her culture.

I don't know
whether that thing was weighing on her
or whether she was really . . .
I really don't know
but I think about it now.

And on the way home
I would say to my grandmother,
"I don't like what you're doing."
She said: "Why?"
"Because you go over there and you pray
and everything else,
and they're going to call you a *kahuna!*"

We never knew much about the good *kahuna*.

And she said,
"No, I had to go, because that is MY job.
It was given to me to go and help.
And that's why we go."
So I said, "Oh, OK. That's fine then!"
You know.
[Tūtū laughs.]

[Others laugh.]
(TŪTŪ 'ŌHI'A: 507–575)

It's really hard to tell
and yet
maybe
we will be all right,
I don't know.
If they would listen,
and I find that
whenever they have meetings
that will help a person,
our Hawaiians don't go there to listen.

Kahuna, healers and practitioners of traditional Hawaiian religion, were at this point in time seen as "ungodly" and potentially dangerous. Tūtū alludes gently to the idea that she was being encouraged to deny or dismiss positive aspects of Hawaiian culture. Tūtū's grandmother indicates to her that she has received a calling to visit another *kupuna* and constructs it as help for others.

This ability and calling is god-given, not a consequence of her *kupuna's* own skills or decisions. This constitutes the moral of the story.

This is in response to a question about the future.

Tūtū 'Ōhi'a creates a sense that our future is based on our behavior now. Tūtū 'Ōhi'a uses the inclusive phrase "our Hawaiians."

You know?
I was asking Jane
about these Hawaiians
who moved to the mainland.
I asked her,
"Are they all doing well?"
She said, "No.
Some of them are not doing well."

And it's the same thing with the Indians.
Over three hundred nations.
Some are doing well,
some are not.
Now we are talking sovereignty.
Now
maybe if we become a sovereign nation
perhaps our people might be helped.

I don't know. It's hard for me to tell.
'Cause I don't know
what the future holds for us.

But I feel
that we who are in the light
and can see
some of the things that can benefit us
and some of the things that will hurt us,
like teachers,
Sunday school teachers,
even workers in health,
might help our people to, to wake up.

Because some of them want to have,
whenever you ask them,
"What do you want for your children?"
They say education.
But they don't work at it!

Tūtū 'Ōhi'a is referring to her daughter, Aunty Jane, who has connected to, and researched the situation of off-island Hawaiians. She includes these Hawaiians in answering her question about whether "we will be all right."

Tūtū 'Ōhi'a sets up an even more inclusive construct of indigeneity that includes "Indians." It is also a construct that includes nationhood—over three hundred nations.

Sovereignty isn't framed as a political or economic construct, but rather as a possible "help" for "*our* Hawaiian people." "Our people" seems to incorporate genealogy, indigeneity, and a notion of nationhood, in Tūtū 'Ōhi'a's sequence of talk. She is referencing claims that are often viewed by others as "political," but using a language of caring and collectivity, on behalf of the welfare of Hawaiians.

Here "them" is "some of our people." Tūtū rarely discusses oppressive forces from the outside as causes of social change. Instead she seems to root causes for social change in "our people." Education is a central issue for Tūtū.

You see what I mean?
So the desire is there
but this thing that pulls them this way
is stronger.

Here, Tūtū motions with her hands, to show two forces pulling away from each other.

I always say we are poor people
but we can be rich.
In whatever we do.
Respect of the land,
respect of our families,
and us for them.
We'll be there.
We'll be there. You see?

So
it's a hard thing for me to know.
How they would fare in the future.
If they listen.
They are full of the teachings.
If they would only listen.
Because in this ear coming out the other one
doesn't do any good.
Waste your time!

Listening to Tūtū, after a while I began to notice a fluctuating pattern of identification and disassociation. Tūtū seemed to talk about some of "our Hawaiians," particularly younger people, or urbanized, less traditional people, as "they"; sometimes "they" became all of "our people," sometimes the people "of old." There was never a clear polarized "we" and "they" equation. At any point, part of "they" in Tūtū's discussion could become part of "our people." She never seemed to sit in judgment on any particular "they" in her discussion. Her talk always seemed somehow to be inclusive of others.[5]

[Others laugh.]

If they would listen and try.
(Tūtū 'Ōhi'a: 611–731)

[Tūtū, what do you think
about the Hawaiian women?]

The Hawaiian what?

[The Hawaiian women. Hawaiian women
like us.
You know, where do we go from here?]

This was Kalo's own question. It came at the very end of the interview. She had not discussed it with me as a "question to consider asking." Kalo seemed to be asking Tūtū as *tūtū*, not as a person she was interviewing. It seemed to be a question Kalo had on her mind. Perhaps Kalo was asking Tūtū's advice on what her own "place" was.

I think the Hawaiian women are
going to be the ones. To lead.
Because many of them are educated,
and many of them know
the weaknesses of raising a family,
of life.

More women should get into politics.
Because we need honesty.
And women, when they go into positions,
their gains are not for themselves.
It's for whoever they work for.
For the company, the community.

Tūtū does not reference external notions of economic
or political power as much as the ethical and community
standards for leadership that she values. She associates
honesty and selflessness with women.

I have a very healthy idea, that the women
will someday lead. Our Hawaiian women.
See, all of this time they have been
taught to hold back.
They feel,
"Oh, I don't know as much as that person."

No! You do!

At this moment Tūtū seemed to be aiming her answer
directly at Kalo. When she said "No, you do!" I felt this
very strongly, although Kalo did not mention this particular
moment later. I felt she was telling Kalo to go ahead and
be a leader.

Even our women who are not, who have not
had as great an education as some who have
gotten degrees and all of that.

Like the Trask girls.
Well, they are leaders now.
Controversial, of course.

This is an allusion to Haunani-Kay Trask, professor in
Hawaiian Studies at University of Hawai'i at Mānoa, and
her sister Mililani Trask, who founded *Ka Lāhui Hawai'i*
(The Hawaiian Nation), a sovereignty organization. It was
said affectionately and with some humor.

[Laughter]

The only thing we can do now,
if we can get our women, our mothers,
to realize if they want their children to have the
education so that they will come up the ladder,

is to be modest, be humble,
and in whatever they do, to teach their children
the best in life.
Lead them in the way that is good.
Not neglect them.
I think many of our Hawaiian children
are neglected.
That's why they act the way they do.
And we blame them.
We should not blame the children.
We should blame the adults.
[TŪTŪ 'ŌHI'A: 789–834]

During the interview a number of Tūtū 'Ōhi'a's
grandchildren and great-grandchildren
dropped by:

Her grandson said, "Oh, what are you guys up to?"
Tūtū said, "Oh, we are just talking about things."
He quickly glanced at the tape recorder and seemed
to recognize we were doing an interview. After a
polite interval and much reassurance that they could
surely stay, they all left, promising to come back
later. (MANA'O: 2034–2042)

Shortly after the interview, an event took place
that left me shaken and confused. It started just
after the interview:

After the interview as we sat in Kalo's car and
headed back to her home, Kalo's mom said, "You
treasure that tape. That was a true gift." (MANA'O:
2053–2055)

On the way home (later with Ivan) I replay the tape
from Tūtū. Big chunks of it are gone. Something

This section underscores Tūtū's constant reference to the relationships between generations and the responsibilities each generation holds. The future again is constructed as contingent on whether we "are full of the teachings" and listen, rather than on external material conditions. When she uses the encompassing word "we" here, as in other areas, she (as other interviewees) pulls us in—inclusion intensifies her lesson.

Tūtū did not say we were interviewing her, or even that we were asking her questions. This very humble answer amplified the strong feeling I had that she was sharing great wisdom. It also brought home to me her discussion about *ha'aha'a*.

was wrong with the tape recorder. I can't remember when she had said what, so I am not sure what is missing, and I am too devastated, too hysterical to allow myself to listen to the whole tape. I am too afraid nothing will be there. Ivan is driving, trying to console me. I keep saying over and over again, wailing really, tears rolling down my face, "Oh my God, what have I done, what have I done? She's ---- years old." Ivan says, "Can't you go back and get it again?" I say, "Oh God, Ivan, you don't understand. It wasn't just an interview. I can't explain it. It's not like just being a sociologist and collecting a nice story. It's her heart, it's her heart. It was such a gift, such a gift and I'll never get it back, I'll never get it back." We have to stop the car. I am sobbing bitterly. (MANA'O: 2081–2112)

As soon as I arrived at our accommodations I wrote down some *"mana'o"* to calm myself, then called a fellow student in Toronto, who calmed my hysterics and told me to record all I could remember of the interview. Three hours later, when I was calm enough to play the interview tape entirely, I discovered that there was actually only a small portion missing, from around the time after her visitors came. I remember wondering how I could be so torn apart, and what was happening to me.

After the time was up for my "fieldwork," I returned to Toronto. Although fieldwork was intended as a preliminary process, I had hoped to get more interviews than I did. Kalo had become ill when we were getting ready to set up additional interviews, and offered to set up more interviews without her participa-

In retrospect, it surprises me that I couldn't think of my fellow student's suggestions for recovering the "lost data" myself. Evidently, Tūtū's words had taken on a weight for me that far surpassed that of "data." "Data," or information, seemed to be something that you synthesize, reformat, and add to other data. In contrast, what I felt I had lost was multilayered stories containing deep messages and offering me a way to think about my own life.

Tūtū 'Ōhi'a constructs stories about the land that celebrate abundance and seem to pull us into synchronic time. Prayer emerges in relation to the abundance she experiences. Tūtū 'Ōhi'a does not construct her own survival, or that of her values, as a struggle. She constructs self-determination and the survival of Hawaiians as a process that is

tion. The idea of conducting interviews with Kalo's *kūpuna,* but without her participation felt wrong. Since I was not related to these *kūpuna,* I felt as if I would be invading their space. I also felt that without Kalo the interviews would not be the same at all.

In Toronto, my dissertation supervisor felt that the interviews and field notes offered numerous accounts of people sharing knowledge.[6] He suggested that I follow up with comparative data taken from academic sources in Canada in order to compare the form, content, and process of academic knowledge-making to the Hawaiian context. He also wanted to know how indigenous knowledge is studied and taken up in academic contexts. He suggested that I use "fieldwork" and interviews in academic contexts in Canada to examine similarities, contrasts, and relationships between indigenous and academic knowledge-creation. I conducted the interviews and fieldwork in Canada in the same way that I had in Hawai'i.[7] Data collection in Canada was an easy and worry-free process.

I assumed that everyday talk that people produce in the Hawaiian community and in the academy would tell me about the routines, procedures, and formulations that emerge from those sites of knowledge-making. I wanted to understand how people in the academy might also "reproduce" land, identity, and the universe story in their talk. I also wanted to compare the way that they created knowledge in their talk to the interviews that took place in Hawai'i. I was especially interested in the grounded cosmologies and epistemologies that emerged in the talk of Canadian (Western)

spiritual. Money is merely a tool, used to help others and contained by Tūtū 'Ōhi'a's abundance paradigm.

Tūtū 'Ōhi'a constructs her experience in terms tied to *'āina.* Her talk is saturated with *'aloha 'āina* and *mālama 'āina.* In many ways, her stories remind me of Kalo's talk of connection in her initial interview.

Tūtū 'Ōhi'a's stories complicate readings of history to do with colonization by collapsing them into lessons about spiritual and ethical integrity. She constructs the future as contingent on the timeless Hawaiian qualities of spiritual integrity and right action. She lends incredible agency to her listeners, to Hawaiian people in general, and to *'āina* in her talk.

Tūtū 'Ōhi'a shares her knowledge through a relationship with those who learn from her. As she includes us in her comments and pulls us in, we are apt to attend more carefully to her message. This is a powerful form of address and, I believe, the key to her influence as a teacher. Prayer, reflection, respect, and humility are key components in Tūtū 'Ōhi'a's knowledge-making. In her talk, through masterful strategic moves, Tūtū 'Ōhi'a enacts the connections between Hawaiians and their families, Hawaiians and *'āina.* Through imagery that activates her talk easily in the memory of the listener, Tūtū 'Ōhi'a passes knowledge down to Kalo.

Tūtū 'Ōhi'a imbues the knowledge from her experience and from her *kūpuna* with the emotional weight of those experiences and those *kūpuna.* She creates, from the fabric of her experience and the stories of her *kūpuna,* a context of acceptance and validation.

academics as compared to Hawaiian *kūpuna*.[8] When I began my fieldwork in Canada, the dreams stopped.[9]

I am not sure exactly why, but as a result of my experiences speaking with Tūtū 'Ōhi'a, Aunty Limu, the caretaker at the Royal Mausoleum, and others, before leaving Hawai'i, I had decided to return to Child and Family Services to request more information on my family history. Perhaps the concern that these individuals had shown for me had strengthened my resolve to try to get information one more time. When I visited Child and Family Services, they said that they would write me if they could give me any additional information.

As I was doing my fieldwork in Toronto, I received a letter from Child and Family Services. The letter repeated much information from the earlier letter I had received in 1985 from them. Yet it gave some new information that increased my knowledge and shape-shifted my "origin myth" into a birth narrative. Now the inclusion of first names, dates, siblings, and information on my birth father made my birth narrative (and me) seem more real.

. . . The following is non-identifying information concerning your birth parents . . . (which was) obtained from your birth mother during her contact with our agency. She was very protective and hesitant in disclosing information. . . . "Barbara,"[10] your birth mother, was a thirty-year-old divorced woman of German, French, and Hawaiian ancestry. She was born in 1922. . . .

A conversation, that in odd ways reminds me of our interview with Tūtū 'Ōhi'a, emerges in an article on the front page of *The Honolulu Advertiser* (Krauss 1994) titled, "Wails and Prayers for Missing Bones." This article refers to two *kā'ai* (woven caskets) in which the bones of deified chiefs were encased. These *kā'ai* were taken from the Bishop Museum and apparently returned to Waipi'o Valley—where it is believed they were originally interred. A conversation within the Hawaiian community regarding this act was included in *The Honolulu Advertiser*:

They marched at dusk with torches lighted, wailing Hawaiian chants in a ceremony said to have last been held a hundred years ago. Thirty-one members of The Royal Order of Kamehameha I assembled yesterday at the Royal Mausoleum in Nuuanu—the resting place of Hawaiian royalty—to ask forgiveness of the gods for the removal last week of sacred bones from the Bishop Museum. "Our purpose was to bring the bad news to our *ali'i* ancestors and to demand return of the bones," said Wayne Davis, genealogist for the order, founded more than 125 years ago by Kamehameha V (Lot) in honor of his grandfather, Kamehameha I.

No spectators or reporters were allowed on the grounds during the ceremony. But people watched from over the fence and listened to the unusual chanting, sobs and moans of despair. Order member Leighton Tseu performed the most *kapu* (private) part of the ceremony out of view, drinking of the 'awa before his *ali'i* ancestors. "I was crying," he said later. "I was asking forgiveness because we were reporting bad news. I was asking unity of all Hawaiians." Davis said that the order's members

Unfortunately, any names (of forebears) we provide you with could lead you to your birth mother, which in turn would be legally damaging to our program. We can tell you, however, that we have checked with one Hawaiian historian who confirms that if your mother reported valid names of relatives, you do indeed have royal blood.

Barbara married in December of 1941 and had three children, Donald, born in 1942, Barbara, born 1944, and Bruce, born 1945. Ten years later, in October of 1951, your birth mother divorced her husband. It was after her divorce that she met your birth father.

Your birth father was reported to be five feet eight inches tall, with a ruddy complexion. He was reported to be of Caucasian ancestry. Your birth mother felt that he may have also been part Spanish or Italian. Barbara had dated him on two separate occasions. He was in the military and had departed the islands soon after your birth mother's pregnancy. She did not know of his present whereabouts and had no intention of informing him of her situation. The records do not contain your birth father's name. Barbara stated that he was known only to her as "Chick."

On February 2, 1952, our agency received a phone call from Barbara, informing us of a baby girl born in Kuakini Hospital on the night of February 1, 1952. Against the advice of the attending physician, your birth mother left the hospital the following day of her delivery. . . .

Because of her concern that no one discover her true identity, she admitted herself to the hospital under an assumed name and falsified her address and phone number. She requested that the baby be removed and placed into the adoptive home. How-

feel that the bones were taken with the intent of "doing the right thing." "But it was incorrect," he said. "They must be returned." (ibid., A1)

I was first attracted by this article's description of people watching from over the fences. This article constructs those outside the order and its tasks, whether Hawaiian or non-Hawaiian, as denied access to this ceremony. It seems to emphasize the meditative, emotive, and private importance of the march. The Hawaiian language is used, and interestingly, some words are not translated for the benefit of people who don't regularly use them.

Although the word "unusual" betrays the vantage point of the writer, the description of the ceremony on the grounds of the Royal Mausoleum is not taken up as spectacle. The writer quickly moves into comments by the Royal Order members themselves. Non-Hawaiians do not speak about the incident or the ceremony in this article.

Another article referring to *kāʻai* appeared in *The Honolulu Advertiser* (Neil 1994), entitled "Priceless Artifacts Still Missing: Burial Caskets, Known as Kaʻai, Centuries-Old." Līloa was the great-grandfather of Lonoikamakahiki. They were both famous ruling chiefs of the fifteenth and sixteenth centuries. Their bones were placed at the Royal Mausoleum at Mauna ʻAla, then in 1918 removed to Bishop Museum.[11]

ever . . . it was not until September 20, 1952 that
you were placed with your adoptive parents. You
were in a foster home, prior to your placement.
<small>(LETTER FROM CHILD & FAMILY SERVICE)</small>

After I received the letter from Child and Family Services, I was unsure as to what to do with that information. I discovered the Christmas Eve concert program among my papers and was reminded of the genealogist Wayne Keona Davis, to whom I had been introduced. I had set aside that brochure in my journal. Leafing through my journal, I was startled to see the half-forgotten brochure from the performance of Kamehameha Schools Concert Glee Clubs that I had attended as a high school student.

Ivan and I were now married, and we decided that we would move to San Diego that summer. The conditions of the sabbatical were that I return to work in San Diego by that fall. Ivan, a free-lance designer, would be eligible to work in San Diego, while I could return to work and complete my dissertation.

I came across Wayne Keona Davis's name in a *Honolulu Advertiser* article having to do with *kāʻai*. I had kept the article among my papers and, like the Kamehameha brochure and the Christmas Eve concert program, it seemed to end up in my hands over and over again.

I finally decided to write Wayne Keona Davis, although I did not really know him. In my letter I asked him if he would consider being the community member representative on my dissertation committee. I also sent him a description of my adoption history and the

This article quotes Edward Halealoha Ayau, administrator of the state's burial program for Hawaiian remains, who received a message from an anonymous male caller who said, "Chief Līloa is home." It was later discovered that the *kāʻai* had "disappeared from the museum" (ibid., A3). The final paragraph of this article is revealing: "Ayau said yesterday that he understands that many Hawaiians want Līloa's remains returned to the Big Island. But he adds that he thinks the manner of their removal was *pono ʻole* (wrong)" (ibid.).

This article uses the phrase "priceless artifacts" to describe the *kāʻai*. This pulls the description outside Hawaiian discourse, where they do not exist as artifacts. Yet it is also notable that the words "stolen" or "theft" are not used. These articles were "taken" or are "missing." Although he is an administrator for a state agency, Ayau speaks as a Hawaiian with spiritual and ethical concerns. He discusses how he understands Hawaiian desires but references the concept of *pono ʻole*. The concept of *pono ʻole* eclipses that of Western law in this article.

letter from Child and Family Services. I asked for his advice:

March 21, 1995

. . . What I guess I am wondering is . . . should I take up this search for my ancestors? I have no desire to hurt my birth mother . . . if the thought of my existence is a wound for her; perhaps it would not be right for me to want to find my ancestors. . . .

As long as I can remember I have dreamed of three kinds of "ancestors." . . . One is a woman who is heavy set, elderly . . . the other is a gray-haired man, (and) . . . the other is a fish. These three have been a constant source of strength and support. I know I am related to them, but I do not yet know who they might be, or what I should do on their behalf. . . .

And sometimes I feel like there is some knowledge in my blood, which is not knowledge I grew up with, but which is waiting for me. I fully realize that I must sound crazy when I say these things. . . . But I know that whoever my ancestors might be or how little of them I carry within me, there are things I need to do and learn to carry out their wishes in this life.

Sometimes when I am around a place where people are buried, I feel them closer. I wonder if they occupy the graves I visit. And I wish I could visit the places [where] they are buried. Or even stranger, I wonder if I have walked among their bones and not even known of it. Even the special places I visit, places where I feel complete and at peace, fill me with the question: Did I visit this place because it is where my people are? . . . If you have any advice for me I will be very grateful. . . .

(LETTER FROM LEILANI)

An editorial written by Wayne Keona Davis (1994, B3), is entitled, "Do What Is Right: Return the *Ka'ai*." Wayne Keona Davis is described by *The Honolulu Advertiser* as "*kahu ku'auhau*, keeper of genealogy for the Royal Order of Kamehameha I" (ibid.) Wayne Keona Davis says:

Uwe . . . E huna 'ia ko kakou ali'i i ka pouli. Nakeke ana na iwi o ko kakou kupuna i ka la. Uwe . . . uwe, aloha 'ino! (Deep is our grief, for our *ali'i* have been hidden in darkness; the bones of our ancestors are rattling in the sunlight. How sad!)

The chiefs and members of the Royal Order of Kamehameha I believe it is imperative to direct this open letter to those who planned and executed the removal of the bones of our ancestors from the halls of the Bernice Pauahi Bishop Museum last week.

Who were Līloa and Lonoikamakahiki? Līloa was the first of the famous Big Island *ali'i nui* to consolidate and unite that island under one rule. He lived in Waipi'o, Hāmākua, on the island of Hawai'i some 600 years or 21 generations ago.

His son, 'Umi-a-Līloa, continued in the footsteps of his father, as did 'Umi's son Keawe-nui-ui-a'Umi. Lonoikamakahiki was this Keawe's son. The two *kā'ai* taken were those of Līloa and his great-grandson Lonoikamakahiki.

Samuel Mānaia Kalani Kamakau, our own *kanaka maoli* historian of the last century, stated that, "There is not a commoner on Hawai'i who can say, 'Our ancestor was not 'Umi-a-Līloa, and if he does, it is because he is ignorant of his ancestry.'"

By the summer of 1995, I had returned to the community college classroom as an instructor, and was working on my dissertation. We were now living in San Diego, and Ivan was working in graphic design. By September I was a bit frantic, trying to keep the dissertation going along with teaching full time. I also felt tired of thinking about the personal issues about ancestry that the dissertation seemed to awaken in me. At the end of September, I received a forwarded letter Wayne had sent to me in Toronto:

11 August 1995

Dear Leilani—

I hope this letter finds you well and in good health and spirits! I'm sure this comes like a lightning bolt out of the blue, so please forgive me for taking so long in answering your very thoughtful and touching letter of March 21st. I am only too happy to assist, in any way, your work for your college thesis. So, if it isn't too late, I promise to be more timely in my response to any work, papers, etc. that you would like me to look over and comment on. I see, by your letter, that you are planning, if you haven't done so already, to move back to San Diego. Kalo says, she thinks you should just pack up and come "home" to Hawai'i "where you belong!"

. . . With all that said and done—the important stuff! One of the main reasons, two reasons really, that it has taken me so long to answer you is that I wanted to give you some words of "wisdom" (haha), comfort and reassurance regarding the dreams you receive. My wife (she has been the receiver of

. . . We are the living descendants, and we, as a people, will ultimately decide where the final resting place will be for them.

If those of you who have done this are indeed *kanaka maoli*, we of the Royal Order of Kamehameha I believe that you may have meant well and you may have felt that our *kūpuna* needed to return to the land of their birth. However, we do not condone your actions.

The questions raised by your deeds are threefold:

Was it *pono*, spiritually and culturally right, to take it upon yourself to do this?

If it was *pono* to return them to Hawai'i, then was the method chosen by you *pono?*

Lastly, by what right or authority were you chosen to be *kahu* of these ancestral bones—are you and your descendants *pono* for the great responsibility this entails? If you know your history, you know the meaning of this statement. If you, who have taken the sacred bones of our ancestors, are not *kanaka maoli* (of Hawaiian blood), return them NOW! They are not, as the media says, "priceless artifacts."

They are the physical, tangible essence of the existence and continuation of *na kanaka maoli, na Po'e Hawai'i* (the People of Hawai'i).

The answer to the first question is *a'ole*, no! The remains of the *ali'i* were always entrusted to retainers who were specifically chosen for this right. . . . The right to care for the bones of Kamehameha Kunuiakea had belonged to the line of Keawe-a-Heulu, but because the resting place

*her families' messages, warning and guidance from
her ancestors, all her life . . .) and I discussed your
letter at length and she feels that she should talk to
you and share her "mana'o" with you in person.
(I hope you are still coming home for a visit in
December!) However, let me just try to ease your
anxiety and rest your mind, somewhat, by saying
that you're in tune spiritually with your ancestors
or 'aumakua, who are, in their ways, guiding and
maintaining contact with you.*

*They must recognize, in you, an entity that is
strongly devoted to her Hawaiian roots, cultural
identity, and ancestral bloodline—even though
that entity knows very little consciously of these
things! I am not a very good translator of dreams
(but) . . . what I have learned and this came from
(my wife's) grandmother, is that you shouldn't
be afraid of them or get frustrated by your lack of
understanding of the sometimes cryptic messages
that dreams or your 'aumakua are imparting to
you.*

*Being the recipient of these messages means one
has been chosen to fulfill a certain task or duty for
or in representation of the family—those here now,
before and those to come. (My wife) would many
times express frustration for not knowing "what she
was supposed to do." Grandma would always tell
her, "You're young yet, when it is time to know—
you will know!"*

*. . . Now, the second reason it took so long to answer
you and why I hope you will be back soon, has to
do with the search for your birth mother. I realized
right away, once having read your letter, that the
Child and Family Service had . . . given you . . . a
bright trail for a genealogist to follow!*

of Keoua, father of Kamehameha, had been revealed
and was common knowledge, Kamehameha chose Ulu-
maiheihei who, along with his half-brother, Ho'olulu, took
his remains to their final resting place.

Their descendants have never revealed the site. It has
been the privilege of the descendants of Ho'olulu, down
to this day, to be the caretakers of the royal remains at
Mauna'ala, the Royal Mausoleum in Nu'uanu Valley. It is
the only piece of sovereign Hawaiian land left in the world
today.

. . . As to the second question, although it may ultimately be desirable to return the *kā'ai* to the Big Island,
that still remains to be seen and should only be done after
certain criteria are met.

Today it must be remembered that the *'aina* is no
longer in the hands of the *kanaka maoli.* Strangers and
foreigners walk on and control our land. Is it *pono* to return
our *ali'i* to land that no longer is protected by the strict
kapu of our ancestors? Land that may, one day, be bull-
dozed, built over, or invaded by foreigners who have no
respect for the bones of our ancestors and who may take
them and sell them for monetary gain as "priceless artifacts"?

. . . We instruct you, in the strictest sense of the word,
to return the two sacred *kā'ai* of our chiefly ancestors to
the Bernice Pauahi Bishop Museum. Once this has been
done, representatives of *ka 'ohana,* which we consider to
be *na kanaka maoli Hawai'i apau,* all native Hawaiians,
should sit down and decide upon the final resting place,

I charted out the information you had received and determined where I would have to go and what I would have to look for in order to find her. The problem was that I don't always have the time away from my job to do the research that people request of me (and I love the challenge of researching!! It is, I believe my "calling" in life!)

So it wasn't until last week that I was able to do anything about it. Well, anyhow, once I started, it took me about ten minutes to find her. I understand, somewhat, her logic in not wanting contact with you (it isn't "you" so much as the circumstances of your conception—my thoughts only). Her family, though not in any way of political power in present day Hawai'i, and not of the monetarily rich power brokers of today, nonetheless are of very high ranking chiefs of old Hawai'i. Several members of the extended family, even today, feel their duty and obligations to the Hawaiian people in a very real and tangible way. They, in turn, are acknowledged as descendants and present-day representatives of one line of high chiefs, by many Hawaiians today.

Please be patient, Leilani, and allow me to approach "the family" before I reveal her name to you. I am not attempting to hide her from you, believe me, and I will tell you who she is in time. I just ask that you wait a little while longer so that, hopefully, you will be received, in a good way, by at least some of your relatives, if not your birth mother.

I do not know her, but do know one of her brothers and several of . . . your cousins, one of which I am a fairly good friend of. I want to feel her (a cousin) out and get her reaction and mana'o. *It may be you won't meet your birth mother, and maybe you may have to be kept a secret from her, but*

when they shall be removed from the museum, how they shall be removed, and the protocol that must be observed at that time. That is *pono!*

Heed the *mana'o* of the older brother to the younger brother and return our *kūpuna* to the place from which you took them. In that way, that which must be done will be done, with *pono.* (ibid.)

A small piece that describes the Royal Order of Kamehameha I accompanies Wayne Keona Davis's editorial:

The Royal Order of Kamehameha I was founded in 1865 by Kamehameha V (Lot) to uphold the memory of his grandfather, Kamehameha I, to maintain the dignity of the *ali'i* and to be of some help and guidance to the Hawaiian people. The order went underground when the monarchy was overthrown in 1893. Public meetings resumed around 1901. Today there are 300 members. Anyone of Hawaiian blood may join. (ibid.)

Abe Kahinuonalani Kamakawiwo'ole (1994, B3) wrote an article that appeared in *The Honolulu Advertiser* entitled "Another View: It Is Right that Līloa Is Home." He is described as a Kamehameha I descendant who lives on the island of Hawai'i, works on projects that benefit Hawaiians, doesn't know where the *kā'ai* may be, and doesn't want to know (ibid.). His article is in response to the editorial by Wayne Keona Davis:

"Līloa is home." The whole island of Hawai'i is home. The *ka'ai* are not stolen! The present major problem involving the *ka'ai* is the decision by the Office of Hawaiian Affairs and the Native Hawaiian Historic Preservation Council to

maybe you can meet and establish some sort of bond with other members of your extended family — I truly hope so!

Be happy and rejoice in the knowledge that you do have a very rich and noteworthy personal history and that I am sure your ancestors await and will welcome you into the family!

I hope you will not be angry with me for not revealing her just yet, but will understand that I am only trying to save possible heartache and hurt from occurring, on both sides.

Please keep in touch and I will keep you abreast of my progress with your relatives. . . .
(Letter from Wayne)

Although I was happy that Wayne might be able to give me some guidance on my dissertation, on another level, the fact that he knew of my family and my ancestors eclipsed that feeling. It seemed that every day on some unforeseen level, this knowledge sifted through. An amazing sense of calm came over me, along with a sense of blessing, grace, and protection.

The idea that I could actually know the names of my ancestors, and be able to speak of and to them by name had been an impossible dream for me. I felt that if I could speak of and to my ancestors, some hidden emptiness would be healed and complete. Above all, the idea that I could have an actual blood relative who might speak to me was overpowering. Wayne wrote to tell me his plans:

place them in Mauna Ala, the Royal Mausoleum, on the island of Oahu.

The major problem from the past was the decision by the Christian Queen Regent Ka'ahumanu to have the *ka'ai* removed from Waipi'o Valley on the island of Hawai'i. What happened in between these events continues to be the result of the queen's decision. . . . Is it not culturally, traditionally, and spiritually *pono*, right for the *kā'ai* to be returned home with . . . *aloha* and reverence?

There is a spiritual "*ea*" that all Hawaiians must come to understand. It involves *aloha* and forgiveness, if all is to be *pono*. We must pray for the decision-makers to remember the words of our *kūpuna*: "Don't touch! Put that back where you found it." We must open our hearts in order to open doors. We must first forgive ourselves, Queen Ka'ahumanu (who allowed the removal of the *kā'ai* from Waipi'o Valley on the island of Hawai'i), our *'ohana*, and all involved with the *kā'ai* who made decisions that were not *pono*. And we must also look to forgiving those who may be clinging to that which is still not *pono*. The *akua*, gods, the *kā'ai* and the spirits of our *kūpuna* are far "above all." (ibid.)

November 1995

Dear Leilani—

. . . Again I find myself rushing off a letter to you without being able to express much of my thoughts regarding your long search of your own roots. What little information I have thus far shared with you is only a very small part of what I will be able to impart to you. I have not, as yet, had the opportunity since receiving your thesis draft, to speak to your cousin Malie Wahine Keʻaliʻi o ke Kai[12], but once I get this sent off to you I will contact her and relay your aloha *to her. I do know that she is anxious to meet and will be happy to hear that you plan to visit this summer.*

Leilani, I want you to know that my ultimate dream for you is, that someday, your birth mother . . . will be able to accept you and learn of the wonderful, sensitive, and intelligent daughter she has, in you.

Thankfully, Malie Wahine Keʻaliʻi o ke Kai and I are close enough that I trust her judgment in this matter, without reservation. I hope that will comfort your mind in some small way. . . .

Before I forget, you have nothing to feel apologetic about, due to your feeling of a "lack of knowledge." At first I thought, "It's too bad you didn't know your genealogy before commencing your work!" But, as I've thought about it more, I believe, given the situation with your birth mother, it may have created more problems as you tried to establish "connectedness" with your "interviewees" than it was worth.

Besides, as inadequate as you may have felt at times, I think it gave you (an) experience where,

The Davis-Kamakawiwoʻole editorials pull us deeper into the community of concern and into cosmological references that are Hawaiian. There is no attempt to collapse this conversation into a non-Hawaiian discourse. Again, the idea of return of the bones to the land is accepted, but the method is debated. Although they speak from a colonized space, dominated by capital, they do not privilege or even reference its accompanying cosmology.

Davis describes Mauna ʻAla (The Royal Mausoleum) as the "only piece of sovereign Hawaiian land left in the world today" (1994, B3). He also decries the use of the phrase *priceless artifacts*, and constructs the bones as the essence of Hawaiian identity and survival.

During this time frame, outside of these articles, no non-Hawaiian editorial commentary arrives in *The Honolulu Advertiser*.[13] The articles use the words of Hawaiians, within context, imagining the righteousness of intent, but the possible incorrectness of the action itself. The central focus on the ancestors, and the importance of the *kāʻai* themselves, is left intact.

This conversation is neither disauthenticated nor is it reformatted into a language or cosmology alien to it. Rather, ancestral concerns, images, and structures of intention enter a public discursive space.

As it appears in *The Honolulu Advertiser*, this conversation does not include everyone. Those outside the community of concern at this point are not given space to speak. In these articles, a conversation about the disap-

although you were at times uncomfortable, you were truly straddling the line of being a "scholar/researcher" on one hand and a young "woman of Hawaiian ancestry" on the other. I would like to believe that, in this neutral role, you were able to grow spiritually, draw conclusions with sensitivity, while all the while adding to and building on your "ancestry of experience"!

Having said that, I can now express to you how very proud of you I am, little sister, that you have accomplished so much in the way of education. . . . Hopefully, it will be the example of a kanaka maoli *such as yourself that will encourage our Hawaiian youth to "strive for the highest"!* Kūlia i ka nu'u!

(LETTER FROM WAYNE)

pearance of the *kā'ai*, situated within the Hawaiian community, occupies a public discursive space. This occurs despite the fact that Hawai'i is dominated by Western/American concerns, discourses, and intentions. There are boundaries around this conversation that are structured by the silence of those outside Hawaiian ancestral connection.

Tūtū 'Ōhi'a and the *kā'ai* discussants voice cosmologies inscribing beliefs about the nature of *earth*, *practice*, *destiny*, and *knowledge*.

Tūtū 'Ōhi'a and the discussants in the *kā'ai* debate discuss the *earth* with great emotion. Tūtū 'Ōhi'a limits the transforming power of money and compresses narratives of loss, privileging the abundance of life on the land. The *kā'ai* discussants create a convergence among '*āina*, sovereignty, and ancestry. It seems that the *kā'ai* themselves have come to embody that convergence.

Both Tūtū 'Ōhi'a and the *kā'ai* discussants take Hawaiian values as a given, to be *practiced*, and tell stories where outcomes are based solely on integrity and right action.

Both Tūtū 'Ōhi'a and the *kā'ai* discussants construct *destiny* as contingent on right action. They collapse the colonization narrative into a narrative about spiritual and ethical concerns.

Both Tūtū 'Ōhi'a and the *kā'ai* discussants place lineage at the core of Hawaiian identity and *knowledge*-making. The agency and responsibility that accrue to Hawaiians eclipse the effects of colonization.

Tūtū 'Ōhi'a is well known in Hawai'i, and like the *kā'ai* discussants, occupies both private and public discursive spaces. In both Tūtū 'Ōhi'a's interview and the *kā'ai* debate, it seems that social memories centering around the land and ethical questions pertaining to ancestry are carried into the present on behalf of living memory.

6　The Ancestry of Experience: Ha'ina

The Experience of Ancestry: Kaona

Wayne Keona Davis sent me information about my ancestors, describing who they were and what some of them had done in the past. He was brief, saying that he didn't want to overpower me with too much "family knowledge" at once. Wayne also told me more about my cousin, Malie (Malie Wahine Ke'ali'i o ke Kai) and said he would tell her about me when he felt that the time was right.

With Wayne's help and that of my colleagues and mentors, I completed my dissertation. My trip from San Diego to Toronto to defend my dissertation involved a reunion with our circle of students and mentors, all involved with indigenous knowledge. Some of them had interviewed elders in indigenous communities. We celebrated not only the dissertation completion and defense, but also the discovery of my ancestry.

My fellow students were preparing their dissertations and trying to find University appointments. Being ignored by a professor or questioned critically at a seminar presenta-

As Hawaiian language and culture are recovered, the voices of *kūpuna* circulate through powerful discourses that traverse Hawaiian communities. The *kūpuna* Kalo interviewed talked about knowledge and ancestry, while they and other *kūpuna* led me, over time, into knowledge about my own ancestry. These *kūpuna* believed that my ancestors were connecting with me and that my birthsands were welcoming me.

How different from the life history that people off-island told me as I grew up. That life history began with my adoption, centered on the effects of my off-island upbringing, and de-emphasized my ancestry. My birthsands and ancestors were not included as presences, or conversants, but were written over, scratched out. Like some histories of Hawai'i, the ways that ancestry and land might enter into lived experience were not included.

Counter to that version of history, chance meetings, odd moments, and stories told by various *kūpuna* referenced connection and ancestry. Different cosmologies and ongoing languages carrying hidden consequences were given breath.

tion could be an upsetting reminder that their professional futures were uncertain. They were also affected by fierce and complex political battles and professional rivalries. They worked feverishly to produce as many publications as possible in order to gain appointments and create a place for themselves: an acceptable academic genealogy to recite. They were also trying to find a space in "academia" in which they could honor and act on the messages and stories they had received from elders while they were doing their research.

After witnessing the struggles of my fellow students, it was a relief to resume teaching in San Diego. The everyday issues of community college students, their frank reactions to the subject matter, and my attempts to make sociology engaging and useful consumed, yet centered, me.

After some months, I received a letter from Malie:

November 1995

Aloha *Cousin:*

I believe it has now been about four months since . . . Wayne Keona Davis . . . in his caring and gentle way, told me about a person, a woman he was helping. I remember the day, it was raining. . . . I often enjoy and celebrate the rain. Sometimes the sound of rain is exciting, so alive. Waters from heaven to earth are considered gifts of life.

So there we were, my friend and I, in a long overdue conversation. It had been months since we talked and it was good to catch up. . . . Then I heard

The Hawaiian literature, the literature of political economy, the invention of tradition debate, and the voices of the *'ohana*—Kalo, Aunty Limu, Aunty Lau, and Tūtū 'Ōhi'a—inscribe beliefs about the nature of *earth, practice, destiny,* and *knowledge*. It is useful to attend to these various voices and the cosmologies that they enact.

In the Hawaiian literature, Hawaiians are genealogically connected to the universe, which is endowed with transforming power. In political economy, *earth* is symbolically annihilated, and capital is given breath. In the invention of tradition debate, indigenous claims to a genealogical connection to the universe are trivialized, and reconfigured as a reaction to capital.

The *'ohana* debates how to recover land and culture, in a struggle against the debilitating effects of capital. Kalo narrates Hawaiian genealogical connections to one another and to the universe. Aunty Limu, Aunty Lau, and Tūtū 'Ōhi'a tell compelling stories of abundance and life on the land, deprivileging capital and endowing the universe with agency.

him say that this woman also had royal blood. I immediately perceived that the woman Wayne spoke about was surely a member of my family. It was only a matter of minutes and a few words until I understood how close we actually were related. . . .

Wayne patiently sat as he allowed me to read the correspondence between you both. . . . I felt very close to you. Especially when I read about your dreams. I too have had dreams, telling dreams from our ancestors. I understand they are messages of caring guidance. I remember looking up at Wayne and proclaiming the wonderment that continues. The cord that binds us that knows no boundaries of space and time. Our 'aumakua and kūpuna know who we are, where we are. It is fortifying to again realize and feel that mana.

And herein is a great kaona (deep meaning) in the value of knowing one's genealogy. For it is in knowing from whence we came, that we know who we are. Then, in that knowing, we may come to understand where our path opens before us.

. . . I want you to know that my heart welcomes you to our family, your family. . . . I also want to tell you that I understand the delicate matter regarding the identity of your natural Mother. I respect that situation and do not wish to bring hurt to anyone. As long as it needs to be, I will remain discreet. But know that when that need is no longer, I'll probably be the first to shout that I was the first to know!
(Letter from Malie Wahine Ke'ali'i o ke Kai)

After I read the first two words in Malie's letter, "Aloha Cousin," I put the letter down and sat for a few moments, letting my feelings move through me. Later I counted my newly discovered "blood relatives" in the photos Malie

In the Hawaiian literature, humans are tasked to the *practice* of guardianship of other creatures and features of the cosmos, which manifest emotion, intent, and purpose. In political economy, humans alone have agency, as they compete for scarce resources. In the invention of tradition debate, the promotion of human guardianship of other species is not regarded as practice, but as representation, or ideology.

The *'ohana* debates issues to do with right action or practice, as its members struggle against the effects of dispossession. Kalo connects current Hawaiian practices to immutable indigenous values. Aunty Limu, Aunty Lau, and Tūtū 'Ōhi'a tell stories where outcomes are based on ethical integrity and right action. Their stories center on the practice of *mālama 'āina,* and the agency of the cosmos.

In the Hawaiian literature, *destiny* is spiritual, and colonization is the catastrophic overturning of cosmological relationships. In political economy, destiny is economic and capital overturns local modes of production. In the invention of tradition debate, Pacific Island destiny unfolds

had enclosed in her letter. Every person represented another connection, and it was almost too much to take in. I remembered old group photographs, where I stood among members of my nurturing but physically different "Texas family." These recent photographs from Malie included people who did not know me, in particular my biological mother, who did not want to know me. Yet I counted them, naming them, my eyes traveling over their faces, at moments, finding my own.

Overcome with a feeling I still couldn't name, I retrieved childhood photos of my mother and me, blond and dark, spinning on the beach in Hawai'i. I put them up around me, suddenly feeling my mother's presence more than ever.

It felt as if my guts were unclenching. Dreams, odd intuitive flashes, places I had been, all came together, no longer as products of an overactive imagination, but as confirmation of ancestral connection. I had no desire to rush to Hawai'i, or to try to connect to my biological mother, but I did feel a new kind of calm.

I realized that I had previously viewed myself as a kind of cipher—weightless, a nonentity, as if my adoption had emptied out my ancestry. The text of my original birth story had been transformed—its meaning concealed, narrowed to the status of an origin myth. My biological code and ancestral genealogy had been inaccessible, secret systems of signification. Somehow a series of random events, and a long, rich succession of stories, had given me the key.

as local modes of economic and eventually cultural production unravel.

For the *'ohana*, destiny is the sum of everyday actions of Hawaiians in the struggle against the effects of capital. For Kalo, destiny is contingent on sustaining cosmic connections that enfold all Hawaiians. Aunty Limu, Aunty Lau, and Tūtū 'Ōhi'a collapse the colonization narrative into a discussion of spiritual and ethical concerns. They construct destiny as dependent on right action, and for Tūtū 'Ōhi'a: protective relationships among all beings.

In the Hawaiian literature, words, ancestry, and other creatures and features of the universe are central to *knowledge*. In political economy we create knowledge as a response to material conditions, particularly class interests. In the invention of tradition debate, present-day indigenous knowledge, tainted by colonization and the incursion of capital, is ideological.

'Ohana members struggle to retain Hawaiian knowledge forms as their material existence is transformed. Kalo echoes the Hawaiian literature, constructing ancestry and connection as central to knowledge. For Aunty Limu, Aunty Lau, and Tūtū 'Ōhi'a, knowledge comes to us through ancestral lines. For Tūtū 'Ōhi'a words and other creatures and features of the universe bring us knowledge.

In August 1996, as I prepared to travel to Hawai'i, I began to write my thoughts in bits:

I am going back to Hawai'i to meet my cousin, her family, and the man who united us all. I will have a week there, then Ivan will be able to come out for the last five days or so.

Although I have in the past been afraid of flying . . . as I approach the seemingly tiny plane I am overcome with a feeling of calm. I thought that I would be terrified, particularly on this trip. The thought of meeting some accident before I could meet a blood relative had been a nagging fear in the back of my head since speaking and writing to Malie.

And now that fear is gone. It is as if trust has come to me, after forty-odd years of distrust. The air, the sea . . . these elements, though of intense value to me, have not in the past been recipients of my trust. Air currents could prove treacherous, drive your craft careening towards earth. The tide could pull you away from shore, and you could be lost. Traveling over and away from land, on a plane, on a boat . . . sometimes has carried a recurring terror for me. You could never return. You could be lost, adrift.

When I get off the plane I am overcome with a sudden, intense flood of emotion. The familiar scenes with descent into Honolulu, the pause I always take at the airport garden full of its lush foliage, are differently charged. I realize that it is because there is a feeling missing. When I used to get off the plane I used to, on some deep level, feel a sense of dislocation. It was like being in a place at once familiar and hopelessly out of reach.

I would wonder at every encounter with another person, if that person might somehow be related to

The Hawaiian literature traces the contours of its own discursive worlds and imagines descendants to whom it will belong. Those descendants now inhabit a confluence of discursive worlds, each discourse carrying a complex vocabulary, habits, rules, and authorizing credentials. At this confluence we find political economy and the invention of tradition debate, whose authorized languages leach out the presence of earth that often saturates the language of the texts and stories of those descendants.

At this confluence we also encounter the voices of Aunty Limu, Aunty Lau, and Tūtū 'Ōhi'a. These *kūpuna* come from a generation whose parents' stories were silenced, and who were taught to distrust their own stories. They have experienced an unimaginable cultural hammering.

Earth enters their talk as a presence, and sometimes as a conversant. Tūtū 'Ōhi'a and Aunty Lau in particular generate a grounded epistemology wherein knowledge emanates from the dictates of the land and passes through the generations connecting us with *kūpuna* of generations past. Knowledge is embedded in a cosmology that traces our relationship to the cosmos, and a phenomenology that lends subjectivity to all creatures and features of the cosmos.

Aunty Lau and Tūtū 'Ōhi'a speak of connection, atonement, spirituality, and *mālama 'āina*, lending incredible agency to Hawaiians and to *'āina*. As my eyes move over their words, like hands moving over a face, I feel the bones of older discourses, lying just beneath the skin.

me, without our knowledge of relationship. I would wonder who in my family was alive. It was as if relatives, dead and living, flickered in and out of my peripheral vision . . . in a dimension inaccessible to me.

In a way this is my first step onto the islands, because the ground, unlike the ground in the past, does not shift and buckle.
(JOURNAL: AUGUST 1996)

JOURNAL—DAY 1

At Hale'iwa I am staying with Peyton just down the road from Malie. Malie is . . . doing errands for her kids. Peyton takes me across the street to the ocean and I am taken into another awareness. The tide pools, rocky and treacherous, end abruptly in a precipitous drop of at least twenty feet of deep water, and you can see all the way down. . . .

The weightless sense of floating in deep water, of perhaps being sucked away from the shore by some tide, of disconnection still, on some deeper level, terrifies me. Peyton knows a bit about my history, and the upcoming meeting with Malie, who is a dear friend of hers. . . . She says, "You really should float in the water here on this trip. You need to." I feel that too. A need to be weightless, cradled, gentled by the water.

But something echoes inside me: "Sink or swim, sink or swim." I remember . . . the feeling of being alone, out there, somehow betrayed. So for the time being I content myself with sitting in the tidal pool, letting the water rush over me. It is a compromise. The waves, seeming to breathe in and out, moving in a heartbeat, are relentless, unpredictable.

At this confluence of discourses we experience backwash as discourses circulate, undertow as discourses recede, and artifacts washed ashore as old vocabularies get recycled into new formulations. We apprehend various ancestries of experience, various ways to talk about who we are, what we learn, who we want to be, and how we want to structure our practices and lives. As we occupy this confluence, deep inside us, structures of intention shift, imperceptibly. Choices emerge.

The story I have told about this confluence sometimes constructs binary oppositions that, however helpful, neglect the nuances of each discourse and the threshold between them that I occupy. It is easy to pretend that my description offers a clear, complete equation. In reality, my experience at this confluence is incomplete, and every conclusion carries unfinished business.

The "data" I have used here are only a few interviews from a different sort of project focusing on Canada as well as Hawai'i. Others could assert that the reproduction of Hawaiian texts, or Hawaiian ways of doing knowledge, in those interviews is coincidental.

Often at this point, academic writers authorize work by drawing the implications of their writing for "the field." This positions their writing as a resolution that directs future

Malie finds me at Peyton's that night. . . . We go to her place and . . . faces of our ancestors and relatives crowd her wall, along with family artifacts. I am suddenly surrounded by my blood history and it is almost too much. While the family threads in and out of the rooms preparing for bed, preparing a snack, asking one another where some article is, I walk around her home, goggle-eyed. Faces of my ancestors look out at me. . . . I wonder who I resemble, if anyone. This thought surprises me. . . .

I feel myself becoming more present somehow. I have been used to an image of myself that flickered in and out, like backlighting to the real things that go on. . . . I discover that Malie plays music at the restaurant where I met the lei-sellers. As periodically happens in our talks we are momentarily speechless. Then Malie says, "I wonder if I was playing in the restaurant the night that you were speaking with those kūpuna. . . .

JOURNAL—DAY 2

Last night, after the evening at Malie's, I slept, floating in that weightless place where everything is assimilated. Is that weightless place where blood memory lives, where the consequences of family history are enacted? Was it in that weightless place where my ancestors met me? I dreamt of eyes, looking out from walls. Some were mine. I dreamt of leis, woven into chains of ancestral intention and protection.

Today . . . I have little to say of my life, and want to say little. All my energy is taken up in assimilating Malie's everyday life, and realizing that we are related. . . . As well, the things she tells me about

paradigms or syntheses in the academic production of knowledge.

In the real world, the limen created by the collision of my research experience and my life history resists synthesis and resolution. For this reason it is useful to explore the gifts of *kaona*, the subterranean meanings and references that experience yields.

Long before Western phenomenology was a discipline, the use of *kaona* presupposed language not only as an instrument of communication, but also as a method by which speakers bring the world into existence. *Kaona* rests on the idea that the learner's subjectivity is the key to knowing. Long before hermeneutics was a discipline, the use of *kaona* presupposed the craft of interpreting secret, hidden meanings in texts, events, and manifestations. *Kaona* requires the learner to explore deeper layers of relationship and meaning in narrative.

Kaona involves indeterminancy—a discussion of instances when the learner can't figure out exactly what is happening, or what is being said. To look into *kaona* is to ask what knowledge is, where it comes from, how it is

our family, living and most especially dead, are almost too much to assimilate.

We drop Malie off to sing at the restaurant. . . . Malie's friends greet us; and she introduces me as her long-lost cousin. The lei-*makers are not there. . . . We laugh and sing for what seems like hours, then late at night after her gig, we drive back home.*

I wake up in the middle of the night, stomach aching. I have had some sort of dream about my mom or about being adrift in the ocean. Difficult to remember. Peyton is up too, and we begin talking. Suddenly the pains begin moving through my stomach, familiar and terrifying. . . . I have been told that adhesions from old surgeries are what make the intestines cramp, or twist. It has to do somehow with assimilation of food. Of information? I know I am trying to assimilate, to come to terms with chains of coincidences that weave back into my past.

As I am talking I put my hands up in the air and Peyton comments: "That's interesting, that's how little babies look as they lie in the crib." I tell her about my birth dream which has recurred during my life where . . . somebody is carrying me away. . . . As I speak of this recurrent dream to Peyton, some sort of old, old pain wells up in my guts. I feel like weeping but can't. She tells me that I have stopped breathing, and advises me to take deep breaths, saying, "Breathe into the pain." As I do this I abruptly begin weeping in long, almost relaxed, moans. The tears stream down my face. In weeping it seems I surrender to some old feeling that I have never acknowledged. My weeping slows, the pain falls away, and I begin to drift into sleep. I murmur to Peyton that I'm fine now, and she moves quietly out of the room.

justified, and how we know what we know. It is to admit to "not knowing." In phenomenological or hermeneutical research, the learner must interrogate the "selves" she brings to her narrated experiences and her telling of others' stories.

To look into *kaona* is also to interrogate one's practices and responsibilities to the knowledge that continually emerges. The following moments and words resist closure or interpretation, and therefore activate *kaona*.

Malie and I visit Wayne and Roxanna. Wayne greets me, saying, "Aloha, little sister." It is a meeting full of tears as we talk about what brought us all together. . . . We speak for hours but what Wayne and Roxanna said simply lodges in my bones. . . . (We go) ma uka *to a project called the 'Ōpelu Project (a place where they are cultivating taro). . . . Wayne is unable to go the whole way, so he sits in the car. Something about that just does not feel right. I wish aloud that he could come up with us. Yet I know I need to walk up the hill to this project. Roxanna, Malie, and I talk when we have reached the project, up in the mountains. . . . Roxanna then tells Malie and me that we must go down to the sea,* ma kai, *now, before the day is over. . . . Roxanna says there will be signs for us. . . .*

Malie and I head to the ocean together at Pūpūkea at sunset. I remember back to my "dream" about losing my mother. I feel myself floating in the water; it seems to cradle me. Tears come over me, and Malie comes closer to me, putting her arms around me.

And then the feeling washes over me, passes. A feeling of peace and forgiveness washes over me and rain begins to fall. Malie says, "Oh, this is the sign we've been looking for." I feel a new layer of meaning compose itself in my awareness, but I cannot name this layer of meaning. As the rain falls, the sun pours through the clouds and a giant rainbow forms, complete and full. Other swimmers, mostly children, exclaim about it, and another rainbow begins to form behind it. The rainbow and its forming twin stand behind Pūpūkea, on land.

I remember Kalo taking me to that place more than ten years ago. I remember I drifted around that

I'm searching through texts in a very upscale-looking store with Ivan. We are befuddled by all we must do and by the array of things. . . . It seems we are wandering aimlessly. Finally we leave, and he asks, "Do you want to go to the bookstore?" I envision a big warehouse full of books, and I don't want to go. (From my dream)

She says she is so sorry, but no. She is not angry, but seems regretful. She goes on to talk about how Hawaiians don't DO Hawaiian culture like they should. She talks about how Hawaiians are too lazy to do their own stuff—they try to buy the lauhala *and not to make it. (From Mana'o)*

Aunty Limu's "no" to taping her voice and using her verbatim words offers me much to think about. I'm not taking up the possible personal reasons Aunty Limu may have had for saying "no." She could have had many reasons: a feeling of being targeted as an expert when there are many knowledges, a feeling of my not being of that place (as Wayne suggested), a desire not to be asked questions, but rather to give knowledge on her own terms, to name just a few possibilities. I never brought the issue up with her again, and it is not a story that is part of our relationship, which grows and deepens over the years.

I chose the pseudonym for Aunty Limu because of memories of her songs and stories about gathering *limu*, which she had shared with us as she taught *lauhala* and *'ukulele*. Pukui and Elbert (1986, 207) give us several usages for the word *limu*. *Limu* is "a general name for all kinds of plants living under water . . . (and) algae growing in any damp place in the air, as on the ground, on rocks, and on other plants." *Limu* can also mean "tricky, deceiving, unstable" like the octopus that changes its color and waves its tentacles, mimicking the movement of sea-

heiau and finally said to Kalo, "I feel like my relatives are here, but I don't know where. They could be just down the road. But I don't know." Now I think of Kalo and something she said to me over and over: "You are related to the 'āina, and you are related to me."

The children's heads are turned towards Pūpūkea, as they continue to talk about the double rainbow that is forming. Malie and I turn now towards the ocean, looking away from land, and notice that the arc of the rainbow is repeated in a stream of cloud streaking across the horizon. After a time we leave the water and decide to walk back home. As we walk and look towards the ocean, a tribe of dolphins arcs through the water.

JOURNAL—DAY 4

Today I am on my own in Hale'iwa—I sleep 'til about 9 a.m. and then lie in bed . . . . My lassitude must have something to do with all that there has been to process, all the thoughts coming to me. I do errands alone all day. I concentrate on breathing. I empty my head of thoughts. I drift around. I am relieved to be alone, to feel the differences in my body. My body has taken on a different weight. I feel huge; I take up space, I displace the air as I move through it. . . .

The only thing that comes to mind, over and over, is the dolphins, the eyes on the wall, and strangely, the eyes of the pueo. *I imagine the men in their* lavalava, *cradling the* pueo, *with the calm eyes, moving it to protection. I remember the way they named this bird. "Pueo," they said, simply, moving on down the hill, cradling it gently.*

weed in the water. Another meaning for *limu* is: a gust of wind (ibid.).

When I saw her in Hawai'i, Aunty Limu talked about gathering *limu* from the sea. This is "doing" culture, a useful undertaking. Is the practice of gathering talk also a useful undertaking? For me to gather Aunty Limu's talk was accompanied by a failure to take up knowledge on her terms—a failure to take up her practices.

Instead, I chose to gather, classify, and then represent talk using an "academic" vocabulary and lens, a practice historically connected to the Western refraction of indigenous knowledge (L.T. Smith 1999). When *kūpuna* recommend that we take up traditional practices, is an undertaking that adds to those warehouses full of books really useful?

When Aunty Limu gathers *limu*, she uses it or shares it with others just as traditionally as Hawaiians gathered, used, and shared knowledge. Yet when I gather talk and publish it, that talk circulates as currency in the scholarly marketplace. Osorio (2007, 5) notes: "Scholars would do well to ask themselves, before they come to study us and while they write their dissertations, 'Whose loss underwrites my gain?'"

Although Osorio's question seems directed to non-Native scholars, as I explore this *kaona* I would like to address the concerns of both nonindigenous and indigenous scholars.

(Over dinner) we are talking about Hawaiian history. That gut-wrenching feeling again. It hits me in waves. I feel I can't breathe, so I excuse myself and walk in and around the park. . . . Tourists flock here for a look at its representation of paradise and "ancient Hawai'i." The park is emptying of visitors now, and a family of peacocks ranges across the grass, pecking curiously at crumbs. They halt and stand away from me, then one is left behind as the others toddle off. After a moment of this strange sharing of space with this peacock, something moves from me and I feel unwrenched. The peacock toddles off and I return to our table.

Any scholar, indigenous or not, could gather local stories to extend and further authorize her academic genealogy. Research ethics would not take into account how Aunty Limu could contribute to that scholar's gain in the academic marketplace. Instead, they are based on Western notions of property rights and individualism, emphasizing "the right of an individual to give his or her own knowledge, or the right to give informed consent" (L.T. Smith 1999, 118). These notions of "intellectual property" allow well-traveled paths of appropriation to remain open.

Later, (we) speak to Roxanna and Wayne about the events of the day before. . . . Roxanna says, "You know, dolphins always lead us towards land. They always lead us towards home, towards Mother Earth." For some reason, speaking with her on the phone, I feel tears stream down my face. . . . Roxanna then says to me, "If you have questions, you can ask in your prayers and the nai'a *will show you, in dreams. You will meet your mother. It's going to be a half-sibling who will lead the way."*

I meet Wayne at a restaurant, where we sit and talk all day. . . . He has a file on me. He shows me the charts, which show my family tree dating back to the time of Kamehameha. A few of these charts he gives to me. It is his concern that giving me all the information at once may be too much knowledge. . . . Here, where the knowledge revealed lodges in the na'au, *in the guts, it is the relaxed assimilation and processing of knowledge that makes sense . . . the slow and measured unfolding of knowledge, which seems to be contained inside me and outside me at once.*

I am not isolating, categorizing, and describing some pattern that lies outside me; rather, I am spiraling inward, corkscrewing into my own being, while it seems as if the water, the air, and land enfold and cradle me. I do not want to know too much too soon.

JOURNAL—DAY 6

Wayne shows me articles about members of my family, weaves stories together . . . . As I look over . . . (my genealogical) charts, gather the ones to copy up into my bag, get ready to leave the restaurant, I feel the weight of my ancestry. . . .

All scholars must vet their research (product) through a scholarly discourse community—colleagues with similar interests, theories, and paradigms understood only by a select few (Orr 1992, 144). The agency of Earth; the land on which the campus rests, may be rendered invisible through landscaping, architecture, and everyday practices.[1] Such communities may also embed hierarchical rituals and the chanting of academic genealogies of authority in everyday talk.

Theoretical paradigms and data may assume the same sort of agency as Earth in the Hawaiian literature. "Academic capital," measured via book deals, academic kudos, and research funding, may assume the same sort of agency as "capital" in the literature of political economy and the invention of tradition. Appropriation, personal gain, and the danger of reformatting might not be a primary concern within such communities.

For nonindigenous scholars this setting conditions research that may tell an incomplete or faulty story about "the other." It constitutes a "problem in research." For indigenous scholars, this setting constitutes distance from community, family, ancestors, and land. It constitutes a "problem in living." The stakes are, therefore, different for many indigenous scholars who want to do right by their own ancestries of experience.

In one respect my abandonment of Aunty Limu's instruction in favor of academic settings and "gains" is a loss for Aunty Limu. *Kūpuna* "do knowledge" their own way, create meaning on their own terms, and shape their own discourses. They have their own knowledge agendas and wishes for us within those agendas.

Academic institutions often lie far off from those

That evening, Malie and I are talking together, and I speak a bit about my feelings growing up in a non-Hawaiian atmosphere in Ohio. What to her comes naturally—the music, the hula, the language, the culture—and is readily available, did not really exist for me in Cleveland. When did I meet Hawaiians? she asks. . . .

I talk about how my parents took me, when I was in high school, to see the Hawaiian kids from the Kamehameha Schools Concert Glee Club. . . .

They were so happy together, it seemed, so confident in who and what they were. And their songs, their dances were so beautiful. The crowd went wild over them. I tell Malie that I remember looking at the brochure, which contained the names of the choir members, and thinking: "I could be related to any one of these kids and not know it." Over the years, I tell Malie, I would pick up this brochure and put it down again, look it over, read over the names, wonder if I would ever know who my family was.

Malie has become quiet, her eyes getting larger. "What year did they come?" she asks me. I tell her I'm not sure; it must have been in the '70s—I was a senior in high school, I think. She pauses, then says, "When I was a junior in high school I went on a tour of the Midwest with Kamehameha Schools Concert Glee Club." She asks me if I still have the brochure and I say I do; in fact, I know just where it is at home. We call Ivan, who is still in San Diego. He retrieves the brochure from my journal. Malie's name is on it.

JOURNAL—DAY 7

My dream from last night is so strange. Streams of paper pop out of a copy machine, each filled with

agendas and the strategies of knowledge-making they contain. Studying indigenous knowledge-making from within academia often involves entering a system of knowledge in the absence of the practices of knowledge and language connected with it (Dei 1999).

Briggs's (1986) analyses of the interview routine suggests that it displaces everyday practices, using preconceived questions that shape the discourse. An interviewer outside the community may not detect, and may consequently delete, interviewees' cues about how they do knowledge. The researcher might lift words out of context to extract themes fitting her theoretical paradigm.

This reformatting may leave us with a deceptive imitation of the movement of talk. What we believe to be the *limu*—gathered knowledge—is actually an octopus—a mimicry of discourse.

For nonindigenous scholars, this is a way in which the community of "the other" experiences a loss that contributes to scholars' gain. Indigenous scholars may also feel a sense of personal loss as the local knowledge of their own communities is "miss-taken," trivialized, or effaced.

1970 MAINLAND TOUR

THE KAMEHAMEHA SCHOOLS
CONCERT GLEE CLUBS
HONOLULU, HAWAII

*little boxes or grids. Within each box or grid is the
notation of a vagina size and a picture of a small
pencil. When I wake up the sun is streaming through
my window and I feel odd and unsettled. Peyton,
who has come into the room, sits on the bed.*

*After I tell her about the dream, she asks me:
"What parts of you are represented in the dream?"
I realize that the sight of generations of my family
moving back into time has stayed with me. Suddenly, all these blood relatives. We talk about the
vaginas, and I realize that each grid on the genealogical charts, which contains a name, represents
another birth. Centuries of births, recorded on a grid,
in pencil . . . a surfeit of connection, as if a web containing me in the darkness is suddenly illuminated.*

*Malie's daughter and I go to Kamehameha
Schools so that she can drop off her registration
materials. The Kamehameha Schools Concert Glee
Club is practicing in a nearby building. . . . I look
out over the ocean and hear the Kamehameha Schools
Concert Glee Club singing, voices drifting across the
lawn towards me.*

JOURNAL—DAY 8

*Today Ivan and I (go) with Wayne and Rox-
anna . . . to the* heiau *at 'Aiea. They take with them
two of their granddaughters. We drive up into the
heights, the air getting cooler, damper, turn in on
a road leading into a park area. There is the* heiau*,
a well-cared-for enclosure of rocks. A shaded, cool
picnic area, surrounded by paths leading up into the
hills. We eat and talk, then laze around in the shade,
talking some more.*

Roxanna says, "Outside entities ('uhane*) are
watching over you. Ask God for guidance. Look for*

Now I'm thinking about the *limu* as a gust of wind. In
my dream about the forest inhabited by eyes, the inhale
and exhale of the forest is like a gust of wind, moving
through the clearing. This reminds me that the *kūpuna*
gave breath to deeply textured lessons devised on their
own terms. They created pedagogical events where I was
made aware of the relevance of their words to my situation. They reminded me to be patient, wait, and attend to
knowledge when it comes. They invited deep, multilayered readings of their words over time. In contrast, academic communities require that their members aggres-
sively and rapidly "produce knowledge."

The ancestry of experience for indigenous scholars,
which sometimes speaks through stories, dreams, and
"intuition," may not be given a hearing in academic communities. Indigenous scholars may be invited to speak
in languages ill-suited to their pursuit of knowledge.
Whether on the basis of being too indigenous or not
indigenous enough, they may be invited to be silent.[2]

In such academic communities, ethical issues
emerge as a list of rules rather than as a deep discern-
ment of one's obligations. I believe that as our new generations of indigenous scholars create ways to meet their
obligations, their methods will eclipse that list of rules.
The knowledge of their ancestors is one place in which
they will find clues to alternative paradigms, agendas,
and settings to create—ways to frame their own practices
in academia.

In the Hawaiian literature words, ancestry, and creatures and features of the universe bring us knowledge.
This reminds us to fully attend to the talk of our "interviewees," resisting urges to write over their words with
theoretical paradigms. It reminds us that nested within
talk or text are grounded epistemologies that retell the
cosmos and create consequences. It reminds us to work
out of a sense of connection and to resist the disconnection we encounter in academic settings. It reminds us to

*the deeper meaning in things. Say a prayer." She
intimates that we all must forgive and yet we all
must look into our lives and hearts and ask for forgiveness. Wayne says, "You have a deep connection,
spirit, and background. Now you are receiving your
spiritual education." . . . When we leave it is very,
very difficult. In particular, leaving Wayne is difficult, because he has somehow become a brother to me
in this short time. . . .*

JOURNAL—DAY 9

In the morning I go up to the heiau *at Pūpūkea
with Ivan. We drive up the hill leading there, which
is just down the road from where Malie lives. . . . (it)
is still the same for the most part. There are differences that seem to echo shifts in my own life, in my
own perceptions.*

First, the enclosures are so huge. The size of the
heiau *is amazing. I had not remembered how vast
this space is. Second, it seems that the underbrush
has been cleared away from the perimeter of the hill.
I look down over Waimea Bay and realize that this
is the scene of my dreams. This is the place that the
man in my dream took me to, where he spoke of a
great place, a place where there is a confluence of
two tides.*

After I returned from Hawai'i, Wayne wrote
me:

23 August 1996

Dear Leilani . . .

*Time sure flies by fast! It's going on two weeks
since you left Hawai'i already. I hope now that*

discard scarcity paradigms and forms of research that are
not *pono.*

My dream reminds me that some indigenous scholars,
though they may be silent/silenced, occupy an interface—
a confluence where important practices take place. Their
ancestors and birthsands nest within them, in deeply textured layers. They are staking their claims, and doing what
is right by their ancestors.

JUNIOR AND THE FUTURE

*. . . I'm on a ship, traveling through Polynesia. The tourists
on the ship are taking videos . . . transfixed by and perceptually stuck to their viewfinders. I'm aware that to them,
later, it may seem like we were silenced/silent. . . . These
tourists move through the world perceptually stuck inside
big, barely permeable bubbles.* (From my dream)

Leilani: What's the future of the Hawaiian people?
Junior: Nothing! It's so screwed up! (Voice rises.) Yeah!
*Kalo: So, if it's screwed up and you could fix it, how would
you fix it?*
Junior: I don't know. (Silence)
Aunty: Think!
*Junior: I thinking, I thinking. Everybody says, think, think.
Help me think! Help me think!*
(From 'Ohana)

Junior's silence stands in contrast to his forceful exclamation: "Nothing! It's so screwed up!" His silence transfixes
me, yet his experiences and the meanings he makes of
them are obscured. The future is something that Junior
has inherited and may, at some point in time, experience
without the adults who now surround him.

As Junior is questioned about how to change this

you're home, the trip and all that you were able to experience, learn and connect with hasn't smacked you one and knocked you off your feet like some steam-rolling wave at Waimea Bay!! I know you will be going over in your mind, for some time to come, all the things you experienced and knowledge you gained in the short time you were here. . . .

I think of you folks constantly and pray for nothing but the best for my "little" sister and her husband, Ivan. Your visit really brought home to me how amazing the guidance of our 'aumakua are as they guided and entwined us all together one to another. The search for your birth mother has also given us all additional family members which, at least for me, is very real, tangible, and is destined to last a life time. I don't think I could feel any closer to a full-blooded biological sister than I do to you, Leilani. I will never forget, in my mind's eye, the sight of you holding my hand with tears streaming down your face because of your concern over my heart attack and how I will take care of myself. . . . (LETTER FROM WAYNE)

Later, he sent me some sound advice:

22 October 1996

Dear Leilani . . .

. . . Just let things, feelings, messages, etc. flow through you, "look" at them and put them aside to "look" at them again—don't "dwell" on things and don't try to analyze and seek meanings and answers in everything at once. Be "casual" in your approach to all these things—savor, but don't stuff yourself with too much at "one sitting." (LETTER FROM WAYNE)

future he has inherited, his plea "Help me think! Help me think!"[3] causes me to feel that an impermeable bubble invisibly walls off his view of the future from mine. It seems that he is alone at this point, and that more questioning will not help me to understand how or why he sees the future as hopeless.

Since I have asked Junior a question about the future, it is useful to reflect on what it *is* that I have asked about. The term for future is *ka wā ma hope* (Pukui and Elbert 1986, 448). *Ma hope* can refer to the time afterwards or behind (ibid., 82).

In a sense, Junior emerges from and faces toward the past. When he looks to the future, his gaze must be directed backward, toward what lies behind him. What resources will help him to face history, which lies ahead?

Junior tries to describe why the teaching of Hawaiian culture and Hawaiian history is not working for him. He is trying to explain why *ka wā ma mua* is not remembered for him.

Junior conveys a sense of disconnection from the school curriculum. He doesn't seem to have access to the discourse of *kūpuna* who are part of Kalo's life. These *kūpuna* create a context of acceptance and validation, gently pulling us into reflection on our own responsibilities

In the summer of 1997 I joined a seminar on the politics of culture in Hawai'i. I was one of two people of Hawaiian ancestry in attendance, although a number of members had ties to Hawai'i. The first night, seminar members recited their "academic genealogies," reckoning how their work, their mentors, and their professional contacts related them one to another. As a community college instructor I didn't trace such relationships and found myself connecting to the other seminar member of Hawaiian ancestry, also at a community college. Soon we were telling stories about our lives. We were joined by a (non-Hawaiian) woman who taught at a local community college, who told some stories of her own.

In the seminar we discussed the invention of tradition debate. We read Linnekin, Keesing, Trask on Keesing, Keesing's reply to Trask, Hereniko, Hau'ofa, Hanson on Hereniko, Sahlins, Obeyesekere, Dening, and various comments on the Linnekin/Trask/Keesing debate. The debate felt terrible as it was conducted face to face by humans.

Something in our language separated us into "Hawaiians" and "academics." I wanted to believe that these "camps" were artificially constructed, and that our identities were stereotyped. Yet when our seminar members discussed the authenticity of various "traditional practices," a rift yawned open. At those times, I looked at the "transcripts" from Tūtū 'Ōhi'a that I had brought along and was engulfed with a rage that I could not explain.

in the world. Their stories reaffirm Hawaiian past practices and pull us into synchronic time where past and present occur simultaneously.

They tend to answer questions about *ka wā ma hope* (the future) by talking about *ka wā ma mua* (the past). They construct the past not as a catastrophe, but as a timeless ethical moment. These formulations give us hope for the future and also find their way into Kalo's talk.

We need to ground these stories about past practices, specifically subsistence practices, as a powerful form of practice in themselves (Hensel, 1996). More than functioning as an ethnic marker, recreating past practices works to reconfigure the future as a range of possibilities based on the continuation of an ethical moment.

Responding to questions about *ka wā ma hope*, these *kūpuna* face *ka wā ma mua* and describe what they see. This pulls us into the notion of trajectory, the idea of being propelled backwards into the future, while the past continues to manifest before us.

As I reflect on Tūtū 'Ōhi'a's vision of what lies before her and her descriptions of what she did *not* know as a child, I am reminded that Junior occupies a trajectory—that he has a future. Whether through mentors, or *kūpuna*, or a class that he takes somewhere, knowledge of his past may help him to create his future.

Silva (2004, 3) suggests that documenting the actions of everyday Hawaiians in the past helps present-day Hawaiians to "recover from the violence done to their past by the linguicide that accompanies colonialism." She

I visited the home of some Hawaiian friends and told them about the debate, thinking that they would laugh about it. Instead my friends angrily said: "They think we have no culture—they are the ones who have no culture."

I felt that I was not able to inhabit that rift with integrity because the words I used sounded so full of self-righteous rage. Seminar talk seemed infused with the recitation of credentials that authorized one to speak.

The phrase "our interlocutors" was used often instead of the equally problematic term, "informant," which made me want to grind my teeth. I found in my dictionary that an interlocutor could be a conversant, or the man in a minstrel show who questions the others.

I thought about the Tuamotuan man I had met in the Marquesas, casually crossing imaginary boundaries. He had held a volume of Tuamotuan stories and chants, surmised that one of the "informants" might be in his family, and used it to remember his chant-lines. Meanwhile, I held Tūtū 'Ōhi'a's words in my hands but could not make them exist.

At times I felt that I was experiencing my great-grandfather's memories on the cellular level. Wasn't it possible that cells could remember deeper realities than eye or hair color? At those moments I felt like I was a container of memory, activated by the movements of leaves on trees I glimpsed through the window. That feeling was at the core of the terrible feeling I had sitting in that room.

states that much written history constructs Hawaiians as passively accepting oppression, while stories generated in oral tradition often give Hawaiians a different, affirming history and sense of agency. Validating stories aids in recovery from "the wounds caused by that disjuncture in their consciousness" (ibid.). Kame'eleihiwa (1992, 22–23) notes:

It is interesting to note that in Hawaiian the past is referred to as Ka wā ma mua, or "the time in front or before." Whereas the future, when thought of at all, is Ka wā ma hope, or "the time which comes after or behind." It is as if the Hawaiian stands firmly in the present, with his back to the future, and his eyes fixed upon the past, seeking historical answers for present-day dilemmas. Such an orientation is to the Hawaiian an eminently practical one, for the future is always unknown, whereas the past is rich in glory and knowledge.

At night I read impatiently, violently cramming information into my brain. Or I met with my two seminar friends, and we just told stories. Or I danced, learning from a local *kumu hula*, and another sort of information coded itself in my cells. Dancing, I imagined myself as a node in a species, itself a node in an ecosystem, itself a node in a cosmos, signals exchanged, and memory replicating down ancestral lines.

Israel Kamakawi'wo'ole died, and his ashes were scattered into the sea at Mākua. People paddled toward the ashes on surfboards and splashed their cupped hands in the water. The water sprayed up, meeting the ashes as they paused in mid-air.

Seminar members put new spins on the ever complexifying, intensifying debate that seemed to have disconnection as its premise and disconnected us into "camps." At the same time, *kumu hula* were getting ready for the Prince Lot Hula Festival. Energies were being directed; there was a confluence. As I sat in a classroom overlooking Mānoa Valley, talking about postmodernist deconstruction, I felt as if my greatgrandfather's shadow moved through the trees.

One day, I snaked a slippery path to Mānoa Falls, the sound of fruit falling and birds calling to one another in the green peace. Unforgiving stones met me early on the path. The wind rustled through me, and jittered through the forest canopy whispering my great-grandfather's name. Sliding, body slick with sweat, I imagined my great-grandfather; running, running. "Watch your step," I chanted to myself. When I reached the falls, I splashed water over my face, feeling cleansed. I was back from the falls

KALO: FROM THE SAME POI BOWL

Through the door he sends me the thought: "What is the ancestry of experience?" I have never heard this phrase before, but I know it is important for me. I take his question to mean: How do my ancestors prefigure my experience, in their voices, brought into historical memory that I've heard, danced, coded? But the question means more. There is at least one other layer that I do not yet understand. . . . (From my dream)

But the fact that you ARE Hawaiian
and you ARE 'ohana
and that we eat out of the same poi *bowl.*
And that we come from the same roots.
And that's the connectedness that people don't understand,
that brings all Hawaiians together,
no matter how much Hawaiian they have by blood quantum.
Wherever they live,
if you are Hawaiian, you are Hawaiian.
And you are accepted into the 'ohana.
Unconditionally.
There are no, no restrictions,
no limitations, no obstacles, no barriers.
The fact that you are Hawaiian,
you're part of the 'ohana.
(From Kalo)

Kalo creates a compelling, inclusive *'ohana* lying outside blood quantum and based on Hawaiian ancestry. I chose to name Kalo for the taro, since she and I spent so much time eating poi together. At Hawaiian Club *lū'au* we would stand next to "non-*poi*-eaters" and scoop up their rejected servings of *poi*.

before I could think about it, passing the level final path, the mountain ridge rising up in front of me. "You are missing things," I chanted to myself.

One day I walked up Pūpūkea Road to Pu'u o Mahuka Heiau, meeting a small tree stump that looked dead, but for shy young green growth, sprouting from its underside. At the *heiau*, I looked down at the bay at an apparent confluence of tides, then drifted around in the silence. I left an offering and started to leave, then suddenly turned back to the *heiau*, saying, "Thank you. I didn't know it, but you were always there for me, from the very first!"

Pukui and Elbert (1986) note that all parts of the *kalo* (a food staple since ancient times) are eaten, the root as *poi*, and the leaves as *lū'au*. They note that *kalo* is the name of the first taro growing from the planted stalk, and also references the "names of generations as listed for Hawai'i island" (ibid., 123). "The taro corm that grows from the older root, especially the stalk called the *kalo*," is called the *'ohā*. *'Ohana*, from the root word *'ohā*, means "family, relative, or kin group" (ibid., 276).

When I returned from the NEH seminar, I was relieved to be back to community college teaching. The seminar subculture seemed based on a scarcity paradigm. Seminar participants who had university appointments seemed stressed, while those looking for jobs seemed afraid. "Knowledge production" seemed literal, with a conveyor belt and anxious workers, stepping up the output.

I had given Malie a list of questions when I was in Hawai'i for the seminar. She later taped her answers and mailed them to me. It was months before I finally transcribed the tape. I had viewed this as a continuation of the interviewing process that went on between Kalo and her *kūpuna*. When I listened to the interview from Malie, I realized that it was more than an interview—it was a personal message. Malie talked to my half-sister, who at that point felt a need to keep my identity secret in order

It is useful to reflect on the *'ohana*, who present Hawaiianness as a genealogical link to one's roots, to which we must "trace ourselves back," and who consistently resist the notion of blood quantum. They, like Kalo, assert that being a descendant of a Hawaiian (ancestry), rather than fitting a notion of blood quantum, is the key to Hawaiian identity. As *'ohana* members interrogate the notion of blood quantum, I think it is clear that they, like Kauanui (1999a), view it as abstract, restrictive, and alien to traditional Hawaiian genealogical practices.

Yet it is not hard to detect the relentless drive to erase ancestry from the experience of Hawaiians. When we erase ancestry from the Hawaiian experience (whether legally or symbolically), we disauthenticate Hawaiians and we render their ancestors invisible.

Osorio (2001) and Kauanui (1999a) discuss the history of Native entitlements in Hawai'i, which involved reliance on the legal device of blood quantum by non-Hawaiians. Kauanui (ibid.) asserts that the Hawaiian Homes Comto protect my birth mother. I understood her motives but felt sad.

Part of the transcription is included here on the left below. Although I heard Malie's words as poetry and included line breaks, I did not feel a need to write commentary on her words, which felt straightforward and deeply personal.

"Where do the land and ancestors come into your life and your life's work and what do you want to tell your ancestors?"

Knowing my genealogy,
I am able to walk the land that they've walked,
breathe the air that they've breathed,
and be in the ocean that they have been in.
So the land does not belong to me,
I belong to the land. I belong to the land.
I belong to the wind and the air
that surrounds that land
and the ocean that embraces that land.
And I belong to the fire
that is the spirit of that land.

We've been talking about the ancestors,
the kūpuna *who have gone before us.*
This question is about the kūpuna
who are here. (Sighs.)
You know, when I think of kūpuna,
my kūpuna *are my family, my ancestors.*
Kūpuna *is a term that is family.*
It does not mean that because someone
is of an elder generation that they are my
kūpuna.

mission Act obscured the dispossession of *all* Hawaiians by authenticating only Hawaiians of fifty percent or more blood quantum as entitled to receive various "benefits." Blood quantum redefined Hawaiianness in ways that further dispossessed Hawaiians and enriched non-Hawaiians. It also wrote over the notion of Hawaiian ancestry.

In 2000, the U.S. Supreme Court ruled in Rice versus Cayetano that the ancestry qualification for voters of the Office of Hawaiian Affairs was unconstitutional because it violated the Fifteenth Amendment of the U.S. Constitution. This ruling redefines indigenous self-determination as a form of racial preference. It invokes race to construct Hawaiians as a "race" receiving "unearned benefits" rather than as an indigenous group that has been dispossessed. In this way dispossession continues as a process. Also, in this way, our ancestors are written over, rendered invisible.

Kauanui discusses another pattern of disauthentication that occurs for off-island Hawaiians—deracination, the notion that Hawaiians aren't an actual "race." This is not to say that Hawaiians are constructed as an indigenous group. Rather, the notion of "race" is invoked to construct Hawaiians as a "non-race" and to write over ancestry.

What is a puna?
Puna is the wellspring.
Kupuna is the one who is that wellspring.
I speak of my own family who are my kūpuna.
They are the wellspring I will choose
to drink from, to learn from.
So the role my kūpuna *play to me,*
is just that.
I am their moʻopuna. . . .
Those are the voices we listen to
. . . the kūpuna
who play a part in our lives.
Those who are our blood
who come to speak to us
in our dreamtime.
Moemoeā. *Dreamtime.*

I want to tell you that you are
one blessed being.

It's incredible.
It's just a miracle, just a miracle. . . .
So the moral of the story is,
even though the odds
seemed stacked against
you knowing where you've come from,
our ancestors would not let you be forgotten.
It's incredible, Leilani.

You know
I have always believed in my ancestors.
I've felt them,
I've heard them,
I've even seen them. . . .
And I feel their messages.
And meeting you was just another sign,

Kauanui (1999b, 3) says:

On the one hand, there is an all too common misunderstanding that any and all who once lived in Hawaiʻi are, therefore, "Hawaiian." And on the other hand, when Hawaiians who have never lived in Hawaiʻi identify themselves as Hawaiian, the politics of reception is often such that others will expect them to have been "born there." The confusion between (or conflation of) nativeness and nativity is persistent. . . .

Kauanui notes that deracination is produced through a lack of historical knowledge about Hawaiian outmigration, the appropriation of Hawaiian identity by off-island non-Hawaiians,[4] and the popular notion that Hawaiians are a "hybrid" or "mixed" race (ibid., 3–8).

Disauthentication as a pattern of exclusion contrasts with Tūtū ʻŌhiʻa's fluid definitions of "they" and "us," which invariably return to inclusive phrases like "our Hawaiians." Tūtū ʻŌhiʻa does not construct Hawaiian identity through markings of difference and exclusion. She connects her listeners to one another, to land, to the relevance of a particular moment, and to their responsibilities to that moment. Like Kalo, Tūtū ʻŌhiʻa seems to see us all, off- or on-island, as connected, as eating out of the same *poi* bowl.

Eating out of the same *poi* bowl posits a universe ordered on the basis of connection. It enacts Hawaiian cosmology; taro holds the genealogical place as elder male sibling to the Hawaiian people. Hawaiians are all related, tied to our ancestors, tied to Hawaiʻi, and in particular, tied to *ʻāina*. Kauanui (1999a, 138) notes:

a proof of their divine presence.
All in the grace of God.

It was once shared with me,
the translation of the word mana, *is grace.*
How incredible.
Do not think of mana *as power but as grace.*

So, the one day,
I know I've shared this with you,
and it's in the letter I wrote to you.
Remember the rain?
And the call from Wayne Davis?
Telling me about you? . . .
I knew you so well at that point.
My spirit knew your spirit immediately.

And I know that when I wrote you
and told you about some of my dreams,
I believe you felt the same way.
Because we immediately knew each other,

Leilani, we were never strangers.

We've only been on earth
for forty-something years.

What is that?
It is barely a bat of an eyelash
when you think of the thousands of years
that our ancestors have walked this earth.

And now, you know who they are!

You know them by name, now.
You've felt them,

Where blood quantum is always about individualization of particular bodies (already said to be "diluted"), Hawaiian genealogical practices enlarge the collective and social.

This struggle with disauthentication is not only legal and cultural, but also spiritual. Genealogy works to disable a cosmology based on disconnection and individualization. When we are reminded of our genealogies, we are reminded that we, and our ancestors, truly exist as a connected collective.

This issue is important for diasporic Hawaiian young people, those born outside Hawai'i and those who have migrated outside Hawai'i. Kauanui (1998, 691) notes that the term "transplant Hawaiian" addresses something important for *all* Hawaiians—the familial and genealogical connections between on- and off-island Hawaiians. Diaz and Kauanui (2001, 320) further theorize Hawaiian indigeneity, using the *huli* transplant (cutting from the *kalo* stalk) for Hawaiians who have migrated off-island, and the *'ohā* (offshoot from the larger corm) for Hawaiians born off-island. These notions ground off-island indigeneity in genealogy and land.

Kauanui (1999b, 18) calls for "multiple diasporic frameworks that reckon with indigeneity, the persistence of homeland, and Hawaiian connections to other people who have their own claims to Hawai'i as home." It may be a while before we fully perceive the impact, contributions, and ancestral *mana* of our current younger generation of transplant Hawaiians. From within academia, transplant and home-grown indigenous students are fashioning the lenses that will help us to see.

you've seen them,
and you've heard them.

But now you know them by name!

All those years you thought you were alone.
. . . Honey, you were being carried.

You were being carried right home, here.
. . . Now it's given to you.

And I love you.

From a letter to Wayne:

Another thought is of not only your presence with
me, but Roxanna's presence as well. Since all these
events, and our visit, I have often felt the both of
you around me, and thought of you. Even though
we spent so little actual time together, it is as if we
spent years talking. Perhaps because every word
meant something. There is a thread that ties us all
together, dear brother. That thread transcends space
and time. I may not write, or seem near, but I am
always beside you. (LETTER FROM LEILANI)

Shortly after my birthday in 1998, I heard that
Wayne Davis had died. I was numb for days,
able only to register that his passing had left
a hole in my life. All I could think about was
our visit to Keaīwa Heiau, at 'Aiea, where we
had felt such a powerful sense of presence
and healing. I thought, too, of Pu'u o Mahuka
Heiau, at a confluence of tides, where early on I
had felt the presence of my ancestors. I remembered seeing at my feet a seemingly dead

AUNTY LAU AND THE MŪ

The kupuna *knows the answers. He has given me a*
kaona, *a phrase with multiple meanings. I open the door*
and (he) . . . is there, still sending thoughts. . . . He tells
me that we can talk story, or I can sleep while we travel to
the . . . heiau/marae. It is at the confluence of two different
tide systems (where) important practices related to atone-
ment take place. (From my dream)

> And she said
> "Until they undo what they did
> to these people that were formerly here,"
> she said,
> "they'll never be happy."
> She said,
> "You see how they *hukihuki?*
> *Hukihuki.*"
> She said "They'll never."

tree trunk, with new growth, young and green sprouting from it.

Weeks later I had a disturbing dream. Before I went to sleep, I worried about my writing. I felt that Wayne was not only a mentor who had helped me find and understand my ancestry, but also an elder brother. I also felt that I had not repaid Wayne for all that he had done for me.

She told me,
"You teach your children that.
So they know what love is."
(From Aunty Lau)

Asked about the future, Aunty Lau speaks about the enslavement and slaughter of the *mū* in the past, focusing on an age-old injustice for which an accounting must be made.

I wrote down my dream:

Ivan and I went to meet Wayne at a restaurant: it was empty inside except for a few tables. Wayne came in, looking ill. It was raining outside and he was wet; his white clothes clung to him. He looked confused, then he left. I ran out alone, desperate to find Wayne. I was running up a hill, toward the place Roxanna and Wayne took us to, the ʻŌpelu Project he couldn't go to.

Rain was coming down, and I was crying, calling his name. People along the way were pointing the way, saying, "He's OK." Finally I got to the project that Wayne never got to with me, where Roxanna and Malie and I had sat without Wayne. I was standing a little below the project. Slowly a blanket rose off a wooden bench in front of the project and Wayne was under the blanket. He smiled at me. I started crying again and ran up and hugged him fiercely. He hugged me for a long time. Then he said, "Let's walk together." His body seemed lighter, healed.

We walked rapidly down the hill, saying nothing, then we were in a kind of patch of plants. I couldn't see them clearly. We had to pass over the plants but they were covered with a big grid of wires. We were supposed to walk over this grid and I started to, very gingerly. Wayne too, but then he started bouncing on the wires. He was getting bruised, not moving forward, not getting off this grid of wires, bouncing way up, using it as a trampoline. Many of the wires had sprung and were sticking into his body. I was upset, terrified. It seemed he was doing it on purpose.

Finally he stopped, and the grid was in shreds. I looked underneath the grid and it was a taro patch. Wayne was lying there on top of the grid, bleeding.

Aunty Lau suggests that Hawaiians look at their behavior, question their ethics, undo unethical practices, and learn how to love. Aunty Lau's story about the *mū* creates a cycle of atonement that pulls me into synchronic time, where past and present seem to fuse. As we've seen, the term *mū* refers to the "legendary people of Lāʻau-haele-mai, Kauaʻi." *Mū* can also mean "silent; to shut the lips and make no sound" and "gather together, of crowds of people." The *mū* was also the public executioner who "procured victims for sacrifice and executed taboo breakers" (Pukui and Elbert 1986, 254–255).

When I gave Aunty Lau her pseudonym, I was thinking of a shortened version of the *lauhala* that she weaves. But it is useful for me to look at the term *lau* itself. *Lau* means "leaf, frond, leaflet, greens; to leaf out." *Lau* can also mean "to be much, many; very many, numerous," and *hoʻolau* can mean "to make numerous; to assemble, as of numerous persons or animals" (ibid., 194).

The idea of a gathering, and of a silence, reminds me of the *kāʻai* debate, another atonement story capable of pulling us into synchronic time. In 1828 Queen Kaʻahumanu (having converted to Christianity) destroyed two Big Island temples and reinterred the *kāʻai* to a cave. In 1858, King Kamehameha IV reinterred them near ʻIolani Palace near their relatives. In 1865 Kamehameha V moved them to the mausoleum at Mauna ʻAla, and in 1918 Prince Kūhiō sent them to Bishop Museum.

This series of chapters in the recent history of the *kāʻai* is marked by displacement. While Prince Kūhiō wanted the *kāʻai* to be studied as Hawaiian cultural accomplishments, they were cocooned in a metal drawer, silent, lips shut, closed off from their progeny and the ʻāina of their birth. In 1994 they were apparently taken back to Waipiʻo Valley, where, some would argue, they have returned home.

Yet he didn't seem hurt. I thought, "Wayne is dead, Wayne is dead." I ran for something to heal him. A first-aid kit—something. I ran back down the hill. Time was collapsing; it took only a dream-minute to get down the hill. I got the kit and ran up; he was sitting back at the project now, but he was already bandaged up, serenely smiling at me. Then I woke up.

For me this dream meant something about the book without Wayne as an advisor and mentor, but it was also a dream containing a message from Wayne. I spoke to Malie about the dream and she said, "Wayne was trying to tell you that it is all right, he is all right. It is time to let go, to let him go."

It is easy to imagine Wayne, having broken through the grids that artificially separate him from this taro patch, this *lo'i*. As a genealogist, Wayne often referred to that first sibling for Hāloa, the Kalo, also named Hāloa. It is easy to imagine Wayne, like Hāloa, inhabiting this *lo'i*, one blood with his elder brother, the Kalo. My body, a very calm space in my guts, is the site where I encounter this dream, which is actually a dream about being embodied in the world, and related, genealogically, through ancestry, to the cosmos.

I drive Aunty Mena to choir practice at her church. She gives me prayers to say to keep safe from the damage that can come from others' thoughts, intentions. I take her to the doctor, and she talks to him about gardening, food, and how she spent her childhood in the *lo'i*.

For the first time in decades my dad revisits Hawai'i. I have never really understood why he has chosen not to return. He describes a

The late Lydia Namahana Maioho, *kahu* of Royal Mausoleum, bewailed the taking of the remains without permission: "They are for all of us. Those *kā'ai* are for every Hawaiian. We have to take care of them." She had hoped they would be in her care at Mauna 'Ala, where other *ali'i* were assembled. However, she also said: "Maybe they really wanted to go back to Waipi'o. We haven't had any rumbling. There was no storm, there was no flooding" (Harden 1999, 82).

The story of the *kā'ai* is a story about the taking of the bones—or it is a story about how the bones came home. Either way, it is a story about *nā iwi*, about bones and about the material consequences of our actions. Ayau (1991, 247) reminds us that *nā iwi* symbolize the link between *kūpuna* (ancestors) and the living:

Nā iwi are placed in the ground to eventually become part of Haumea (Earth), thereby insuring a place for the bones forever. Most importantly, *nā iwi* impart the mana of the deceased to that ground, to that *ahupua'a* and eventually to the island. The entire area therefore becomes sacred with *mana.*

helicopter flight over Kaua'i that he decided to take. The mist seems to rise up as the helicopter swoops over the landscape. I feel as if I, too, am watching the mist rise, a *lei* adorning the uplands. I am beginning to understand that this story is about the presence of forces who watch over and protect me.

For my birthday, Ivan designs a visual featuring a large photograph of my mother that was taken just before she died. She is radiant, looking over her shoulder, probably smiling at the photographer. Near the bottom of that photograph, Ivan has inserted a smaller, older photograph of my thirty-four-year-old mother, looking exultantly at me, a four-year-old on her lap. As my young mother gazes at her adopted toddler, the radiant older woman whose bones were called home, seems to look out of the frame, directly at me. I put this visual by my desk at home where it bursts my aging heart. She smiles at me as if to say: "Here, I think this is probably ready for me to type." I feel her hand, cool on my forehead.

I talk to Malie over the phone, and she tells me that my half-sister has told my half-brother about me. He calls, and his voice, warm and calm, invites me to visit. For the moment we exchange letters and photographs. I remember how Wayne and others told me: "When it is time to know—you will know!" I remember Roxanna telling me: "You will meet your mother. It's going to be a half-sibling who will lead the way."

Yet I remember the *pueo* quietly sitting in the hands of the men at Nu'uanu, observing us.

Rose (1992) notes that the identities of the *kā'ai* are uncertain, not authenticated. Acceptence of their identities as Līloa and Lonoikamakahiki are understandable since these two *ali'i* were progenitors of the reigning Kamehameha family and related to many prominent eighteenth-century families. Cachola-Abad (1996, 226) questions whether it is necessary to know the names of deceased individuals in order to provide respectful burial treatment.

The debate about the *kā'ai* and the *kā'ai* themselves represent a convergence between '*āina*, sovereignty, and ancestry. Ayau sees the proper treatment of *nā iwi o nā kūpuna*, the bones of our ancestors, as an issue related to sovereignty—the right to practice cultural and spiritual beliefs (Ayau 1991, 263). The debate about the *kā'ai* deploys deep memory in service of atonement—healing the ethical present.[5]

In the *kā'ai* editorials in *The Honolulu Advertiser*, the bones are seen as the essence of Hawaiian identity and survival. Nobody in the debate questions their "identity" or "authenticity"; rather, the debate is about whether or not they should "return home."

What do "authenticity" and "returning home" mean for Hawaiian and other indigenous adoptees, who were taken from their communities, ancestry, and land? Patton (2000) notes that transracial adoptees struggle with issues concerning their history, origin, and meaning of their adoption.

I remember Kalo saying, "Every time a *kupuna* dies, I feel the knife cut into me." I imagine the deaths yet to come, in my lifetime. I imagine the wounded *pueo,* circling, circling, circling down, falling from the sky.

While I was listening to Malie's tape, I hit a lot of empty space—some problem with the tape recorder. It reminded me of my hysteria when the words of Tūtū ʻŌhiʻa were temporarily lost on the tape—my sense that the message was irretrievable.

Yet, while I sat letting the empty spaces on Malie's tape go by, it somehow felt as if those spaces were not actually empty. The "white" noise had a voice beneath it, Malie's, that had been inadvertently erased. I felt a strange sense of calm, listening to that white noise, figuring that maybe Malie's voice would return when some button was activated on her side.

This reminds me of the voices of our ancestors, who in my everyday thoughts exist as white noise. They speak clearly to me only in my dreams, hold me while I sleep, and fly down to touch my face.

At a Hawaiian Club event I see Aunty Limu, who is visiting for a while, on her way to Las Vegas. I tell her that I have found my people. She nods and twinkles at me and simply says, "I knew you would." I realize that somebody has already told her that I found them and has told her their identities. She has already reckoned that we are not related in near history. If we were related, she would tell me. I realize that, therefore, who my people are doesn't matter to her at this moment, as much as the

She states that in a society that idealizes "ideologies of authenticity," including biological kinship, adoptees, particularly transracial adoptees, are made to feel as if they are automatically inauthentic (ibid., 171).

For adoptees, the role of biological factors in identity formation is eliminated, leaving only socio-cultural factors. For transracial adoptees, this is a process complicated by issues of race and racism (ibid, 14). Transracial adoption privileges identity as solely socially constructed, yet in the transracial adoptee's everyday experience, biology and race often shape identity. This evidences incomplete attempts to pretend that race doesn't exist, by a race-conscious society.[6]

Indigenous adoption also activates issues about loss of ancestry. "Identity begins in the files of the U.S. child welfare system" (ibid., 21), so that the adoptee's ancestry is obscured.

"The Hawaiian adoptee will be unable to connect to other Hawaiians through ancestry, which has been excised from her experience—the adoptee is a genealogical isolate. Yet the off-island discussion of transracial adoption does not regard ancestry (or genealogy) as an element in identity formation. Media representations of adoptees' experience construct reunion with the birth mother (and occasionally the birth father) as closure for identity issues" (ibid.). The manner in which mainstream adoption patterns destroy

fact that I know and can remember my ancestry. Malie performs here in California, in a big auditorium. I sneak backstage and find her before her performance. As we hug one another I say, "I'll be in that auditorium listening to your voice for the second time. But this time, I know who you are, and I know who my ancestors are, and I know who I am." She hugs me and we just stand there for a moment, holding each other.

Later, Ivan, Aunty Mena, and I sit together, listening to Malie, and I am silent with the wonderment of knowing. Malie introduces me to the audience as her "long-lost" cousin. She dedicates a song to me, and her voice floats out to meet me, collapsing time and space.

After I return home, as I file away copies of the brochure from her performance, I come upon that old brochure from that first performance in Cleveland. I remember throwing it in the trash, then fishing it out. I threw it in the trash, dug it out again, looked at all those names. Those names were voices, were marked as carriers or even rememberers of older voices. Despite those voices, the brochure was the evidence of silence, of separation, a reminder that there was no such thing as ancestry. That is what I thought it was, when I threw it in the trash.

the genealogies of Hawaiian children who are adopted out is excluded from the discourse. The need to know one's ancestry or connect with one's ancestors is not part of the off-island discourse on adoption.

James Clifford (1997) suggests that identity involves a dialectic between roots and routes. Patton (2000, 18) asserts that roots are written over when a social worker maps out the new route for identity, "shaped by a sense of displacement." Without knowledge of biological origins, actual roots exist only as "alien . . . genetic maps sketched in indecipherable code" (ibid., 171). The indigenous adoptee may be defined as "other," but without authentic roots—without a way to decode that original biological map. The adoptee, who grew up "away from indigenous culture," may be labeled as "not really indigenous," or inauthentic.

I get off the plane in Honolulu, walk to the baggage claim, and after a lifetime apart, walk into the arms of my half-brother. He encircles me with *lei* made by his wife, a *lei*-maker. We travel to a friend's ranch, up a hill. That ranch looks out over a tiny island, where, my half-brother tells me, our great-grandfather and some others,

For indigenous adoptees, adoption is also an act of taking the body from the land, of sacrificing "home." For Pacific Islander adoptees, dislocation from the islands to an off-island location may involve a sense of exile. Others may assume that indigenous adoptees miss "home" and want

intent on driving the U.S. Marines off the island of O'ahu, hid the guns.

I visit my sister-in-law's *lei* stand and discover that it was her sister, also a *lei*-maker, who talked to me, a stranger in a bar at Waikiki, and told me, "We're *'ohana.*" There is a huge *pā'ina* at the house of a friend of theirs. We stand in a circle, holding hands, and the host gives thanks that my half-brother and I have found one another. I meet my niece and nephew, and their families. And looking out at me from their faces I see the eyes from my dream of a forest of eyes.

My niece and her daughters pore over their scrapbooks with me, telling me their histories. My half-brother and my cousin fill me with family stories. At a party at my half-brother's house before I leave to come home to San Diego, many relatives stay the night so we can have a last goodbye the next day. When I get back on the plane the next day, I am numb with the enormity of what has just happened.

After I return to San Diego, I fish out that old brochure from that first performance in Cleveland and look at it again.

Did my connections to my ancestors sprout roots, waiting for a fertile *lo'i* to grow in? And what or who provided that *lo'i?* Books? Dreams? Archives? Stories? Professors? *Kūpuna?* The repetitive, precise movement of a debate on cultural production? The repetitive, precise movement of feet and hands in a *hula?*

to return. Or others may assume that they have no relationship to "home." Others may invent an imagined history for the indigenous adoptee, a story of leaving home or coming home, of displacement or salvation. It may be a story that narrates a particular definition of—or erasure of—indigeneity.

Is indigeneity a particular relationship to colonization? Is indigeneity what happens when you live on a reservation, a reserve, an island, a particular area on an island? Is indigeneity an array of values and behaviors learned through socialization in an indigenous community? Is indigeneity having an ancestor who is indigenous? Is indigeneity meeting blood quantum requirements? Is indigeneity a genealogical connection to land? The experience and stories of indigenous adoptees force a complicated reading of these questions and a deeper consideration of the possible answers. I believe that so far, these questions, and their answers, constitute a text whose leaves are not yet opened, a story of bones, cocooned off, shrouded in silence.

In England, Ivan's mother dies suddenly of an infection, after a cancer operation that should have saved her life. He is numb with shock and going through the motions, only able to cry when he is dreaming. He takes early retirement from his workplace, and I take a leave of absence from work so we can work to put her affairs in order.

Then, on a whim, we take up my half-brother on his invitation to travel with his family to Tahiti to see the canoe race: Hawaiki Nui Va'a. Ivan and I are in Ra'iātea, with my half-brother, his wife, and our cousin. Dear friends of my sister-in-law take us into their homes as we await the event.

At the marae *(heiau)* at Taputapuātea I walk with my half-brother and cousin and suddenly the air seems charged, as we stand on these stones, our arms around each other. Our host's home is full of laughter, generosity, and children. They take us to a *motu* (tiny island), where we swim, eat, and talk story. Every evening there is *'ukulele* music, fresh fish, sometimes *hula*. My cousin sings and plays for the ceremony inaugurating the first leg of the race on Huahine. She invites me up for a *hula,* and I dance to the sound of her voice.

The next few days hundreds of canoes are at each start, and we follow the race by boat—traveling from Huahine to Ra'iātea, from Ra'iātea to Taha'a, then from Taha'a to Bora Bora. Every day we track the canoes by boat, as they skim toward the open sea, passing close enough for us to hear the paddlers. Sometimes they seem submerged by the waves. Toward the end of each leg, we speed ahead to the finish line to await the finishers. Each evening

TŪTŪ 'ŌHI'A AND THE 'OHULOA

I am aware that the stones left by the people to show others the way and to make offering will look like part of the landscape. I am fumbling to lock the door. The kupuna says to me, again, "What is the ancestry of experience? . . . (We are) going to a place like Waipi'o on the Big Island, Hawai'i, where there is a confluence, the great falls of Hi'ilawe, the birthplace of Kamehameha. I'm still trying to lock the door. "It is just such a place of confluence. It is a place of importance to you," he says, looking through me. As I wake up his voice says to me, "First, you must make your claims. Stake your ground then, and dig our voices up. We will manifest." (From my dream)

I was all alone with the 'ohuloa.
And when I got home I said to my husband,
"Take me to the doctor, I think I broke my arm."
He said, "How?"
I said, "I felt I was thrown down on these rocks.
I was pulling the 'ohuloa plant."
He said, "You didn't ask for it. You just took it."
"You had no business to just take it
without asking for it."
(From Tūtū 'Ōhi'a)

In Tūtū 'Ōhi'a's story the plant has consciousness and intent. Intentionality is a key concept in the phenomenological analysis of knowledge and experience. Being intentional is not only a characteristic of acts of consciousness; it is the essential characteristic or fundamental structure of consciousness itself. Intelligence is not only located in Tūtū 'Ōhi'a's mind—it is encoded in the 'ohuloa, which sends her a message. The key to Tūtū 'Ōhi'a's knowledge lies in her responsiveness to the message that the 'ohuloa sends and her interpretations of the intent behind that message.

we celebrate with our hosts, eating freshly caught fish, under the stars, playing, singing and laughing almost all night.

Finally at the finish at Bora Bora, at the final celebration, we sit together on a friend's boat, enjoy the sun, and play *'ukulele* before we leave for the airport. When we board the plane, I realize that as the canoes have made this journey, Ivan has inwardly made a journey about his mother's death. Some sadness has begun to leave his eyes. And I see that as the canoes have made this journey, I have come to realize the full impact of my own journey, watched always, by that forest of eyes.

Ivan and I prepare to travel to England where we will clear out his mother's house so that it can be sold. The day before we leave I am taking Aunty Mena to the doctor. Professional and polite when I first met him, the doctor now seems to sparkle when he sees Aunty Mena. He practices his newfound Hawaiian words on her, asking her how her *hula* teaching is coming along. After the doctor's visit and some errands, as I am dropping Aunty Mena at her house, she suddenly turns to me and says, "I should give you that *tī* plant" pointing at a sizeable *tī* plant in front of her house. "You will need this," she says.

I'm a bit surprised since it has been an ongoing joke between us that, because I travel so much, I am a born plant killer. This teasing intensified when one day she said that talking to my plants might help them to survive. I noted what a flourishing collection of potted plants and garden she had, and asked her what

Although the *'ōhi'a lehua* is the most likely candidate for the plant Tūtū 'Ōhi'a described, *kaona* emerges having to do with the term I "heard," *'ohuloa.* 'Ohu can mean "mist, fog, vapor, light cloud on a mountain; adorned as with leis," and *loa* is defined as "distance, length, height" (Pukui and Elbert 1986, 278, 209). I remember my imagined scene of Tūtū 'Ōhi'a gathering plants that grow in the heights as the mist floats about her, and my dream about the mist rising.

These evocative images lead me to reflect on how, through *hula*, dancers embody places. For example, dancers model the behavior of plants that grow on the heights, mist on the mountain. This sort of embodying practice strikes me as a kind of communion: The interior world of the dancer is attuned to the outer world of the earth and the cosmos. In *hula kahiko*, in particular, dancers perform the subjectivity of other (nonhuman)

she said to her plants to coax them so successfully into lushness. She said, "Oh, I just say to them, 'Grow or die.'"

As I prepare to leave, I suggest to Aunty Mena that I pick up the *tī* plant when I get back from England. She seems fine with that, and we talk for a while, before I leave. Our goodbye is especially fond, full of hugs, and I am saddened by the fact that I won't see her over the holidays.

England is wonderful and terrible. Ivan's family is kind and generous, but the grief that he feels is debilitating. We stay in the house and help it to disappear, day by day, item by item. He barely has time to reflect on his history, or decide on the destiny of the memoirs, photos, and much-loved items that inhabit her home. He ships many of her possessions to San Diego.

When we return to San Diego, exhausted and numb with sorrow, I play our voice mails, which I simply haven't had the energy to check. I find that on Christmas Day Aunty Mena had died in her sleep. Two of her students spoke to her the evening before, asking her if she was all right. They were concerned because she seemed tired and had a worrisome-sounding cough. When they asked her if she was OK, she looked at them and said, "Yes. I'm fine. God is with me." Unable the next day to get Aunty on the phone, her daughter Pilialoha, who lived a few hours away, spoke to one of the students and became very anxious. Finally, one student got into Aunty Mena's house and found her body, lying on her bed.

creatures and features of the universe. The movements of the dancers, particularly in *hula kahiko*, remind me of the affect attunement behavior of babies and mothers.

Affect attunement between child and parent involves a matching of some aspect of the other's behavior that reflects the other's feeling state. In *hula kahiko*, the dancer does not imitate the mist rising; she embodies the mist rising. Since affect attunement (unlike imitation) starts with an emotional resonance, it is similar to empathy, but it recasts that resonance into movement (Stern 1985, 142–145). In the case of *hula kahiko*, emotional resonance is recast into dance. Affect attunement does not necessarily become empathic knowledge or response, but is "a distinct form of affective transaction in its own right" (ibid., 145). In *hula kahiko* an emotional relationship arises between the dancer and the cosmos, through the embodiment of mist rising.

Stern (1985) says that feeling states to which we don't attune are experienced in isolation with no interpersonal context of shared experience. We can view affect attunement as a particular sort of conversation or communion. The dancer is in conversation, or communion with the mist as it rises. What is at stake for human-to-human affect attunement is the shape of and extent of the "shareable inner universe" (ibid., 151–152), a connection between the baby and the mother, both nodding.

Aunty Mena wrote her *hula* choreography onto scrolls using a particular method that made her intentions clear. Her scrolls allowed her to avoid relying on her own memory of the choreography. Her scrolls could also counter her students' faulty memories of her choreography. As students, we grew to depend on her scrolls, knowing that when we tried to remember her choreography we were most likely to remember only what worked for us. We faithfully recorded the contents of the scroll for each *hula* we learned, sitting cross-legged on the floor of Aunty's basement, where we danced.

Now Pilialoha visits her mom's house, full of the *hula* costumes she designed, scrolls, CDs, artifacts, hundreds of books: an overpowering legacy. Pilialoha and I seem to share a sadness that we had left Aunty Mena's *hālau*. I know that Pilialoha left, in part because her husband's job was elsewhere. Why did I leave? There was cancer, the divorce, Toronto, back to Grossmont, and the book. I think we both feel that Aunty Mena has no student who can truly carry her *hālau* forward now that she is gone.

Aunty Mena celebrated our lives. Pilialoha tells me that Aunty Mena talked to her about how proud she was of me, speaking of me as her student who taught college students. Aunty Mena told me countless times about how she was happy for Pilialoha but worried about her, especially when Pilialoha had breast cancer.

Both of us remember how Aunty Mena talked to us about family, about work, about our dreams. She did this despite the fact that we were no longer a part of her dream. But I know that we think of Aunty Mena and ask ourselves: "Why did I leave the *hālau*? Why did

Hula, in particular *hula kahiko*, as affect attunement behavior with *'āina*, stands in contrast with Berry's notion of environmental autism (1991). For earth-to-human affect attunement, the shape of the shareable outer universe is at stake. This is a cosmos that is shared between the dancer and *'āina*, shared sites where the mist rises. This fits Casey's notion that bodies and places "interanimate each other" (1996, 24).

This attunement has consequences, one of which is emplacement. Casey notes that we are placelings, emplaced through our bodies, often remembering a place from the point of view of our bodies (ibid., 19–21). Thus "even if such bodies may be displaced in certain respects, they are never placeless" (ibid., 24).

Hula kahiko is emplacing practice. Do societies bereft of emplacing practices result in generations of unemplaced humans, inclined to symbolically and literally obliterate *'āina*?[7] Casey (1987) says that places contain thoughts and memories; they are vessels for recollection. "Habitual body memory" involves remembering in and through the body as the past becomes "actively ingredient" in the bodily movements that are used to accomplish a particular action (ibid., 149). *Hula kahiko* is a form of remembering which involves knowledge of *'āina* experienced in and through the body. The body becomes a container for place, which is in turn a powerful container for historical memory.

Practitioners of *hula*, in particular, *hula kahiko*, transform their bodies into sites of historical memory as they embody *'āina*. The body becomes a container for place, even if the body has been displaced, a container for historical memory, even if written history has textually displaced memory.

I leave you?" When we ask one another this on the phone we break down, and there is sobbing on both ends of the line. Who did we think we were? Where did we think we were going?

Every time Pilialoha comes down to San Diego to work on Aunty Mena's house, Aunty Mena's students gather there, play tapes of her singing and playing, and dance her *hula* together. Each time the group gets bigger. Meanwhile, after speaking with Pilialoha, I have begun to meet with Aunty Mena's students who were in their first year of *hula* when she died. We work on the *hula* and methods that Aunty Mena would have worked with them on, had she lived. Since they have joined other *hālau hula*, our purpose is to provide an ongoing sense of connection to Aunty Mena. It is obvious that we all need to meet together to dance Aunty Mena's *hula.*

For about six years, I let *hula* with Aunty Mena languish and then die out while I worked on this book. And after a while I just let the book, like *hula*—languish.

Instead, I focused on creating and teaching a class in Pacific Islander studies at my college. Undergrad anthropology majors, Pacific Islander students, surfers, members of *hālau hula*, and "seekers-of-the-right-general-education-class-time-slot" signed up. We critiqued classic and current ethnographies, held an occasional round table Q and A about the Pacific Islander diasporic experience, and when *hālau hula* members in the class were so inclined, got to see some excellent *hula*.

When I think back to Tūtū ʻŌhiʻa's story of the plant, knowledge is not the discovery of new information, nor is it activated solely from within Tūtū ʻŌhiʻa. Rather, it is the repetition of an older pattern, the result of Tūtū ʻŌhiʻa's knowing how to connect with *ʻāina*, and, therefore, how to connect with historical memory.

Casey (1987, 192) describes how the "lived body" appropriates familiar places and activates knowledge about those places that is "bred of familiarity." This is not new knowledge, but is the repetition of old patterns. If, in *hula kahiko*, the body can become a site for powerful pre-Contact rememberings of *ʻāina*, then it is *ʻāina* that appropriates the "lived body" and activates knowledge. And by taking up identity as a link between the body and *ʻāina*, by invoking pre-Contact themes and deep memory, *hula kahiko* enacts a powerful cosmology for sovereignty.

Stillman (2001) notes that poetic texts of *hula* evoke collective memories, which are central to discourses about identity. She notes that "for Hawaiians, the *hula* encodes and transmits key knowledge about the historical past through which they define themselves" (ibid., 189). As the connection between body and place is amplified, the connection between body and the memories held by place is amplified. Enacting the past through *hula*, in particular *hula kahiko*, can thus involve an interrogation of the present and a wayfinding process for the future.

I am invited to speak on a panel with an amazing gathering of Hawaiian scholars—all women. As a community college instructor who has not published any work, I wonder why I have been asked. When I meet them they offer their acceptance, support, and advice. As I listen to their presentations, currents of memory and intention begin to move inside me. One of them (who was, it turns out, a reviewer for my book) takes me aside and urges me to find a way to publish it.

I return home and hold the manuscript in my hands. I am suffused with sadness. Why did I leave this manuscript? Why did I leave you? Who did I think I was? Where did I think I was going?

And then my father, at the age of ninety-four, loses his energy and becomes very frail. *Hula*, the Pacific Islander class, the manuscript—all forgotten, I visit him often, thankful that he lives nearby. He finally stops driving, and now I am around even more, taking him on errands, especially to the doctor. My father talks about the past much more now, and he reminds me of the day that he and my mother first saw me. He asks about the book, and about my newfound relatives.

He becomes ill, and in the hospital we find that it is congestive heart failure, kidney failure, and it is time to let go. As he begins to slide under I say to him, "I love you, Dad." And all he can say, over and over again until he is gone is, "My sweet daughter. My sweet daughter." And I realize where I was going, all this time. I was just going full-circle, having a life, connecting, reconnecting, doing what matters.

Malie Wahine Ke'ali'i o Ke Kai
Mary the Queen of the Ocean

Stillman (2001) describes how vital *hula* repertoire disappeared from public circulation and was institutionalized in archives, cocooned off from those who should have inherited it. She notes that "performers and audiences alike were increasingly cut off from engaging with processes of remembrance" (ibid., 190). When these texts were entombed, much of the repertoire of *hula* was dismembered and Hawaiian intergroup memory was interrupted.

Stillman notes that *hula* texts enable us to remember "what poets of the past wanted, or needed, to express" so that it can be "remembered" or "embodied" in the bodies of performers" (ibid., 201).Yet, she notes, the result of institutional practices is that performers who could embody these texts are prevented from engaging "processes of memory invited by those very texts"—a form of dispossession (ibid., 201–202).[8]

Stillman asserts that bringing these institutionalized *hula* texts out of the archives represents "a way to begin decolonizing knowledge" (ibid.). It seems to me that the story of recovery of *hula* texts, like that of the *kā'ai* and perhaps like my own story, is a story about atonement and the return of *nā iwi*. Like those stories, it is also a story about remembering, which for Stillman is "an act of advocacy . . . asserting determination over historical knowledge" (ibid.).

So now, I return to writing this manuscript—the reason why I left *hula* and why I am going back to *hula*. I begin to ask: How does knowledge happen? Is it created by individuals who follow ideological maps borrowed from imposed socio-economic worlds? Is it guided by *'āina* and ancestors through seeming coincidence, unnamed structures of intention, and odd choices? Is it a list of categories piling up? Is it voices manifesting? Is it a book being laid down? Is it a *hula* being taken up? Is it the mist rising in a forest of eyes?

Like the *kā'ai* and like indigenous adoptees who live in the space in between, these *hula* texts may seem to fall silent. But they have powerful voices that give breath to timeless stories. These stories will be taken up and will be embodied. We will dig these voices up, and they will manifest.

Conclusion

Bones and Voices

I close my eyes for a moment, as I write the last page of this book.

My ancestors are with me momentarily, just behind me. These are not souls I can connect to in this world, yet their presence is more deeply felt than that of many people I talk to every day.

There are losses—my mother, my father, Aunty Mena, Wayne. But there are always new gifts. On my birthday, I access my phone messages and hear a warm voice: "This is your sister, wishing you a happy birthday." My (half-)sister sends me photos of my family and my ancestors, and invites me to visit. A new connection grows.

I close my eyes, and my ancestors are behind my eyes. Their voices are white noise, but that is because my ear is not tuned to hear.

I am largely an outsider to the deeper layers and complexities of Hawaiian cosmology, language, and systems of signification. Yet I do know that there are crucial times when we must dig up the voices of our ancestors, these voices that have not been heard, that arrive from the past; and we must try to understand what they say.

Because the histories we create, made up of connectable incidents, are sometimes not as important as the manifesting of old stories, old voices, old songs. Those voices are reordering the cosmos.

We must manifest our ancestors in the present, not because of historical facts, but because of their being rendered invisible and what that invisibility means in the world. We carry their stories in our bones. The rhythm of those stories, their righteousness—those are the heart stories that we have lost, that are so difficult to read.

I speak in an academic voice for any number of reasons, but that voice falters here, and all I know is that when I was a child, my ancestors came down in the night and touched my face.

My feet are on a particular *'āina*, but that *'āina* does not always come up through my feet and into me. I am not of any particular place, yet I am of a particular place.

I am an outsider, but my ancestors cradle me in their arms still. They fly down to touch my face in my dreams.

I know I will be with them again someday and this frightens me, because it will mean that my time is up for trying to do something good here.

We talk so little about this,
about how our ancestors and those who love us
embrace us, about how we will someday join
them, about how meanwhile, we learn so little
from their good or bad deeds.

About how there is so little time to act on
behalf of their bones.

Appendix A

Cast of Characters

Note: Aunty Philomena Keali'i Waine'e Aranio, her daughter Pilialoha, Ivan Holmes, Wayne Keona Davis, Roxanna Davis, George J. Sefa Dei, and Linda Rose Locklear are named with their consent, since they were in an advisory role as I wrote this book, and reviewed my manuscript. All those who gave interviews or crossed my path in Hawai'i are given pseudonyms to protect their anonymity. My blood relatives are given pseudonyms to protect my birth mother's anonymity.

Aileen Kawahara: A Child and Family Services Social Worker.

Aunty Aho: A kupuna who was interviewed on TV.

Aunty Hala: A kupuna who was interviewed on TV.

Aunty Jane: Tūtū 'Ōhi'a's daughter.

Aunty Kimo: Kimo's wife. Kimo and Aunty Kimo sold leis behind a restaurant I visited.

Aunty Lau: A kupuna who was interviewed by Kalo.

Aunty Limu: A kupuna who teaches lauhala on O'ahu; she refused my formal interview but I spent quite a bit of time with her, and wrote notes on those experiences.

Aunty Mena: Philomena Keali'i Waine'e Aranio, a kupuna and kumu hula for Hālau o Hale Loke, was born in Honolulu, and spent her early childhood with her tūtū on the island of Hawai'i. She spoke only Hawaiian and they farmed kalo. At age ten she returned to Honolulu where she remembers being slapped on the hand when she spoke Hawaiian. As a young adult she studied hula under Joe Kahaulelio, Henry Pa, and Lokalia Montgomery, and achieved her 'ūniki (graduated) under Joe Kahaulelio.

Aunty Rita: A kupuna living in San Diego who was mentioned by Aunty Limu.

Barbara: (Pseudonym) my birth mother, also the pseudonym of my half-sister.

Big Sis: Niece to Kalo, interviewed by Kalo in the 'ohana interview.

Bruce: (Pseudonym) my half-brother.

Dad: Brother-in-law to Kalo, interviewed by Kalo in the 'ohana interview.

Donald: (Pseudonym) my half-brother.

Eemee Face: The elderly Chinese woman in my dreams, who may have cared for me according to my origin myth.

Gard: Kalo's husband, who is haole and college educated.

George J. Sefa Dei: My graduate advisor and thesis (dissertation) chairperson at Ontario Institute for Studies in Education/University of Toronto.

Grama: Kalo's mother, who was interviewed by Kalo in the 'ohana interview.

Ivan Holmes: My husband, whom I met in the Marquesas.

Junior: Nephew of Kalo, interviewed by Kalo in the 'ohana interview.

Kalo: My friend from San Diego, living in Hawai'i, whom I interviewed, and who interviewed kūpuna.

Kimo: Aunty Kimo's husband. Kimo and Aunty Kimo sold leis behind a restaurant I visited.

L'il Sis: A niece to Kalo, interviewed by Kalo in the 'ohana interview.

Malie Wahine Ke'ali'i o ke Kai: (Pseudonym) "Mary the Queen of the Ocean," my cousin. I asked Aunty Mena to give her a pseudonym. On waking one morning, Aunty Mena was inspired with this pseudonym, which she wrote, and which I have used, exactly as written.

Mom: Kalo's sister, interviewed by Kalo in the 'ohana interview.

Peyton: A friend of my cousin who lived down the road from her at Pūpūkea, and with whom I stayed while I was visiting Hawai'i.

Roxanna Davis: Wife of Wayne Keona Davis, genealogist.

Tūtū 'Ōhi'a: A kupuna, interviewed by Kalo, whose daughter is Aunty Jane.

Wayne Keona Davis: Genealogist for The Royal Order of Kamehameha I, husband of Roxanna Davis.

Appendix B

A Hula for Aunty Mena

Following is a hula choreographed in honor of Aunty Mena. In the absence of live music, it works to use "Ka Loke Polena: *The Yellow Rose*" by Anthony "Tony" K. Conjugacion, as performed by Raiatea Helm on her CD: Raiatea.

Ka Loke Polena: *The Yellow Rose*

Break: wāwae ki'i right uwehe: left hand at hip, right wave out to right side (reverse footwork and hands)

VERSE: 1 (2X)

Kaulana i ka nani o ku'u pua: *Famed is the beauty of my blossom*

Left hand up, right hand move left side to front, palm down, turn palm over; both hands to eyes and up, palms in
Kāholo right, left
Left hand on hip, right hand wave at self 2X; pick flower right, waist-high with both hands, then lift to right
Step brush uwehe right, left

He nani 'i'o nō ia loke polena: *A true beauty is this yellow rose*

Left hand on hip, right hand to eye (wave 2X); right hand up, palm out, then move slightly down, palm in
Kāholo right, left
Hands pick rose right, chest-high, hold up; open blossom, then move hands down to waist level
Step brush uwehe right, left

VERSE: 2 (1X)

Hōli'o ko maka me ka 'ōlinolino: *Dazzling are your eyes that sparkle*

Hands up to the right wave 2X (palms out); wave 2X at eyes
Kāholo right, left
Hands out and "twinkle" (flick in and out) at eyes 4X
Step brush uwehe right, left

He mino'aka kou poina 'ole ia: *And your smile so unforgettable*

Hands to mouth, then out, flip over so palms are up
Kāholo right, left
Left hand on hip, right at chest; look down over right shoulder
Left hand at chest, right hand up, shake head, forefinger back and forth
Step brush uwehe right, left

VERSE: 3 (1X)

Ho'ina i ka mana'o hāli'ali'a: *A fond recollection comes to me (of you)*

Hands out, pull in and cross at self, left arm held chest-high, right elbow at left hand, right hand point at temple
Kāwelu left side, then right side
Gather hands from right (high) to self, then left (high) to self
Kāholo right, left

Kāwelu i ke aheahe a ka makani: *Swaying gently amidst the gentle breeze*

Left hand on hip, right at chest, then reverse
Kāwelu left side, then right side
Left hand out left side, right over head, then out right (reverse)
Kāholo right, left

VERSE: 4 (1X)

Ke kani hone a nā manu o Lehua: *The sweet voices of the birds of Lehua*

Hands 2X at mouth, hands wave at shoulders 2X
Kāwelu left side, then right side
Swooping bird, left hand high (in back of head), right low dip twice at
    knee level (reverse)
Kāholo right, left

Hū a'e mai ke aloha i ke ahe eaea: *Swelling up with love, lilting on the air*

Swoop hands down, scoop up, then wave 2X at heart
Kāwelu left side, then right side

Hands cross each other in air (palms out, then in), then wave down to
    self and give out from self
Kāholo right, left

VERSE: 5 (1X)

He aheahe ka makani o Wai'ōpua: *Gentle as the Wai'opua breeze*

Hands up to right, left (palms out); left hand front, right overhead, then
    out
Hela right left, right left
Hands make waves down 2X right, then make island (dip hands once
    front, then circle hands out front)
Kāholo right, left

Ke'ala onaona e moani nei: *Attractive is your sweet wafting scent*

Left hand up, right hand to nose, wave 2X, out front and turn palm up
Hela right left, right left
Zigzag hands from up left, across right, down left, down right; put left
    hand on hip, draw right hand out right
Kāholo right, left

VERSE: 6 (2X)

Neia ku'u mele o ku'u pua: *This is my song of my beloved*

Left hand at chest, right hand at mouth and out right (reverse)
Hela right left, right left
Left hand on hip, right hand wave at self, pick flower right waist-high
Kāholo right, left

Ka pua loke polena poina 'ole ia: *The yellow rose, so unforgettable*

Both hands pick rose waist-high, hold up and raise higher; open
    blossom, then move hands down
Hela right left, right left
Left hand on hip, right at chest, look down over right shoulder
Left hand at chest, right hand up, shake head, forefinger back and forth
Kāholo right, left

nonwhiteness as an exclusion of whiteness, an accusation of whiteness, and a rebellion against racism. Perhaps my story unravels here, because I am only narrating my own search for "self."

14 Wayne Keona Davis (1995) suggests that Kamakau may have meant that at the coming of foreign Christian missionaries, the Hawaiian religious/social order was in disarray and the gods had been "overthrown." He notes that over forty years had passed since Cook had first arrived and in that time a whole generation of Hawaiians had been born and attained middle age. It was by then common to see a foreigner breaking a *kapu* without apparent punishment from gods or *ali'i*. For instance, sailors regularly ate with women, and these same women often ate food traditionally reserved for men, without apparent punishment.

Because of these foreign influences, along with death-dealing sicknesses, it appeared that their gods were forsaking the Hawaiians. According to Wayne Keona Davis, it is then not surprising that at the death of Kamehameha I, champion of the old ways, lingering doubts of the people in the old system/religion surfaced with the "official" breaking of the eating *kapu* by Liholiho, his mother Keopuolani, and Ka'ahumanu. These events led to the upheaval of the old gods. Within a year the missionaries arrived.

15 I am using my *kumu hula*'s text, since it's taken from her knowledge line. For a more "orthographically correct" version, and different translation, see Beamer 1987, 58.

Chapter 2

1 Marx's view of nature combines naturalism and humanism (Bottomore 1983, 215) and could be described as modern. Although Grundmann (1991, 91–92) critiques "ecologists' attacks on Marx," he acknowledges that Marx's view of nature is essentially modern. Merchant (1989) talks about the genesis of the "modern" view of nature in Europe, as the subsistence economy was largely replaced by the accumulation of profits in an international market. The death of nature, according to Merchant, was the most influential "accomplishment" of the scientific revolution. Along with it came a system of values based on power, and very much in sync with the goals and projects of commercial capitalism. Merchant notes:

Living inanimate nature died, while dead inanimate money was endowed with life. Increasingly capital and the market would assume the organic attributes of growth, strength, activity, pregnancy, weakness, decay, and collapse obscuring and mystifying the new underlying social relations of production and reproduction that make economic growth and progress possible. (ibid., 288)

Shiva (1988) asserts that epistemologies attending the death of nature resulted in violence against nature and violence against organic systems of knowledge, which were rejected as irrational. The disconnected consciousness mirrored material disconnections created in relation to land, inviting an erasure of indigenous epistemologies.

2 Political economy is particularly helpful in describing how the state dispossesses indigenous peoples (Povinelli 1995). Kulchyski (1992) uses Marx's idea of totalization to discuss Canadian indigenous peoples' attempts to reestablish or sustain their own ways of life, on their own land. Totalization is a process in which the capitalist state attacks all social forms impeding it and destroys pre-capitalist

social relations. Social relations are reshaped to fit the expansion of the commodity form, and land, people, objects, and symbols are transformed into commodities (Kulchyski 1992; Ollman 1993). Serialized space and time are imposed on indigenous peoples and individualization works to obliterate cultural differences between groups and communal connections within groups. Yet, from the margins of dominant society, indigenous peoples may find ways to subvert the totalizing effects of capital. Resistance may be "deeply coded" and may live "more in the everyday than in any sphere of existence" (Kulchyski 1992, 174, 188). Kulchyski's work is helpful in understanding how present-day indigenous knowledge gets produced from within, yet embodies resistance to capitalist formations.

Silva (2000) uses political economy to discuss the ban on *hula*. She argues that the desire to ban *hula* reflected a confluence of a Puritan work ethic imbued with a disdain for Hawaiian practices and an economic need for laborers imbued with the notion that *hula* "encouraged idleness" (ibid., 31, 33, 39). *Hula* was seen as depriving plantations of cheap native labor. Silva relates the banning of *hula* to the project of establishing colonial capitalism and establishing control over Hawaiian labor.

3 Some writers collected, described, and authenticated ancient Hawaiian oral tradition, working with Hawaiian informants. For early writing, mostly by non-Hawaiian anthropologists, see Emerson (1893, 1965, 1978); Fornander (1969); Handy (1927, 1940); Handy and Handy (1972); Handy and Pukui (1972). For writing outside of anthropology or by Hawaiians, see Beamer (1987); Kahananui (1962); Kanahele (1979, 1986); Pukui (1983); Pukui, Haertig, and Lee (1974a, 1974b). Pukui, a scholar who possessed great family knowledge of Hawaiian tradition, worked with anthropologists and scholars in other fields. For further discussion on cultural production, see Barrére, Pukui, and Kelly (1980); Charlot (1987); Kaeppler (1993); and Pukui and Korn (1973).

Others discussed modern-day Hawaiians, writing about acculturation, cultural differences, or how ancient traditions are articulated in the lives of present-day Hawaiians. See Beaglehole (1937); Boggs (1985); Gallimore, Boggs, and Jordan (1974); Gallimore and Howard (1968); Howard (1974); Shook (1985). Much writing honored the divide between pre-Contact (or ancient) and post-Contact (or modern) Hawaiian culture.

Descriptions of Hawaiian culture/cultural production also functioned as entry codes into theoretical issues. Scholars advanced the notion of a dialectical relationship between structure and history (or agency) in relation to Hawaiian (and Polynesian) responses to contact. See Dening (1980, 1988); Obeyesekere (1992); Sahlins (1981, 1992); Valeri (1985). A critical anthropology of colonialism and political economy emerged, discussing the effects of colonialism on Hawaiians and the ways that Hawaiians accommodated, negotiated, and resisted Western expansion. Local forms of response to global capitalism were a central focus of this writing. One thread of this discussion built on Sahlins's (1981, 1992) suggestion that the everyday reenactment of cosmology could affect societal structure. While political economy conceptualizes praxis as setting the conditions for cultural structure, Sahlins used the example of Hawai'i to posit cultural structure as setting the conditions for praxis. He thus bent the lens of political economy in order to analyze Hawaiian cosmology.

4 For core arguments, see Handler and Linnekin (1984); Hanson (1989); Keesing (1978, 1989, 1991, 1994); Linnekin (1983, 1985, 1990,

1991a, 1991b, 1992); and Linnekin and Poyer (1990). In rebuttal, Friedman (1992a, 1992b) interrogated the accuracy of inventionist claims and the degree to which these claims enacted issues to do with power. Trask (1991) offered a rebuttal coming from Hawaiian vantage points. This debate offered contesting views of Polynesian cultural practices and identity. In Hawai'i's case, where a cultural revival had been taking place for over a decade, debates often concerned the enactment of identity within cultural practice.

5 Linnekin (in Linnekin and Poyer 1990, 161) discussed how "false cultures" which are static are produced by tourist industries, nationalists, and scholars, while, in contrast, Jolly (1994) opened up a space to view tourist performances as dynamic, rather than static. Jolly argued that a process of turning culture into a "thing" might be termed "an intensification rather than a complete rupture with pre-colonial practices" (ibid., 257).

6 Linnekin also said that "the theme of such stories is that the dead vouchsafe family property to their descendants, who are to be caretakers in their turn" (1985, 85). I don't think this formulation quite gets to the role of land. As a consequence, there is not much space for a deeper analysis of how land and practice are related. Linnekin's description of the probable future of the Hawaiian community she researched attended to political, and most especially economic, variables. She focused on the continuance of economic exchange, reproducing Marx's economistic notions.

7 Thomas (1997, 10) suggested that Hanson called up exogenous images which worked to expose the Maori cultural renaissance as politically tarnished:
> We are invited to visualize a handful of power-hungry Maori activists sitting around a table in a smoke-filled room, flipping through the pages of discredited texts of colonial ethnology and cynically figuring out what it might be most convenient to invent next.

Thomas asserted that Hanson's binary notion of tradition versus change constituted Western ideology, discussing how exogenous artifacts come to symbolize the power of capital to transform indigenous values:
> Thus, a tribe amongst whom grass skirts are still worn will be seen as comparatively untarnished by foreign intrusion, while it is obvious that Samoans or Tongans who wear digital watches and possess radios or videos have leapt across the gulf between the traditional and modernity and can no longer be expected to have any distinctively native culture. (ibid., 172)

Exogenous images offer a visual shorthand for the belief that capital taints cultural production, distilling and deploying the cosmology of political economy. In another context, Stead (1994) critiqued four Pacific Islander authors by deploying exogenous elements in their lives (using faxes, traveling in Europe, and winning awards) in order to detract from their "authenticity" as indigenous authors (xvii). This strategy, which wouldn't "work" on nonindigenous authors, is enabled by pre-existing notions about destiny, in relation to indigenous peoples.

In contrast, Sahlins discussed a successful indigenous artist, whose life uncynically encompassed exogenous elements, thus creating his own indigenous space within dominant culture. Sahlins called this "the indigenization of modernity" suggesting that indigenous people use exogenous objects to shape their own destinies (1994, 390). While the discussion of "nonnative" elements in "native lives" narrowed the discursive space within which indigenous artists and writers could voice indigenous cosmologies, Sahlins's work widened that space.

8 For a critique of claims made about colonization, see Jolly 1992 and Thomas 1997. Sahlins, unlike most other discussants, drove the discussion toward issues of cosmology by bringing up the topic of prophecy (1994, 387). Prophecy, the cosmological "other" of European arrival, works to disable notions of destiny as linked to European agency and the movement of capital. By mentioning prophecy, Sahlins contained the European presence and its accompanying cosmology, conferring agency on indigenous people and an indigenous cosmos. Trask also ruptured the notion of destiny, saying: "When compared with Hawaiian self-governance for over 2,000 years prior to annexation, the few decades of American control are paltry indeed" (1993, 38, 39).

9 Claims about knowledge and power spanned a wide continuum, shifting onto the topic of academic identities and discursive authority, and becoming part of a larger discussion about how ethnography enacts power. Linnekin downplayed the possible consequences of cultural construction, and felt that it was inclusive of nonscholarly voices (992, 250). Jolly believed that writers should avoid "a style of writing that presumes Western scholars have the truths and Pacific politicians are perpetrating illusions or self-delusions." (1992, 63). Tobin stated that Hawaiians are treated only as potential "informants" and that their voices were "shut out" (1994, 125). Thomas (1997) discussed cultural construction as an attempt to regain academic authority.

10 Since this time, work on indigenous epistemologies, particularly taken up by Pacific Islander scholars, has emerged. This work focuses on the experiences and formulations of everyday Pacific Islanders. For work on Hawaiian mentors, centralizing 'āina, experience, and genealogy as epistemological themes, see Meyer (2001). For work on indigenous knowledge in regards to identity, place, and addressing Pacific Islander colonial history, see Gegeo (2001).

11 This dream was the first time I heard the phrase "ancestry of experience." Davis (1995) speaks of ancestry as having to do with the steps, levels, strata, or generations through time past to the present and the future. He likens the phrase "ancestry of experience" to the term "wisdom of ages." He notes that when kūpuna are asked, "How and when will I know?" they say, "You will know someday when you are ready." Davis asserts that:
> This implies not only mental maturity in order to understand, but also time to learn "through experience" or through various little or seemingly unconnected experiences, that, over time, add to and build upon total experience and through that—knowledge. This, I think, also teaches one patience and humbleness (ha'aha'a) or not being a "know-it-all" or having a "big head" while keeping one attuned to his/her experiences. (ibid., 3)

12 For a discussion of how both modernist truth-value and postmodernist deconstruction are woven through this debate, see Linnekin (1992). For links between the postmodern project and capitalist modernity, see Friedman (1992b). Although there were tensions between modernist (political economy) and postmodern arguments, both vantage points shared a cosmology that excises

ancestry and land (or cosmos) as potential sources of present-day knowledge.

13 I believe that it is impossible to talk about indigenous identity without positing the subjectivity of land as related to ancestry. This is not to say that Hanson, Keesing, and Linnekin routinely obscure land and ancestry in all their work. It is possible that as they narrate their fieldwork, in certain cases, despite an economistic frame, they can construct land and ancestry as key to indigenous identity. For instance, the focus of Hanson's (1970) work on Rapa was how Rapans "own and exploit property to secure their material livelihood." Using a framework of political economy he attempted to understand cultural meanings associated with "things economic" such as the sentimental value of land, and the relationship between land and ancestry (ibid., 40–48). This work can be seen as Hanson's attempt to understand Rapan worldviews and notions about land, using an economistic frame.

Chapter 3

1 The sociology research protocol of having people sign forms giving their "informed consent" to use their words and guaranteeing their anonymity before I could tape their words made sense. However, my initial plan to tape events or other conversations felt wrong, so I decided that in those cases, I'd just write down the experiences I had as *"mana'o"* (my own thoughts).

Anonymity ensures confidentiality for the people who as interviewees spoke to me about their personal experiences and feelings. Interviewees' signatures gave their permission for me to quote their descriptions of their experiences and feelings and ensured their anonymity. Their stories, which would normally be circulated only by them, are into wide (and unknown) circulation, sometimes divorced from the context of their telling. Under these conditions I feel that their privacy should be ensured.

There are others who were not quoted from interviews, but whose experiences and words are now into circulation, though as a less formal part of my narrative. Therefore, their privacy is also protected by anonymity. Field notes and interviews were transcribed from tapes. When excerpts from field notes and interviews are used in this work, the name of the tape and the line numbers are listed.

2 Other ideas outside ethnomethodology focus on everyday talk. Sociolinguistics (linguistics) discusses the distribution of talk; pragmatics (philosophy) discusses speech acts characterizing speaker-hearer relations; conversation analysis (sociology) discusses rules governing conversation; and the ethnography of talk (anthropology) discusses how language represents social relationships.

Practice theory (Bourdieu 1990) and structuration theory (Giddens 1984) see dispositions or structures as the basis for the repetitive patterns in talk. Traditional ideas about talk and culture have reified these structures or dispositions as "culture." Discourse analysis involves the study of the structures of texts or (in the U.S. in particular) everyday conversation or talk from an ethnomethodological perspective.

These ideas are similar to ethnomethodology in that they focus not so much on cultural norms as on practical, repeated everyday precedents. I believe that as we find ways to explain our lives and account for ourselves, the stories we tell organize our experience and shape our behavior. We voice experiences that fit, and exclude

those that don't. The way we interpret our experience powerfully shapes our lives.

3 Critiquing this idea, Davis (1995) noted:
I thoroughly understand your feeling at the time of your various interviews and "near" interviews. I believe that your "cultural/bloodline" sub-consciousness was at work. "Connectedness" or relationship (by blood or otherwise) is and always has been an important introductory step . . . to establishing a basis for conversation or acceptance into one's "circle." "What part of my life experience or genealogy do you fit? What common ground do we have so that we may be comfortable with each other and not feel threatened by any implied or unknown influences?". . . Your discomfort was due to this gap in your life: Although you are of Hawaiian blood, in what way could you explain your "connectedness"? As it turns out, today you could establish "relationship," I'm sure, with many whom you felt then as "not in any way related!" You were correct in knowing you needed "Kalo's" physical presence to establish your "connectedness" then.

4 This was quite a reduction in questions, considering that I had initially proposed more than twenty specifically worded questions, which would have taken the interviews in a more focused, yet less deep-delving direction. These questions covered three general areas: people's views of their Hawaiian ancestry/identity, how they related to and experienced cultural production and events, and how they related to and experienced *kūpuna*'s stories.

5 The sense of being on two different topics, yet actually being on two different sides of the same story, relates the process of knowing that seems to go on in the *'ohana*. It seems that family members are sharing in the construction of this story from different vantage points. In this interview, meaning seems to be created through participation (Borofsky 1994, 338). In this particular case, and in others throughout the interview, the notion that there should be some static, agreed-upon corpus of knowledge owned by all family members is not only problematic, but misses the point. The central point, for me, is that the *'ohana* perform knowledge and create spaces to think critically about their experiences. They are not reciting a static corpus of knowledge; rather they are creating a process of "coming to know."

6 The chaining that members do, as they complete one another's sentences, is notable. Borofsky (1994, 338) notes that:
We might focus . . . on the conditions that structure knowing into knowledge. . . . People, in interacting with one another, come to share certain ways of communicating, or associating, with one another.

The *'ohana*'s talk involves chaining some formulations and rupturing others. In this way they shape a debate that reveals the complicated spaces that can exist in post-Contact Hawai'i, as it struggles to decolonize. Yet, for the *'ohana* that debate exists in a context of acceptance and close connection. That debate constitutes a process of knowing, a meaningful and purposeful activity of knowledge creation.

7 This juncture in the interview involves comments that lead me to feel that Mom, Kalo, and Dad are interrogating the notion of blood quantum. Their questions and answers don't strike me as a search for information. Rather, it seems that they are artfully performing

the limitations of the concept of blood quantum. When Mom asks, "How much you need to be Hawaiian?" I think that she is asking about (and perhaps unmasking) the legal concept of blood quantum. Dad's answer, "Quarter maybe," carries that same feel, and his offhand tone seems to render the "fraction" unimportant.

As I read their formulations, I am very aware of my presence in the interview. I sit on the couch between them, awkwardly holding the tape recorder and turning it this way and that to catch a whispered phrase or distance the noise of a baby crying. I am definitely in the role of the audience, and their social performance is at least as important as the informational content of the interview.

8 This notion of having one's identity structured by others and of being divested of the opportunity to name one's world is explored by Wood (1999, 9) who discusses "the violent rhetoric of names," referencing the terms Hawaiian and Kanaka Maoli. He notes that the term Kanaka Maoli grounds Hawaiianness in the land, while Euroamerican emphasis on blood-quantum "makes it reasonable for foreigners to claim that Hawaiians will continue to exist even if, for example, they are all forced to relocate and live far from their ancestral islands" (ibid., 13). For me, this formulation by Wood echoes Dad's formulations. In the 'ohana's discussion, the topic of language loss often segues into the topic of loss of land.

9 Dad consistently resists the invoking of "blood quantum," which includes a discourse about loss of Hawaiianness due to inter-marriage. This discourse typifies policy definitions of Hawaiian indigeneity and consequently has been taken up among Hawaiians. People with Hawaiian ancestry who identify themselves as Hawaiian through family connections and genealogical ties to Hawai'i will find it necessary to challenge the idea that anyone who lives in Hawai'i is Hawaiian. This reflects the different locations and privileges between people who label themselves as Hawaiian by virtue of residency and by virtue of Hawaiian ancestry (Kauanui 1998).

The discourse of "blood quantum" does not validate who Dad is as a person, or who his 'ohana is, as a family. Kauanui states that these notions "actually go against Hawaiian cultural genealogical practices, forms of self-definition, and family structures" (ibid., 683–684). Kauanui's statement is relevant to Dad's half-joking performance of whiteness, which works to complicate the dialogue about haole. Like earlier speakers who talk about unhelpful ali'i or unscrupulous Hawaiians, Dad challenges the immutability of victim and perpetrator roles.

Lisa Hall (2005, 405) offers a deeper way to view Dad's resistance to the idea of "blood quantum." She notes:

The indigenous conception of Hawaiian identity is very different. Hawaiian identity lies in a genealogical relationship to 'aumakua (ancestral spirit), 'āina (the land), and kānaka (other Hawaiians). Hawaiians are linked through 'aumākua, ancestral spirits, and through mākua, our parents. . . . Our genealogies explain our relations to other Hawaiians and—most importantly—where we came from. Though these elements may be interpreted differently, with them we are Hawaiian no matter what else we might be. Without these elements, there are no Hawaiians. Concepts such as "part" and "full," fifty percent, or more and less than fifty percent, are colonial constructions that threaten to divide Hawaiians from each other.

10 Kalo uses metaphor in ways that anchor pre-Contact cosmologies. In Ito's discussion of Hawaiian "talk story," she says that through metaphor "Hawaiians express, create, and retain their culture-as-lived" (1999, 6–7). She notes that metaphors reveal a worldview and a moral system. I certainly got this feeling, as Kalo spontaneously wove metaphors into a community of images that evoked connection. In her conclusions, Ito critiques the "invention of tradition" argument, having found in her study of Hawaiian everyday talk ongoing "cultural ties that bind and define Hawaiians" (ibid., 149).

11 A prime example of this is L'il Sis's quandary having to do with the opportunity open to her. That opportunity had to do with obtaining land, yet for L'il Sis, it also involved violating her own sense of Hawaiian ethics. Given that Hawaiians occupy less than ten percent of the housing units in Hawai'i, while they make up about twenty percent of Hawai'i's population, the issues facing L'il Sis are high-stakes issues (Stannard 2000, 17).

Chapter 4

1 I am treating myself as a subject here. The mana'o tapes were made right after the interviews or events described, so they give an idea of what I chose to highlight or remember. They also indicate the tension between interviewer versus learner roles that I experienced.

2 Why did I take up hula rather than lauhala? Kaeppler (1993) notes that hula has flourished, not only as an art form and as tourist entertainment (or "airport art") but also as an ethnic identity marker. Off-island, dance seems to be very accessible as an ethnic marker. It could be that I simply searched for such a marker—perhaps remembering my brush with the Kamehameha Schools Concert Glee Club, perhaps because I was so inept at lauhala weaving.

Kaeppler also notes that hula has functioned "as a vehicle for understanding Hawaiian culture" (ibid., 233). I think that this was the more powerful drive influencing me to take up hula. As a practice it might have seemed to offer an "entry code" into Hawaiian "culture."

3 There is a similarity between Aunty Limu's view and Linnekin's (1985, 1991a, 1991b) view of practice versus representation in that both privilege everyday practices on the land. However, I'm not sure if they would agree once we got down to the specifics of "what shapes Hawaiian identity."

4 In regard to this point, Davis (1995) noted:
. . . I believe although she knew you on the mainland, Aunty Limu was expressing a reluctance to your interview because now you are in "her place" and you are not firmly established here. I think her attempt at "finding" your birth-mother was her way of trying to find a tangible link to you through your Hawaiian "connectedness." On the other hand, it was a very Hawaiian sign of closeness to you as a friend to offer to pass on her knowledge of lauhala.

5 For example, Davis (1995), in reading this piece, stated:
You are different from those that "have stolen knowledge, Leilani. You are Hawaiian, you are of this 'āina and today you can prove it, you can recite your genealogy."
When I first read this, I was at a point in my journey where I needed this validation, yet I wondered if his words were just wishful thinking. As Dei (2000, 122) notes: "There are dangers of

unproblematically privileging the subject position which one occupies." Perhaps it is useful for the sake of research ethics to continue to inwardly feel this uncertainty and to act as if all researchers are by definition complicit. Yet, this presents a problem: the only way to completely escape complicity is to not write; yet if we don't write, we silence ourselves. And isn't that silence its own sort of lie—one that creates complicity as well?

6 Adoption was an important part of traditional Hawaiian culture, and continues as a practice among Hawaiians (Pukui, Haertig, and Lee 1974a, 49–51). *Hānai* involves rearing the child as one's offspring, with the rights and obligations that entails. In *hānai* it is assumed that the child will know and even maintain close contact with his or her birth parents. The mainland pattern of adoption, which focuses on the severing of genealogical ties, inverts Hawaiian practices in *hānai.*

 In clear contrast is the fact that off-island adoption has historically relied on the obliteration of the child's genealogy. This has made it impossible for the child to connect to other Hawaiians based on ancestry. It (in a way) has served to sever ancestry from the experience of the child. It seems that the off-island discussion of transracial adoption does not usually take this notion of ancestry (or genealogy) as a central element in identity into consideration.

7 What does Aunty Limu's rage against these bikini-clad *haole* women represent? Teaiwa's (1994) discussion deepens my understanding of the metaphors in play here. Teaiwa identifies the body as the site of physical and social experience. She describes how missionaries clothed the bodies of Pacific Islanders and how this functioned as a device of colonial social control. Aunty Limu calls up that process when she says, "All your ancestors, those missionaries, came and took us, we were naked, and made us wear long dresses." We could take the bikini as an artifact that stands in for the erasure of Pacific Islander bodies and the consequent forgetting of that erasure, manifest in its flip-side of the near-naked *haole* body. So Aunty Limu says, "And now you come here dressed in nothing."

Teaiwa (1994) discusses how the bikini, named for Bikini Atoll, which was traumatized by nuclear testing, is a celebration and a forgetting of nuclear power and its erasure of Pacific Island history (ibid., 87). Without intending to make light of Teaiwa's discussion, I would like to apply it to Aunty Limu's claim, which arrives in a "nonnuclear" context. Teaiwa notes that a *haole* woman in a bikini can be marked as "exotic," and a "natural" prop in a scene of leisure (ibid., 93). I think that Aunty Limu takes up such scenes in exactly that way. On her way home from her job teaching *lauhala* she finds this woman getting on the bus, fresh from Waikīkī beach or the International Market Place. This bikini is a false prop masking the histories (and everyday lived experiences) of those for whom Waikīkī is decidedly not the visitor's leisure paradise. It is part of a process of forgetting.

Teaiwa notes that the bikini "valorizes woman as Nature," in harsh contrast to what Teaiwa calls the "abom(b)ination of Nature" (ibid., 101). While Teaiwa identifies the abom(b)ination of Nature as manifested by military and scientific technology, we could say that it is also manifested in the appropriation of land and the usurpation of sovereignty. Ultimately, it is manifested in the marginalization (and trivialization) of ancient Hawaiian cosmology. And Aunty Limu, authoritative and unyielding, coming home from work in her mother hubbard, and confronting a bikini-clad *haole* woman, interrogates that process.

In Aunty Limu's statement, time collapses. In her talk, I hear a refusal to forget Hawai'i's particular abom(b)inations. Is her "Shame on you!" only about what this woman is showing? Or is it for the offenses of history and consequent addition of insult to injury?

8 I am not sure which story to weave. It is helpful to revisit Kulchyski (1992: see Chapter 2, Note 2), who notes that indigenous peoples may find ways to subvert the totalizing effects of capital. Resistance may be "deeply coded" and may live "more in the everyday than in any sphere of existence" (ibid., 174 –188). Kulchyski's work is helpful in understanding how present-day indigenous knowledge gets produced from within, yet may often embody resistance to capitalist formations. It does seem notable to me that Aunty Limu takes an event that is usually emblematic of the scarcity paradigm—asking for a loan—and reshapes it into a story full of connection, delight, and abundance.

9 It may be important that Kalo knows both Michael and the *kupuna* whom Aunty Lau is discussing. In another story, Aunty Lau discusses a relative of that same *kupuna*. Borofsky's (1987) comments on the way that Pukapukans create knowledge cause me to think about the personal messages that Kalo, Aunty Limu, and Aunty Lau convey to their listeners. I think that the listener's job is to understand the personal messages inherent in the story. Borofsky says:

In collecting data, for example, Pukapukans tend to be less direct than anthropologists. They concern themselves far more with subtleties of personal relations and the contexts of interaction. Anthropologists, with their interviews, censuses, and maps, collect their data in a more systematic, straightforward manner than Pukapukans. They also do it in a far shorter period of time. Though aware that status rivalries exist, anthropologists tend (as outsiders) not to be as involved in them. (ibid., 146)

I think that Aunty Lau is purposefully (albeit gently) addressing the behavior of a *kupuna* whom Kalo knows and admires. In this respect she is indirectly referencing a long-standing relationship between Kalo and this other *kupuna*. Since Kalo was engaged in time-consuming projects on behalf of this other *kupuna*, Aunty Lau may have had concerns about Kalo being over-extended. I think that Borofsky's phrase "status rivalries" is too strong to apply to this interaction. However, I also believe that at certain junctures throughout the interview Aunty Lau creates a way for Kalo to let go of her own unquestioning acquiescence to this other *kupuna*. There is a kind of "status leveling" that takes place, allowing Aunty Lau to encourage Kalo to be more mindful of her own health and her own needs.

10 Aunty Lau creates a compelling sense of acceptance and inclusiveness. Her stories about Michael and about wet versus dry *kalo* cultivation construct unconditional acceptance of the experience and consequent knowledge of others. For a Pacific scholarly example of this inclusionary voice, see Hereniko's *Woven Gods: Female Clowns and Power in Rotuma* (1995, 11). For a Pacific scholarly example of disauthentication of an indigenous background, see Hanson's (1996) review of *Woven Gods: Female Clowns and Power in Rotuma.* Hanson interrogates the validity of Hereniko's intuitive accounts as a Rotuman by questioning the length of his experience in Rotuma— thus disauthenticating his indigeneity. Howard (1997) responds to Hanson's review by authenticating Hereniko's indigeneity, defending the book's contents and insights, and commenting on

the disdain marking Hanson's review. In Hanson's critical review, he questions Hereniko's status as an insider to Rotuman culture. White and Tengan (2001) critique Hanson's focus on Hereniko's expatriate status. Hanson made much of the fact that Hereniko left Rotuma at sixteen and teaches at the University of Hawai'i. White and Tengan assert that Hanson's position is absurd, stating: "Apparently, if travel abroad for education doesn't disqualify you from cultural status, then teaching at the University of Hawai'i is surely fatal. . . . For Hanson, the operative metaphor for culture is that of an island, remote and bounded, requiring long-term, settled, localized fieldwork" (ibid., 403).

In contrast, Aunty Lau's operative metaphor for culture seems to be an ocean of *lo'i*—each different, some wet, some dry, each conditioning a particular experience. Hanson assumes that relocation negates one's knowledge—knowledge is not continuous or self-perpetuating. Once passed down, knowledge is fragile and shaped by future experience. In contrast, Aunty Lau sees knowledge, in her story of Michael, and her story about the *lo'i*, as continuous and self-perpetuating. Once passed down ancestrally, knowledge is robust and shapes future experience. While Hanson's idea of knowledge is anthropocentric and denies the power of ancestry, Aunty Lau's idea of knowledge is very '*āina*-centric, privileging the power of ancestry. Hanson's story of Hereniko shapes Hereniko as powerless—once he leaves his island, his knowledge shrivels and should be invalidated. Aunty Lau's story of Michael shapes him as powerful—though he left Moloka'i, he keeps the knowledge of his *kūpuna* and it should be validated.

Konai Helu Thaman (2003, 14) urges academics in Pacific studies to ". . . examine our own ways of thinking and knowing and explore how they might be changed in order to create a Pacific studies that is Pacific in orientation and inclusive in its processes, contexts, and outcomes." I think that Aunty Lau, and many other *kūpuna* are excellent models for the politics of inclusion. In her conclusion, Thaman directs some reflective questions toward Pacific studies academics: "What relationship do your ideas have to locally recognized concepts of knowledge and wisdom? And how are globally available, academically generated ideas able to articulate with the needs of Oceanic peoples and communities such that they can foster a better way of living at this time, let alone the future?" (ibid.).

As I reread Aunty Lau's discussion about the localized creation of knowledge in responses to the land, and her discussion about the articulation between her grandson's use of a text and her own knowledge, I think that she models responses to Thaman's questions. In her own interactions, Aunty Lau consistently works to construct a relationship between her ideas and the ideas of others. She finds ways to understand their needs and to make her knowledge helpful to them. She consistently privileges disparate local knowledge—whether emergent from other *kūpuna* or from the dictates of the land. Aunty Lau and her grandson work to use an academic text to further their knowledge-making. As Aunty Lau discusses the future by deploying an ancient story about the *mū*, she makes it known that the stories of her own ancestors constitute an applied knowledge that gives us clues to our own future as Hawaiians.

11 Kalo privileges everyday talk among Hawaiians in her life, and stories that *kūpuna* tell her carry great pedagogical weight. It is useful to ask how Kalo would be viewed, in regards to the oft-appearing notion of "Westernized elites" in the invention of tradition-debate. Given that she is a Western-educated activist and school adminis-

trator who is financially well-off, would she be classified as part of the "Westernized elite?" It is clear that Kalo finds a deep connection with *kūpuna* who advise and mentor her and above all, tell her stories. The conditions of Kalo's "childhood" were far from "Westernized" or "elite." Yet in relation to the invention of tradition-debate, her present-day social position and recent schooling might be viewed as more salient than her history, or her connections to *kūpuna*. Her Western education might be viewed as more powerful than her talk story with *kūpuna*. The notion that ancestral knowledge is part of her everyday experience might be overtaken by the idea that her identity is dictated by her socioeconomic status (or relation to capital). In this way, the transformational pedagogy of the *kūpuna* who advise her, and those *kūpuna* themselves, could be rendered invisible.

Chapter 5

1 I think that Tūtū 'Ōhi'a's stories about living on the land are more than just stories. She talks about subsistence in a way that reaffirms Hawaiian identity, and centralizes '*āina* as central to Hawaiian identity. Hensel (1996), who writes about the Yup'ik of Southwestern Alaska, states that the values associated with subsistence have become key symbols of Yup'ik identity. He notes that subsistence is in particular an ethnic marker for Yup'ik, providing and validating a local identity for those who are involved in the cash economy. He argues that subsistence, although not necessarily a central economic activity, is important as a symbolic activity. Hensel views talk about subsistence and subsistence activities as linked practices:

> Subsistence discourse is privileged over the actual practices of hunting, fishing, gathering, and processing because it is constantly available for strategic use in ways in which the physical practices of subsistence are not. (ibid., 4)

It seems important to ground stories about past practices, and even more specifically subsistence practices, as a powerful form of practice in themselves. Hensel asserts that discourse is "among the most, if not the most, important form of practice" (ibid., 4–5). He notes that subsistence and its discussion ground individuals in the past, particularly an indigenous vision of the past. I think that subsistence discourse, as taken up by Tūtū 'Ōhi'a (and other *kūpuna*) is a powerfully articulated and strategically complex situated practice.

2 A question is raised about the type of plant Tūtū 'Ōhi'a is describing. I heard the name *ohuloa* and as I play back the tape this is what I continue to hear. It could be that she is speaking of the *'ōhi'a'ula*, an *'ōhi'a'ai* (type of *'ōhi'a-lehua*) that has red fruit (Pukui and Elbert 1986, 278). The *'ōhi'a lehua* has many forms; from low shrubs to tall trees. The *lehua mau loa* (globe amaranth) and *'uhaloa* (Waltheria indica var. americana) are other possibilities.

I am advised by Malie Wahine Ke'ali'i o ke Kai to consider the *kaona* (hidden meaning) that could emerge. Pukui and Elbert (1986, 278, 209) define *'ohu* as "mist, fog . . . light cloud on a mountain; adorned with leis" and *loa* as "distance, length, height, distant; far."

One way to take this might be to imagine Tūtū 'Ōhi'a gathering plants that grow in the heights where the mist floats about her. There is an allusion to the *ali'i* whom she speaks of; those who are high up to be adorned with *lei*. Another way to take this is as a reminder of my dream about the mist rising and about knowledge. These options give me plenty to reflect on as a learner: first, my lack of knowledge about Hawaiian plants; second, the purpose of her errand and the historical role of the *ali'i;* and finally, the mist on the mountain, rising to reveal knowledge. And the (literally) teeth-grinding intensity of that image as it visited my sleeping self.

3 In Tūtū 'Ōhi'a's talk, when it comes to practices on the land and *mālama 'āina,* it seems that a construction of Hawaiian vs. non-Hawaiian rarely occurs. She attends to the experiences, practices, and values of Hawaiians, rather than the behavior of non-Hawaiians. This reminds me again of Hensel (1996, v–vi), who states that:
    Although ethnicity is overtly constructed in terms of either/or categories, the discourse of Bethel residents suggests that their actual concern is less with whether one is Native or non-Native than with how Native one is in a given context.

4 Malie Wahine Ke'ali'i o ke Kai notes, "This sounds like spiritual *ho'oponopono,*" which Pukui and Elbert (1986, 341) define as:
    To put to rights, to put in order or shape, correct, revise . . . rectify . . . mental cleansing; family conferences in which relationships were set right (ho'oponopono) through prayer, discussion, confession, repentance and mutual restitution and forgiveness."

5 Tūtū 'Ōhi'a's inclusivity calls to mind Hensel's (1996) discussion of ethnicity among Yup'ik people. Hensel notes that their discourse calls for "a new treatment of ethnicity as a negotiated category" (ibid., 14). Hensel notes that in discourse the Yup'ik don't construct ethnicity as an either-or (white or non-white) set of categories. Rather they negotiate and reenact ethnicity, constructing and maintaining images of themselves.
    I think that Tūtū 'Ōhi'a creates a continuum of Hawaiian-ness, in order to instruct us, as she tells stories. I am reminded of her strategic moves, when Briggs (1987) discusses elders' speech as pedagogical events. In studying elders' oral tradition having to do with Hispanic land-grant research, Briggs found that in elders' talk three major themes emerge. These are moral imperatives of selflessness, religiosity, and knowledge about or practices on the land (ibid., 246–247). He notes that in their talk elders subtly manipulate linguistic forms as well as the social situation, saying that "a good speaker thus makes the listeners aware, explicitly or implicitly, of the relevance of the remarks to the present situation" (ibid., 248).
    Tūtū 'Ōhi'a is a clear example of this ability to connect her listeners to the relevance of a particular moment. I think that part of her ability to do this is due to her resistance to a polarized "we" and "they" and creation of a sense of inclusion in her talk. It leaves us free to look at occurrences from any number of vantage points, and question our own practices without laying blame on ourselves or others. It is clear to me that those I interviewed were accomplished in that regard.

6 In Hawai'i I interviewed Kalo, who in turn interviewed two mentors and was reinterviewed for comments on her interviews with her mentors. Transcripts averaged from thirteen to sixteen pages, and interviews averaged about two hours in length. When talk-story was added (for which the tape recorder was off but for which I took notes), the length ran to about three hours. I also conducted a focused interview with Kalo's *'ohana.* I interviewed an additional mentor in three separate meetings of about an hour each.
    My plan had initially been to examine two different sorts of events and productions, for primarily local audiences and for tourist audiences. I taped and wrote field notes on six formal public community events and an additional four private, casual events.

Although I attended and taped four events staged for tourists, I did not take field notes on these events, nor did I use them for my research. My field notes from events, informal interviews, and informal gatherings ran to about sixty pages.
    In addition, Kalo and I had spent many hours together, discussing each interview, discussing her and my role in the research: doing errands related to her career, community work, and family involvements; and just talking story. I wrote copious notes on our discussions. In this preliminary research, I had, with Kalo's help, gathered interviews that were not focused on events, but on identity and knowledge creation. I was now very interested in how events and talk shared within the Hawaiian community might be pedagogical in nature.

7 In Canada I interviewed three students studying indigenous knowledge, who each in turn interviewed professors who were their mentors. Students answered (in their own order) the interview questions; then I positioned myself as a listener while students interviewed their mentors. I then reinterviewed the students for comments about how they took up the knowledge of their mentors. Transcripts averaged from ten to thirteen pages, and interviews were about one and a half hours long. I also conducted a focused group interview with four students which lasted two and one-half hours.
    I made slight revisions to the questions I had used in Hawai'i for use in Canada. My revised list of questions was:
1 How did you come to be interested in indigenous knowledge? Why are you interested in it?
2 What do you feel is important to convey to others about indigenous knowledge, and to whom should this information be conveyed?
3 a. What dangers are indigenous peoples facing today, and what strengths do you feel indigenous peoples have in facing those dangers?
    b. What dangers are nonindigenous North Americans facing today, and what strengths do you feel nonindigenous North Americans have in facing those dangers?
4 a. What do you think is the role of indigenous spirituality and indigenous knowledge about the land as we move into the future?
    b. Do you experience any difficulties addressing issues about indigenous knowledge in an academic community? If so, what are those issues and how do you negotiate them?
5 A lot is happening right now—are you hopeful for the future?
    In Canada I also attended and took field notes on five formal public events involving the academy and five casual, private events. My field notes from events, informal interviews, and informal gatherings ran to about fifty pages. I coded and analyzed sequences and frequencies of particular themes, comparing Canadian and Hawaiian transcripts. This allowed me to talk about how indigenous knowledge is approached and shared, in community and academic settings.

8 The struggles of Canadian academics to find ways of privileging indigenous knowledge were central to their talk. They often constructed a "scarcity paradigm" about knowledge, learning, and the future of indigenous peoples that I had not found in my interviews in Hawai'i. This "crisis cosmology" entered the talk, regardless of the nature of the interview question. Interviewees worried about scarce resources, pressures to publish, and the (non-)acceptance of indigenous knowledge in academia. Knowledge was shared (predictably) through assertions, categories, and summaries, rather

than through stories. The grounded cosmologies and epistemologies that emerged in the talk of Canadian (Western) academics reflected the cosmology of political economy.

9 Fieldwork in Hawai'i was an emotionally exhausting, worrisome process in which my own ancestry was implicated. Yet the inclusion I felt and the way people opened up to issues about my ancestry made it a rich and emotional experience. I also experienced disturbing tensions that seemed related to local (Hawaiian) and academic (nonindigenous) locations.

Fieldwork in Canada was predictably free of these sorts of tensions. There was no disjunction between research and community protocols, because the community was a research community. I experienced a worry-free fieldwork process, marked by an "easy" process of data gathering. I felt understood and uniformly well received by others in this process. Yet the process in Canada was accompanied by the strange sensation of recording everyday activities taking place in and around the academy. It seemed as if I was constantly writing about structures and hierarchies having to do with money (funding), time, panel structuring, and worries about conference organization. Much of my talk in my field notes is taken up by processes of faxing, word processing, phoning, leaving messages, and so forth.

The tensions that appear in my fieldwork in Canada have to do with attempting to be part of a collective within a structure that does not appear to allow for much collectivity. Also, a great deal of talk arrives in my notes about individuals' struggles with their own search for "expert status" or fears that their authority to speak might be undermined by others.

10 Pseudonyms are used for birth family members, in order to protect my birth mother's privacy.

11 For a history of the multiple moves of the *kā'ai* see Rose (1992), who notes that they were assumed to be from Hale o Līloa, the old mausoleum associated with the *pu'uhonua* (place of refuge) of Paka'alana, in Waipi'o. They have resided on the grounds of 'Iolani Palace, and in the Royal Mausoleum at Mauna 'Ala in Nu'uanu Valley, and finally, at the Bishop Museum. According to Rose, their association with the fifteenth- or sixteenth-century high chiefs Līloa and Lonoikamakahiki hasn't been validated, nor has their original "home" at Hale o Līloa.

12 Malie Wahine Ke'ali'i o ke Kai is a pseudonym given to my cousin by my *kumu hula*, Aunty Philomena Keali'i Waine'e Aranio. I have kept Aunty Mena's diacritics as written.

13 Other articles discussing the *kā'ai* appeared in later time frames. See Tangonan (1994) for a later article submerging the Bishop Museum's legal standpoint in themes about Hawaiian spirituality.

Chapter 6

1 Scholars may be conditioned to be indifferent to the campus as an environment, which is expected to be clean, convenient, attractive, and in good repair—supplied (by "others") with resources. Orr notes that the result is "no great understanding of the place, or in the art of living responsibly in that or any other place" (1992, 103). Berry addresses this by noting that "our difficulty in appreciating the earth community as primary educator is that we have little

sense of or feeling for the natural world in its integral dimension" (1988, 90).

2 This invitation to silence through being too indigenous or not indigenous enough does not go unnoticed. Linda Tuhiwai Smith (1999, 14) notes that it is said of native scholars and activists that "our Western education precludes us from writing or speaking from a 'real' and authentic indigenous position" and "those who do speak from a more 'traditional' indigenous point of view are criticized because they do not make sense." Discussing her experiences in the academy, Teaiwa (1995, 60) notes, "As native students we felt that we were anomalies; on the one hand the academy seemed to operate quite happily by assuming the authenticity of our absence; on the other hand, our presence in the academy was enabled by the absence of our authenticity as natives." Travel, relocation, or being born elsewhere is also used to disauthenticate indigenous peoples, signifying "displacement" and forfeiture of "roots" (Diaz and Kauanui 2001; Gegeo 2001). Gegeo (2001) discusses his experiences of being marked as nonindigenous by an editor, since Gegeo lives in the USA. He notes that those same standards mediating authenticity for indigenous scholars are not applied to the "metropolitan citizen who lives in another culture or is born abroad" (ibid., 495).

These comments call up the ways in which being a scholar and/or activist automatically rendered "nativity" inauthentic in the stories and images attending the invention of tradition-debate. A more nuanced view is emerging. White and Tengan (2001, 399) suggest that this way of theorizing indigeneity is challenged as indigenous scholars enter the academy in greater numbers. Linda Tuhiwai Smith (1999, 14) assumes trajectory and change for indigenous scholars:

For each indigenous intellectual who actually succeeds in the academy. . . there is a whole array of issues about the ways we relate inside and outside of our own communities, inside and outside the academy, and between all those different worlds.

In discussing Hereniko's experience of disauthentication, White and Tengan (2001) described Hanson's metaphor for culture as "an island, remote and bounded" (403: see Note 10, Chapter 4, 130–131). In contrast, Hau'ofa calls for a Pacific identity based on movement along ocean pathways through a sea of islands "unhindered by boundaries" (1993, 8). Hau'ofa (1998, 409) again invites us to consider the ocean relative to Pacific identity, when he notes "the sea is our pathway to each other and to everyone else, the sea is our endless saga, the sea is our most powerful metaphor, the ocean is in us." Derné (1998) poses some questions for anthropology, in his work on the role of water as related to the sensory construction of time and space. One of his questions is: "How do particular sensory understandings shape people's lives?" (ibid., 6). A related question might be, "How do particular sensory understandings shape academic disciplines?" The ocean as a metaphor is not only symbolic in a literary or textual sense. Hau'ofa (1998) presents a metaphor with powerful sensory understandings—a metaphor that is lived in and by the body. Ocean (water) as a metaphor that is to a great extent "embodied" by Pacific indigenous peoples serves to powerfully recenter the discipline and emplace Pacific indigenous peoples within it.

3 Junior searches for the verbal collaboration that will "help him think." He approaches thinking much like Abraham Piianaia, a mentor Meyer interviewed (2001, 135), who said, "Thinking is also having others tell you what they think." Rather than saddling each "individual thinker" with an isolated monologue, the

'ohana co-produces knowledge through patterned strategic moves, chaining or rupturing others' formations, in a process of sharing knowledge. Junior may be in crisis, but it is a crisis shared via fluid and flexible dialogue, rather than an isolated static monologue. The monological and personalized strategies privileged by modern/Western pedagogies enjoin us to "think for ourselves." In contrast, the strategies of dialogue and validation used by 'ohana members might allow Junior to see himself through the lens of others (ibid., 136).

4 Kauanui (1999b, 10–13) notes that non-Hawaiians often define themselves as Hawaiian once they are off-island, sometimes describing themselves as "the ones saving Hawaiian 'culture' more so than Hawaiians." Wood (1999, 41) observed that Caucasians living in Hawai'i grew to think of themselves as kama'āina with more knowledge about "authentic" Hawaiian culture than the Hawaiians themselves. Wood suggests that the Euroamericans living in Hawai'i envisioned themselves as "guardians and pre-servers" of Hawaiian culture (ibid., 45–47).

5 This debate, like other such discussions, opens up into what Simon (1992) might call "a critical pedagogy of remembrance." Simon defines remembrance as "the practice in which certain images and stories of a collective past are brought together with a person's feelings and comprehension of their embodied presence in time and space (ibid., 149). Simon discusses how a critical pedagogy of remembrance would be responsive to "the spiritual desire to under-stand our presence in both historical and cosmic time" (ibid., 151). I think the kā'ai debates accomplish this.

6 Transracial adoption opens up issues of race and power—in particular, the power of being marked (Patton 2000, 19). Before they are cognitively ready to understand adoption or their life histories, transracial adoptees living in predominantly white communi-ties often hear comments about their skin color, their adoption, and their cultural background. Issues of racial identity become entangled in complex and problematic ways, with adoption issues. Transracial adoptees experience "a disjuncture between the ways they experience themselves in their families and the racist treat-ment to which they are subjected in public (ibid., 13).The "racial differences" between them and their families are commented on, so their adoption is always a visual reality that they cannot escape. Steinberg and Hall (2000, 11) note that:

Many transracially adopted adults have told us that they have never been able to think about adoption as an issue separate from race. For children adopted across racial lines, race and adoption often become inextricably connected.

7 In the context of conservation and resource management Berkes (1999, 176) describes Western science as utilitarian—aimed at pre-dicting and controlling nature, through the paradigm of positivist-reductionism. Berkes notes how positivist-reductionism has tended to dominate ways of thinking about conservation and resource management. In asking questions about the role of traditional ecological knowledge and in resource management, he notes that indigenous knowledge systems are at odds with the positivist-reductionist paradigm, which "displaced traditional knowledge in the first place." Berkes speaks of the challenge of creating new "ethical principles for ecology and resource management," despite the fact that positivist science has focused on "the notion of man's dominion over nature." While Berkes finds that the science of ecology begins to approach the "community-of-beings worldview" of what he calls "traditional ecological knowledge," he finds that "the materialist tradition, and the Newtonian, machinelike view of ecosystems" are still a part of ecology (ibid., 181–182). This discus-sion speaks to the role of cosmology in social action, or social policy regarding "the environment." It also, I think, speaks to the conse-quences of a culture that might be said to be bereft of emplacing practices.

8 This dispossession exists in the midst of the Hawaiian Renaissance, which has activated "a process of research and rediscovery"—hula students have turned to kūpuna, "who in turn sifted through memories, recollections, and knowledge—much of which had lain dormant for years and even decades" (Stillman 2001, 197). These kūpuna didn't have access to the archived texts, so they could only pass down the knowledge that had been passed to them. Stillman notes the tension between oral narratives passed down and newly disinterred written accounts: "It is possible that more missing pieces relevant to Hawaiian music and dance will surface, forcing us to revise cherished notions of stories related to us in their absence" (ibid.). With newly discovered texts, the hula community will be challenged to respect the efforts of kūpuna "to hold onto what they could even if new research discoveries show their stories to be incomplete. The narratives they told were stories that con-nected the pieces they had" (ibid., 200).

Glossary

I have used the *Hawaiian Dictionary* (Pukui and Elbert 1986); *Ka Poʻe Kahiko: The People of Old* (Kamakau 1964); and *The Works of the People of Old: Na Hana a ka Poʻe Kahiko* (Kamakau 1976) as sources for this glossary. They are also used as guides to usage, except for quotes by others, whose usage and diacritics are unchanged.

ʻahi: Hawaiian tuna fish, particularly yellow-fin tuna

ahupuaʻa: Plots of land, running from the mountains to the sea and shared by *ʻohana* or extended family.

ʻai: Food or food plant. Often *ʻai* refers specifically to *poi*; harvest, taste, bite, edible; various ways of eating may qualify *ʻai*.

ʻāina: Land, earth.

aku: Bonito, skipjack (fish); an important food item.

akua: God, deity.

ʻale wiliau maka lae: Swells which break agitatedly against points or capes of land.

aliʻi: Royalty, chief, chiefess, king, queen, noble.

aliʻi nui: High chief.

aloha: Love, affection, compassion, mercy, pity, kindness, greeting, hospitality.

aloha ʻāina: Love of the land.

ʻaʻole: No.

ʻaumakua: Family or personal god.

ʻauwaʻalalua: Spanish man-of-war; fleet of canoes with two sails.

ʻawa: The kava, whose root is the source of a narcotic drink used for ceremonies and healing.

ea: Air, breath, respiration; sovereignty, rule; independence; life.

hā: The breath of life. To breathe, exhale; breath, life.

haʻahaʻa: Humble, unpretentious, modest, unassuming.

haʻina: Saying, declaration, statement, explanation; answer. The last verses of a song that usually begin with the word *haʻina* and that repeat the theme of the song, or the name of the person to whom the song is dedicated.

hālau: Long house, as for canoes or *hula* instruction.

hālau hula: Place of learning for *hula,* usually ancient *hula* (*hula* school).

hana: Work, labor, job, duty, activity, action, deed, service.

hānai: Informal adoption, usually within Hawaiian families.

haole: Whites, foreigners, white person, American, Englishman.

heiau: Ancient temple, pre-Christian place of worship.

holoholo: Travel around, to take someone out for a drive or excursion.

holokū: Loose dress with a train, patterned after the mother hubbard dresses of the missionaries.

hoʻoponopono: To put in order, correct, mental cleansing. Family conferences in which relationships were set right (*hoʻoponopono*) through prayer, discussion, confession, repentance, mutual restitution, and forgiveness.

hui: United group, club, association, society, corporation.

hukihuki: Fight, have conflict; pull or draw frequently, or by many persons as in a tug-of-war game.

hula: Hawaiian dance.

hula ʻauana: Modern *hula, hula* which "wanders" or drifts from place to place.

hula kahiko: Ancient Hawaiian dance.

ʻili ʻili: Small stone, as used as instruments in dance.

ipu: The bottle gourd, a wide-spreading vine; a drum consisting of one or two gourds.

iwi: Bone. The bones of the dead were cherished and hidden. *Iwi* sometimes means "life, or old age."

kāʻai: Sennit container for remains of a chief. Sennit casket alleged to contain the bones of Līloa and Lono-i-ka-makahiki.

ka hana a ka poʻe kahiko: The works of the people of old.

kāhea: To call, invoke, greet. Recital of the first lines of a stanza by the dancer as a cue to the chanter.

kahiko: Old, ancient; old person.

kahu: Human acting as guardian of *ʻaumakua,* honored attendant, keeper; administrator.

kahu moʻokūʻauhau nui: Keeper or administrator of genealogy, historian.

kahuna: Healer, priest, minister, sorcerer; expert in any profession.

ka lāhui Hawai'i: The nation of Hawai'i: *lāhui* means nation, race, people, nationality.

kalo: A plant which provides a staple, particularly in the form of *poi*. In English, taro.

kama'āina: Native-born, children of the earth .

kanaka: Human being, mankind, person, individual.

kanaka maoli: True Native Hawaiian person. *Maoli* means native, indigenous; genuine, true, real.

kaona: Hawaiian technique of using hidden meanings for a word or phrase. Concealed reference to a person, thing, or place.

kapu: Religious law, taboo, prohibition, sacred, holy, consecrated.

ka wā ma hope: The future, afterwards, by-and-by, later, hereafter; behind.

ka wā ma mua: The past, before; ahead, forward, in advance.

kī: (or *tī*) A Hawaiian plant. Leaves are used for clothing and to wrap articles. Green *tī* leaves are believed to afford protection from spirits. In English, *tī*.

ko'i mū: Legendary people of Kaua'i often called "banana-eating-*Mū*" also term used for a public executioner; children were told the *mū* would get them. *Ko'i* means axe, adze, adzelike, sharp, projecting, as a forehead.

kōkua: help, assist, support.

kūkākūkā: Confer, speak, talk, discuss.

kuleana: Right, property, responsibility, jurisdiction, authority, interest, claim; ancestral plots of land.

kūlia i ka nu'u: Strive to reach the summit (Queen Kapi'olani's motto).

kumu: Master, instructor, source, teacher; also means base, foundation, basis, main stalk of a tree.

kumu hula: Master or instructor or source of *hula*.

kumulipo: Origin, source of life, name of the Hawaiian creation chant..

kūpikipiki'ō ka po'i ana: A swell that twists about and breaks here or there.

kupuna: Elder, grandparent, ancestor, relative of the grandparents' generation; starting point or source.

kūpuna: Plural.

lau: Leaf, frond, leaflet, greens, to leaf out.

lauhala: Pandanaus (or screwpine) frond, especially as used for weaving or plaiting items such as mats, baskets, and hats.

laua'e: A fragrant fern, also spelled *lauwa'e*.

lehua mau loa: Globe amaranth, everlasting *lehua*, so called because its flowers do not wilt.

lei: Garland of flowers, leaves, shells, ivory, feathers, or paper given as a symbol of affection.

lei hulu: Feather lei, formerly worn by royalty.

limu: A general name for all kinds of plants living under water, both fresh and salt.

lipo: Deep blue-black, as of a cavern, the sea, the night, or dense forest.

loa: Long distance, length, height, distant, long, far.

lo'i: Irrigated terrace, used especially for growing taro (*kalo*).

lōkahi: Unity, agreement, accord, unanimous.

lū'au: Hawaiian feast, named for the taro tops that are served.

Māhealani: The sixteenth day of the lunar month, the night of the full moon.

māhele: Portion, division, section, quota, precinct, share; land division of 1848 (the great *māhele*).

mahimahi: A type of fish, dolphin; a gamefish up to five feet long.

maka'āinana: Commoner, populace, people who attend the land.

makahiki: Ancient festival beginning about the middle of October and lasting about four months, with sports, religious festivities, and a taboo on war.

makua: One generation below *kupuna*, parent generation, parent, any relative of the parents' generation.

mālama 'āina: Protection of the land; *mālama* means to care for, or preserve.

mana: Spiritual essence, supernatural or divine power.

mana'o: Thought, idea, opinion, theory, meaning.

ma uka: Inland, upland, toward the mountain.

menehune: Legendary race of small people who worked at night building fish ponds, roads, and temples.

moemoeā: To dream, dreamtime; a dream of a cherished wish.

mō'ī: King, sovereign, monarch, majesty, ruler, queen.

mo'o: Serpent, lizard, reptile, dragon, water spirit; also succession, series, genealogical line or lineage; story, tradition, legend.

mo'opuna: Grandchild, great-niece or nephew; relatives two generations later; descendant.

mū: Public executioner, he procured victims for sacrifice and executed taboo breakers; children were frightened by being told that the *mū* would get them.

mu'umu'u: A loose gown.

na'au: Intestines, bowels, mind, heart, "guts."

nā kanaka maoli Hawai'i a pau: All native Hawaiians.

nai'a: Dolphin (porpoise).

niu: Coconut, two coconut halves used together as a percussive musical instrument.

noho: Possession of a medium by a spirit or god, possessed, to possess, to summon a spirit to possess.

'ohā: Taro corm growing from the older root, especially from the stalk called *kalo*; tender plant, shoot, or branch (offspring, youngsters).

'ohana: Extended family, family, relative, kin group; related.

'ohe-hano-ihu: Nose flute, also called *kōheoheo*.

'ōhi'a: Two kinds of trees; *'ōhi'a 'ai* and *'ōhi'a lehua*.

'ōhi'a 'ai: The mountain apple.

'ōhi'a lehua: Also called *lehua*, the plant has many forms. The flowers are red, rarely salmon, pink, yellow, or white.

'ōhi'a 'ula: An *'ōhi'a 'ai* with red fruit.

'ohu: Mist, fog, vapor, light cloud on a mountain adorned with lei.

'ōpae: General name for shrimp.

'ōpelu: Mackerel, scad.

'ōpio: Youth, youngster, child generation, one generation below *makua*.

'ōpule: Type of fish (a wrasse).

pa'akikī: Hard, compact, difficult, stubborn, obstinate.

Pākē: Chinese.

pa'i: To slap, clap; pounding, usually of the *ipu*.

pā'ina: Dinner, small party with dinner.

palaoa: Sperm whale.

papa kaula: Order of prophets. *Papa* means native born, especially for several generations; *kaula* means seer.

pau: Finished, ended, completed, over, all done.

pilau: Rotten, stinking, spoiled, putrid, decomposed.

po'e Hawai'i: People of Hawai'i.

po'e kahiko: People of old, ancestors, ancients.

poi: Traditional Hawaiian food; the Hawaiian staff of life. Made from cooked taro (*kalo*).

pono: Goodness, uprightness, morality; correct or proper; well-being; true condition or nature; proper, just, fair, beneficial.

pono 'ole: Wrong, not fitting or just; *'ole:* without, not, lacking.

po'o pa'akiki: Obstinate, stubborn, literally hard-headed. *Po'o* means head.

pua: Flower, blossom.

pueo: Hawaiian short-eared owl, sometimes regarded as a deity.

pū'ili: Two split bamboos, used as a percussive musical instrument.

puka: Hole, entrance, gate, slit, vent, opening.

puna: Wellspring.

pu'uhonua: Place of refuge, sanctuary, asylum, place of peace and safety.

tūtū: Grandparent.

'uhane: Soul, spirit, ghost.

'ukulele: Literally "leaping flea," a stringed instrument brought to Hawai'i by the Portuguese.

'ūlili: Three gourds filled with seeds, used as a musical instrument by pulling a string to twirl the gourds.

'ulī 'ulī: Two gourd rattles decorated with feathers, used as percussive musical instruments.

'ūniki: Graduation exercises, as for *hula* (probably related to *niki,* to tie, as the knowledge was bound to the student).

wahine: Female, woman, lady, wife, sister-in-law.

References

Andrade, Ernest. 1996. *Unconquerable Rebel: Robert W. Wilcox and Hawaiian Politics, 1880–1903*. Niwot, Colorado: University Press of Colorado.

Ayau, Edward Halealoha. 1991. Native Hawaiian Burial Rights. In *Native Hawaiian Rights Handbook,* edited by Melody Kapilialoha MacKenzie, pp. 245–273. Honolulu: Office of Hawaiian Affairs.

Barrère, Dorothy B. 1964. Foreword. In *Ka Po'e Kahiko: The People of Old,* by Samuel M. Kamakau, pp. vii–viii. Translated by Mary Kawena Pukui, arranged and edited by Dorothy B. Barrère, Special Publication 51. Honolulu: Bishop Museum Press.

Barrère, Dorothy B., Mary Kawena Pukui, and Marion Kelly. 1980. *Hula: Historical Perspectives*. Pacific Anthropological Records No. 30. Honolulu, Bernice Pauahi Bishop Museum.

Bauman, Zygmunt. 1996. From Pilgrim to Tourist—or a Short History of Identity. In *Questions of Cultural Identity*, edited by Stuart Hall and Paul du Gay, pp. 18–36. London: Sage Publications.

Beaglehole, Ernest. 1937. *Some Modern Hawaiians*. Honolulu: University of Hawai'i Research Publications 19.

Beamer, Nona. 1987. *Nā Mele Hula: A Collection of Hawaiian Hula Chants*. Lā'ie, Hawai'i: The Pacific Institute, Brigham Young University.

Berkes, Fikret. 1999. *Sacred Ecology: Traditional Ecological Knowledge and Resource Management*. Philadelphia: Taylor and Francis.

Berry, Thomas. 1988. *The Dream of the Earth*. San Francisco: Sierra Club Books.

Berry, Thomas. 1991. *The Ecozoic Era*. E.F. Schumacher Society Lectures, October 19.

Boggs, Stephen T. 1985. *Speaking, Relating and Learning: A Study of Hawaiian Children at Home and at School*. Norwood, NJ: Ablex.

Borofsky, Robert. 1987. *Making History: Pukapukan and Anthropological Constructions of Knowledge*. Cambridge: Cambridge University Press.

Borofsky, Robert. 1994. On the Knowledge and Knowing and Cultural Activities. In *Assessing Cultural Anthropology* edited by Robert Borofsky, pp. 331–348. New York: McGraw Hill.

Bottomore, Tom, ed. 1983. *A Dictionary of Marxist Thought*. Cambridge, MA: Harvard University Press.

Bourdieu, Pierre. 1990. *The Logic of Practice*. Translated by Richard Nice. Stanford: Stanford University Press.

Briggs, Charles. L. 1986. *Learning How to Ask: A Sociolinguistic Appraisal of the Role of the Interview in Social Science Research*. Cambridge: Cambridge University Press.

Briggs, Charles. L. 1987. Getting Both Sides of the Story: Oral History in Land Grant Research and Litigation. In *Land, Water, and Culture: New Perspectives on Hispanic Land Grants*, edited by Charles L. Briggs. and John. R. Van Ness, pp. 217–268. Albuquerque: University of New Mexico Press.

Briggs, Charles. L. 1996. The Politics of Discursive Authority in Research on the Invention of Tradition. *Cultural Anthropology* 11 (4): 435–469.

Buck, Elizabeth B. 1993. *Paradise Remade: The Politics of Culture and History in Hawai'i*. Philadelphia: Temple University Press.

Cachola-Abad, C. Kēhaunani. 1996. Review of *Reconciling the Past: Two Basketry Kā'ai and the Legendary Līloa and Lonoikamakahiki*, by Roger Rose. *The Contemporary Pacific* 8 (1): 224–226.

Casey, Edward S. 1987. *Remembering: A Phenomenological Study*. Bloomington: Indiana University Press.

Casey, Edward S. 1996. How to Get from Space to Place in a Fairly Short Stretch of Time: Phenomenological Prolegomena. In *Senses of Place*, edited by Steven Feld and Keith H. Basso, pp. 13–52. Santa Fe, NM: School of American Research Press.

Charlot, John. 1987. *The Kamapua'a Literature: The Classical Traditions of the Hawaiian Pig God as a Body of Literature*. Lā'ie, Hawai'i: Institute for Polynesian Studies, Brigham Young University.

Clifford, James. 1986. Introduction: Partial Truths. In *Writing Culture: The Poetics and Politics of Ethnography*, edited by James Clifford and George Marcus, pp. 1–26. Berkeley: University of California Press.

Clifford, James. 1988. *The Predicament of Culture: Twentieth-Century Ethnography, Literature and Art*. Cambridge: Harvard University Press.

Clifford, James. 1997. *Routes: Travel and Translation in the Late Twentieth Century*. Cambridge: Harvard University Press.

Davis, Wayne Keona. 1994. Do What is Right: Return the Ka'ai. *The Honolulu Advertiser* March 6: B3.

Davis, Wayne Keona. 1995. *Personal Communication*.

Dei, George J. Sefa. 2000. Rethinking the Role of Indigenous Knowledges in the Academy. *International Journal of Inclusive Education* 4 (2): 111–132.

Dening, Greg. 1980. *Islands and Beaches.* Honolulu: University Press of Hawai'i.

Dening, Greg. 1988. *History's Anthropology: The Death of William Gooch.* Washington, DC: University Press of America.

Derné, Steve. 1998. Feeling Water: Notes on the Sensory Construction of Time and Space in Banaras. *Man in India* 78 (1&2): 1–7.

Diaz, Vicente M., and J. Kēhaulani Kauanui. 2001. Native Pacific Cultural Studies on the Edge. *The Contemporary Pacific* 13 (2): 315–342.

Emerson, Nathaniel B. 1893. The Long Voyages of the Ancient Hawaiians. *Hawaiian Historical Society Papers* 5: 1–28.

Emerson, Nathaniel B. 1965. *Unwritten Literature of Hawaii: The Sacred Songs of the Hula.* Rutland, VT: Charles E. Tuttle.

Emerson, Nathaniel B. 1978. *Pele and Hi'iaka, A Myth from Hawaii.* Rutland, VT: Charles E. Tuttle.

Fornander, A. 1969. *An Account of the Polynesian Race, its Origins and Migrations, and the Ancient History of the Hawaiian People to the Times of Kamehameha I* (Vols. 1–3). Rutland, VT: Charles E. Tuttle.

Friedman, Jonathan. 1992a. Myth, History, and Political Identity. *Cultural Anthropology* 7 (2): 194–210.

Friedman, Jonathan. 1992b. The Past in the Future: History and the Politics of Identity. *American Anthropologist* 94 (4): 837–859.

Gallimore, Ronald, Joan Whitehorn Boggs, and Cathie Jordan. 1974. *Culture, Behavior and Education: A Study of Hawaiian Americans.* Beverly Hills, CA: Sage Publications.

Gallimore, Ronald, and Alan Howard. 1968. *Studies in a Hawaiian Community: Na Makamaka o Nanakuli.* Pacific Anthropological Records 1. Honolulu: Bishop Museum Press.

Gegeo, David. 2001. Cultural Rupture and Indigeneity: The Challenge of (Re)visioning "Place" in the Pacific. *The Contemporary Pacific* 13 (2): 491–507.

Giddens, Anthony. 1984. *The Constitution of Society: An Outline of the Theory of Structuration.* Cambridge: Policy Press.

Goldberg, David Theo. 1993. *Racist Culture: Philosophy and the Politics of Meaning.* Oxford: Blackwell Publishers Ltd.

Grundmann, Reiner. 1991. *Marxism and Ecology.* Clarendon Press.

Hall, Lisa Kahaleole. 2005. "Hawaiian at Heart" and Other Fictions. *The Contemporary Pacific* 17 (2): 404–413.

Hall, Stuart. 1996. Introduction: Who Needs Identity? In *Questions of Cultural Identity,* edited by Stuart Hall and Paul Du Gay, pp. 1–17. London: Sage Publications.

Hall, Stuart. 1997. The Work of Representation In *Representation: Cultural Representations and Signifying Practices,* edited by Stuart Hall, pp. 13–74. London: Sage Publications.

Handler, Richard, and Jocelyn Linnekin. 1984. Tradition, Genuine or Spurious. *Journal of American Folklore* 97: 273–290.

Handy, E. S. Craighill. 1927. *Polynesian Religion.* Honolulu: Bernice P. Bishop Museum Bulletin 34.

Handy, E. S. Craighill. 1940. *The Hawaiian Planter.* Honolulu: Bernice P. Bishop Museum Bulletin 161.

Handy, E. S. Craighill, and Elizabeth Green Handy. 1972. *Native Planters in Old Hawai'i: Their Life, Lore, and Environment.* Bishop Museum Bulletin 233. Honolulu Bishop Museum Press.

Handy, E. S. Craighill, and Mary Kawena Pukui. 1972. *The Polynesian Family System in Ka'ū, Hawai'i.* Rutland, VT: Charles E. Tuttle.

Hanson, Allan. 1970. *Rapan Lifeways: Society and History on a Polynesian Island.* Boston: Little, Brown and Company.

Hanson, Allan. 1989. The Making of the Maori: Culture Invention and Its Logic. *American Anthropologist* 91 (4): 890–902.

Hanson, Allan. 1996. Review: *Woven Gods: Female Clowns and Power in Rotuma,* by Vilsoni Hereniko. *American Ethnologist* 23 (I): 199–200.

Harden, M. J. 1999. *Voices of Wisdom: Hawaiian Elders Speak.* Kula, Hawai'i: Aka Press.

Hau'ofa, Epeli. 1993. Our Sea of Islands. In *A New Oceania: Rediscovering Our Sea of Islands,* edited by Eric Waddell, Vijay Naidu, and Epeli Hau'ofa, pp. 2–16. Suva, Fiji: School of Social and Economic Development, University of the South Pacific in association with Beake House.

Hau'ofa, Epeli. 1998. The Ocean in Us. *The Contemporary Pacific* 10 (2): 392–410.

Hau'ofa, Epeli. 2000. Epilogue: Pasts to Remember. In *Remembrance of Pacific Pasts: An Invitation to Remake History,* edited by Robert Borofsky, pp. 453–471. Honolulu: University of Hawai'i Press.

Heap, James. 1990. Applied Ethnomethodology: Looking for the Local Rationality of Reading Activities. *Human Studies* 13: 39–72.

Hensel, Chase. 1996. *Telling Our Selves: Ethnicity and Discourse in Southwestern Alaska.* Oxford: Oxford University Press.

Hereniko, Vilsoni. 1995. *Woven Gods: Female Clowns and Power in Rotuma.* Honolulu: University of Hawai'i Press.

Herman, R. D. K. 1996. The Dread Taboo, Human Sacrifice, and Pearl Harbor. *The Contemporary Pacific* 8 (1): 81–126.

Hess, Harvey. 1979. Aunty Edith—A Coming Together of Life and Art. *Ha'ilono Mele* 5 (2): 2–12.

Hobsbawm, E. J. 1964. Introduction. In *Pre-capitalist Economic Formations* by Karl Marx pp. 9–65. Translated by Jack Cohen. New York: International Publishers.

Howard, Alan. 1974. *Ain't No Big Thing: Coping Strategies in a Hawaiian-American Community.* Honolulu: University Press of Hawai'i.

Howard, Alan. 1997. Hanson's Review of *Woven Gods. American Ethnologist* 24 (I): 191–192.

Ii, John Papa. 1983. *Fragments of Hawaiian History,* revised edition. Translated by Mary Kawena Pukui, edited by Dorothy B. Barrère. Special Publication 70. Honolulu: Bishop Museum Press.

Ito, Karen L. 1985. Affective Bonds: Hawaiian Interrelationships of Self. In *Person, Self, and Experience: Exploring Pacific Ethnopsychologies,* edited by Geoffrey M. White and John Kirkpatrick, pp. 301–327. Berkeley: University of California Press.

Ito, Karen L. 1999. *Lady Friends: Hawaiian Ways and the Ties that Define.* Ithaca: Cornell University Press.

Jolly, Margaret. 1992. Specters of Inauthenticity. *Contemporary Pacific* 4 (1): 49–72.

Jolly, Margaret. 1994. *Women of the Place: Kastom, Colonialism and Gender in Vanuatu.* Philadelphia: Harwood Academic Publishers.

Kaeppler, Adrienne L. 1993. *Hula Pahu: Hawaiian Drum Dances. Volume I. Ha'a and Hula Pahu:* Introduction by Ka'upena Wong. Bishop Museum Bulletin in Anthropology 3. Honolulu: Bishop Museum Press.

Kahananui, Dorothy M. 1962. *Music of Ancient Hawai'i: A Brief Survey.* Honolulu: University Press of Hawai'i.

Kamakau, Samuel M. 1964. *Ka Po'e Kahiko: The People of Old.* Translated by Mary Kawena Pukui, arranged and edited by Dorothy B. Barrère. Special Publication 51. Honolulu: Bishop Museum Press.

Kamakau, Samuel M. 1976. *The Works of the People of Old: Na Hana a ka Po'e Kahiko.* Translated by Mary Kawena Pukui, arranged and edited by Dorothy B. Barrère. Special Publication 61. Honolulu: Bishop Museum Press.

Kamakawiwo'ole, Abe. 1994. Another View: It is Right that Līloa is Home. *The Honolulu Advertiser* March 6: B3.

Kame'eleihiwa, Lilikalā. 1992. *Native Land and Foreign Desires: Pehea Lā E Pono Ai?* Honolulu: Bishop Museum Press.

Kanahele, George S. (ed.). 1979. *Hawaiian Music and Musicians: An Illustrated History.* Honolulu: University Press of Hawai'i.

Kanahele, George S. 1986. *Kū Kanaka Stand Tall: A Search for Hawaiian Values.* Honolulu: University of Hawai'i Press: Waiaha Foundation.

Kauanui, J. Kēhaulani. 1998. Off-Island Hawaiians "Making" Ourselves at "Home": A (Gendered) Contradiction in Terms? *Pergamon* 21 (6): 681–693.

Kauanui, J. Kēhaulani. 1999a. "For Get" Hawaiian Entitlement: Configurations of Land, "Blood" and Americanization in the Hawaiian Homes Act of 1921. *Social Text* 17 (2): 123–144.

Kauanui, J. Kēhaulani. 1999b. Diasporic De-Racination: Tracing the Contours of Off-Island Hawaiian Subjects. Paper for The Twenty-Fourth Annual University of Hawai'i Pacific Island Studies Conference. University of Hawai'i at Mānoa.

Keesing, Roger M. 1978. Politico-religious Movements and Anticolonialism on Malaita: Maasina rule in Historical Perspective. *Oceania* 48: 241–261.

Keesing, Roger. M. 1989. Creating the Past: Custom and Identity in the Contemporary Pacific. *The Contemporary Pacific* 1 (1–2): 19–42.

Keesing, Roger M. 1991. Reply to Trask. *The Contemporary Pacific* 3: 168–171.

Keesing, Roger M. 1994. Theories of Culture Revisited. In *Assessing Cultural Anthropology*, edited by Robert Borofsky, pp. 301–312. New York: McGraw Hill.

Kent, Noel J. 1983. *Hawaii: Islands Under the Influence.* New York: Monthly Review Press.

Krauss, Bob. 1994. Wails and Prayers for Missing Bones. *The Honolulu Advertiser* March 5: A1.

Kulchyski, Peter. 1992. Primitive Subversions: Totalization and Resistance in Native Canadian Politics. *Cultural Critique* 21: 171–195.

Lili'uokalani, Queen. 1978. *The Kumulipo: An Hawaiian Creation Myth.* Translated by Queen Lili'uokalani. Kentfield, CA: Pueo Press.

Lindstrom, Lamont and Geoffrey M. White. 1995. Anthropology's New Cargo: Future Horizons. *Ethnology* 34 (3): 201–209.

Linnekin, Jocelyn. 1983. Defining Tradition: Variations on the Hawaiian Identity. *American Ethnologist* 10 (2): 241–252.

Linnekin, Jocelyn. 1985. *Children of the Land: Exchange and Status in a Hawaiian Community.* New Brunswick, NJ: Rutgers University Press.

Linnekin, Jocelyn. 1990. The Politics of Culture in the Pacific. In *Cultural Identity and Ethnicity in the Pacific*, edited by Jocelyn Linnekin, and Lin Poyer, pp. 149–174. Honolulu: University of Hawai'i Press.

Linnekin, Jocelyn. 1991a. Cultural Invention and the Dilemma of Authenticity. *American Anthropologist* 93 (2): 446–449.

Linnekin, Jocelyn. 1991b. Text Bites and the R-word: The Politics of Representing Scholarship. *Contemporary Pacific* 3 (1): 172–177.

Linnekin, Jocelyn. 1992. On the Theory and Politics of Cultural Construction in the Pacific. *Oceania* 62: 249–263.

Linnekin Jocelyn, and Lin Poyer. 1990. Introduction. In *Cultural Identity and Ethnicity in the Pacific*, edited by Jocelyn Linnekin and Lin Poyer, pp. 1–16. Honolulu: University of Hawai'i Press.

Malie Wahine Ke'ali'i o ke Kai. 2000. *Personal Communication.*

Marx, Karl. 1964. *Pre-capitalist Economic Formations.* Translated by Jack Cohen, introduction by E. J. Hobsbawm. New York: International Publishers.

Marx, Karl, and Frederick Engels. 1981. *The German Ideology Part One.* Edited and with introduction by C. J. Arthur. New York: International Publishers.

McGregor, Davianna Pōmaika'i. 1996. An Introduction to the *Hoa'āina* and Their Rights. *The Hawaiian Journal of History* 30: 1–27.

Merchant, Carolyn. 1989. *The Death of Nature: Women, Ecology, and the Scientific Revolution.* San Francisco: HarperSanFrancisco (A Division of HarperCollins Publishers).

Merry, Sally E. 2000. *Colonizing Hawai'i: The Cultural Power of Law.* Princeton: Princeton University Press.

Merry, Sally Engle 2003. Law and Identity in an American Colony. In *Law and Empire in the Pacific: Fiji and Hawai'i*, edited by Sally Engle Merry, and Donald Brenneis, pp. 123–152. Santa Fe: School of American Research Press.

Meyer, Manulani Aluli. 2001. Our Own Liberation: Reflections on Hawaiian Epistemology. *The Contemporary Pacific* 19 (1): 124–148.

Miles, Robert. 1993. *Racism After "Race Relations."* London: Routledge.

Neil, Christopher. 1994. Priceless Artifacts Still Missing: Burial Caskets, Known as Ka'ai, Centuries-old. *The Honolulu Advertiser* February 27: A1.

Obeyesekere, Gananath. 1992. *The Apotheosis of Captain Cook: European Mythmaking in the Pacific.* Princeton: Princeton University Press.

Ollman, Bertell. 1993. *Dialectical Investigations.* New York: Routledge.

Orr, David W. 1992. *Ecological Literacy: Education and the Transition to a Postmodern World.* Albany: State University of New York Press.

Osorio, Jonathan Kamakawiwo'ole. 2001. What Kine Hawaiian are You? A Mo'olelo about Nationhood, Race, History, and the Contemporary Sovereignty Movement in Hawai'i. *The Contemporary Pacific* 13 (2): 359–379.

Osorio, Jonathan Kamakawiwo'ole. 2006. "Protecting Our Thoughts (A speech delivered at *Voices of the Earth Conference*: Amsterdam, 1993). Center for Hawaiian Studies, University of Hawai'i at Mānoa website: http://www/hawaii/edu/chs/osiorio.html.

Patton, Sandra. 2000. *BirthMarks: Transracial Adoption in Contemporary America.* New York: New York University Press.

Povinelli, Elizabeth. A. 1995. Do Rocks Listen? The Cultural Politics of Apprehending Australian Aboriginal Labor. *American Anthropologist* 97 (3): 505–518.

Pukui, Mary Kawena. 1983. *'Ōlelo No'eau: Hawaiian Proverbs and Poetical Sayings.* Bishop Museum Special Publication 71. Honolulu: Bishop Museum Press.

Pukui, Mary Kawena, and Samuel H. Elbert. 1986. *Hawaiian Dictionary.* Revised and enlarged edition. Honolulu: University of Hawai'i Press.

Pukui, Mary Kawena, E. W. Haertig, and Catherine A. Lee. 1974a. *Nānā i ke Kumu (Volume l).* Honolulu: Hui Hānai.

Pukui, Mary Kawena, E. W. Haertig, and Catherine A. Lee. 1974b. *Nānā i ke Kumu (Volume 2).* Honolulu: Hui Hānai.

Pukui, Mary Kawena, and Alfons L. Korn, eds. and trans.. 1973. *The Echo of our Song; Chants and Poems of the Hawaiians.* Honolulu: The University Press of Hawai'i.

Robillard, Albert B. 1992. Introduction: Social Change as the Projection of Discourse. In *Social Change in the Pacific Islands*, edited by Albert B. Robillard, pp. 1–32. London: Kegan Paul International.

Rosaldo, Renato. 1989. *Culture and Truth: The Remaking of Social Analysis.* Boston: Beacon Press.

Rose, Roger G. 1992. *Reconciling the Past: Two Basketry Kā'ai and the Legendary Līloa and Lonoikamakahiki.* Bishop Museum in Anthropology 5, Honolulu: Bishop Museum Press.

Sahlins, Marshall. 1976. *Culture and Practical Reason.* Chicago: The University of Chicago Press.

Sahlins, Marshall. 1981. *Historical Metaphors and Mythical Realities: Structure in the Early History of the Sandwich Islands Kingdom.* Ann Arbor: University of Michigan Press.

Sahlins, Marshall. 1992. *Anahulu: The Anthropology of History in the Kingdom of Hawai'i. Volume One: Historical Ethnography.* Chicago: The University of Chicago Press.

Sahlins, Marshall. 1994. Goodbye to Triste Tropes: Ethnography in the Context of Modern World History. In *Assessing Cultural Anthropology*, edited by Robert Borofsky, pp.377–394. New York: McGraw-Hill.

Shiva, Vandana. 1988. *Staying Alive: Women, Ecology, and Development.* London: Zed Books Ltd.

Shook, E. Victoria. 1985. *Ho'oponopono: Contemporary uses of a Hawaiian Problem-solving Process.* Honolulu: University of Hawai'i Press.

Silva, Noenoe K. 1998. Kanaka Maoli Resistance to Annexation. *'Ōiwi: A Native Hawaiian Journal* 1: 40–75.

Silva, Noenoe K. 2000.He Kānāwai E Ho'opau I Na Hula Kuolo Hawai'i: The Political Economy of Banning the Hula. *The Hawaiian Journal of History* 34: 29–49.

Silva, Noenoe K. 2004. *Aloha Betrayed: Native Hawaiian Resistance to American Colonialism.* Durham: Duke University Press.

Silvers, Ronald. 1982. Discourse in a Search for a Communicative Relationship. In *Interpretive Human Studies: An Introduction to Phenomenological Research*, edited by Vivian Darroch and Ronald Silvers, pp. 173–214. Washington, D.C: University Press of America.

Silvers, Ronald. 1994. *Personal Communication.* OISE/University of Toronto. December.

Simon, Roger I. 1992. *Teaching Against the Grain: Texts for a Pedagogy of Possibility.* Toronto, OISE Press.

Smith, Dorothy E. 1990. *The Conceptual Practices of Power: A Feminist Sociology of Knowledge.* Toronto: University of Toronto Press.

Smith, Linda Tuhiwai. 1999. *Decolonizing Methodologies: Research and Indigenous Peoples.* London: Zed Books Ltd.

Stannard, David. 2000. The Hawaiians: Health, Justice, and Sovereignty. *Cultural Survival Quarterly* 24 (1): 15–20.

Stead, C.K. ed. 1994. *The Faber Book of Contemporary South Pacific Stories.* London: Faber and Faber.

Steinberg, Gail, and Beth Hall. 2000. *Inside Transracial Adoption.* Indianapolis: Perspectives Press.

Stern, Daniel N. 1985. *The Interpersonal World of the Infant.* New York: Basic Books, Inc.

Stillman, Amy Ku'uleialoha. 1989. History Reinterpreted in Song: The Case of the Hawaiian Counterrevolution. *The Hawaiian Journal of History* 23: 1–30.

Stillman, Amy Ku'uleialoha. 1999. Aloha 'Āina: New Perspectives on "Kaulana Nā Pua." *The Hawaiian Journal of History* 33: 83–99.

Stillman, Amy Ku'uleialoha. 2001. Re-Membering the History of the Hawaiian Hula. In *Cultural Memory: Reconfiguring History and Identity in the Postcolonial Pacific*, edited by Jeannette M. Mageo, pp. 187–204. Honolulu: University of Hawai'i Press.

Tangonan, Shannon. 1994. Hawaiians Say Spirits Urged Taking of Kā'ai. *The Honolulu Advertiser* December 21: A2.

Teaiwa, Teresia K. 1994. bikinis and other s/pacific n/oceans. *The Contemporary Pacific* 6 (1): 87–109.

Teaiwa, Teresia K. 1995. Scholarship from a Lazy Native. In *Work in Flux*, edited by Emma Greenwood, Klaus Neumann, and Andrew Sartori, pp. 58–72. Melbourne: The University of Melbourne History Department.

Tedlock, Barbara. 1987. Dreaming and Dream Research. In *Dreaming: Anthropological and Psychological Interpretations*, edited by Barbara Tedlock, pp. 1–30. Cambridge: Cambridge University Press.

Thaman, Konai Helu. 2003. Decolonizing Pacific Studies: Indigenous Perspectives, Knowledge, and Wisdom in Higher Education. *The Contemporary Pacific* 15 (1): 1–17.

Thomas, Nicholas. 1997. *In Oceania: Visions, Artifacts, Histories.* Durham: Duke University Press.

Tobin, Jeffrey. 1994. Cultural Construction and Native Nationalism: Report from the Hawaiian Front. *Boundary 2 Special Issue:* 21(1): 111–133. Durham: Duke University Press.

Trask, Haunani-Kay. 1991. Natives and Anthropologists: The Colonial Struggle. *The Contemporary Pacific* 3 (1): 159–167.

Trask, Haunani-Kay. 1993. *From a Native Daughter: Colonialism and Sovereignty in Hawai'i.* Monroe, Maine: Common Courage Press.

Trask, Haunani-Kay. 2000a. The Struggle for Hawaiian Sovereignty: Introduction. *Cultural Survival Quarterly* 24 (1): 8–11.

Trask, Haunani-Kay. 2000b. Tourism and the Prostitution of Hawaiian Culture. *Cultural Survival Quarterly* 24 (1): 21–23.

Trask, Mililani B. 2000a. Hawaiian Sovereignty. *Cultural Survival Quarterly* 24 (1): 12–14.

Trask, Mililani B. 2000b. Hawai'i and the United Nations. *Cultural Survival Quarterly* 24 (1): 24–25.

U.S. Congress. 1993. United States Public Law 103–150. *Congressional Record.* 103rd Cong., 1st sess., Vol. 139.

Valeri, Valerio. 1985. *Kingship and Sacrifice: Ritual and Society in Ancient Hawaii.* Translated by Paula Wissing. Chicago: The University of Chicago Press.

Wagner, Roy. 1981. *The Invention of Culture.* Revised and expanded edition. Chicago: The University of Chicago Press.

White, Geoffrey. M., and Ty Kāwika Tengan. 2001. Disappearing Worlds: Anthropology and Cultural Studies in Hawai'i and the Pacific. *The Contemporary Pacific* 13 (2): 381–416.

Wood. Houston. 1999. *Displacing Natives: The Rhetorical Production of Hawai'i.* Lanham, Maryland: Rowman and Littlefield, Publishers, Inc.

Index